HISTORIC DRESS
IN AMERICA

Volume Two   1800-1870

about
Nov. 1804

1804-1

Sophie B. Steel
'06

HISTORIC DRESS
IN AMERICA
1607=1870

ELISABETH McCLELLAN

Illustrations by
SOPHIE B. STEEL & CECIL W. TROUT

Volume Two   1800-1870

1804

Frontispiece (Figure 1).—Picture of an Empire gown worn in Philadelphia, now in the collection at Memorial Hall. The train is of blue satin bordered with a bias fold of white satin embroidered with sprays of roses and leaves in natural colours. Over the short puffed sleeves of white crêpe trimmed with bands of embroidered satin are caps of the white satin with embroidered roses. The same pattern is embroidered above the hem of the white satin under-dress. Around the train and on the hem of the under-dress is a narrow trimming of embroidery in pink and white. The shoulder ruching is made of plaited white crêpe edged with lace. The dress turban of blue satin is embroidered to match the dress and ornamented with two white plumes and one of pink. This beautiful gown is a hundred years old.

ISBN 0-88143-076-5 Volume 2
Set ISBN 0-88143-077-3
First Published 1904-10
Reissued 1969 by
Benjamin Blom, Inc. Bronx, New York 10452
and 56 Doughty Street, London, W.C. I

Library of Congress Catalog Card Number 70-81515

Printed in the United States of America

Historic Dress in America was reissued in 1937 in an unaltered reprint
as *History of American Costume 1607-1870.*

CONTENTS
Volume Two

MANY books have been written on the houses, the furniture, and the decorations of the century we have so lately seen pass into history, but of the costumes chosen and worn by our immediate ancestors very little has been recorded in print. Yet, as Mr. Calthrop, the English authority on the history of dress has aptly said, " To see our ancestors dressed is to have a shrewd guess as to what they were—as to what they did." The present volume is designed to bring us within the charmed circle of intimacy and to reveal to us the tastes and fancies, the pursuits and pastimes, of our nineteenth century grandparents. It goes to press with many thanks to the friends who have lent me their ancestral treasures. · The scheme of illustration has been to arrange the garments on living models and to copy the hair and accessories from contemporary portraits or old fashion plates. As the first years of the twentieth century have witnessed a revival of the scant and clinging skirts, the turbans and scarf draperies, of a hundred years ago, we are reminded of the old verse :

> " Fashions that are now called new
> Have been worn by more than you,
> Other times have worn the same
> Though the new ones get the name."

ELISABETH McCLELLAN.

Philadelphia, November, 1910.

ILLUSTRATIONS
Volume Two

Initials

Other Illustrations

Contemporary Rulers

1800–1870

PRESIDENTS OF THE UNITED STATES

John Adams, of Massachusetts	1797–1801
Thomas Jefferson, of Virginia	1801–1809
James Madison, of Virginia	1809–1817
James Monroe, of Virginia	1817–1825
John Quincy Adams, of Massachusetts	1825–1829
Andrew Jackson, of Tennessee	1829–1837
Martin Van Buren, of New York	1837–1841
William Henry Harrison, of Ohio	1841–1845
(Term finished by John Tyler, of Virginia.)	
John Knox Polk, of Tennessee	1845–1849
Zachary Taylor, of Louisiana	1849–1853
(Term finished by Millard Fillmore, of New York.)	
Franklin Pierce, of New Hampshire	1853–1857
James Buchanan, of Pennsylvania	1857–1861
Abraham Lincoln, of Illinois	1861–1869
(Term finished by Andrew Johnson, of Tennessee.)	

KINGS OF ENGLAND

George III and the Regency	1760–1820
George IV	1820–1830
William IV	1830–1837
Victoria	1837–1901

RULERS OF FRANCE

Napoleon, First Consul	1800–1804
Napoleon, Emperor	1804–1814
Louis XVIII, King	1814–1815
Napoleon, Emperor (100 days, March 20–June 22)	1815
Louis XVIII, King	1815–1824
Charles X, King	1824–1830
Louis Philippe, King	1830–1848
(Republic proclaimed February 25, 1848.)	
Louis Napoleon, President	1848–1852
Louis Napoleon, Emperor	1852–1870

WOMEN'S DRESS
1800–1870

"The Morning Post may now display unfurl'd
Four columns of the Fashionable World,
And not confin'd to tell of war's renown,
Spread all the news around of all the town.
While gay gazettes the polish'd Treasury writes
Of splendid fashions, not of vulgar fights.
Proud to record the tailor's deeds and name
And give the milliner to deathless fame
Who first shall force proud Gallia to confess
Herself inferior in the art of dress.
Oh, join to pray and hopes may not be vain
Commence gay Peace a long and joyous reign.
May Europe's nations by thy counsels wise
Learn e'en thy faults to cherish and to prize
And shunning glory's bright but fatal star
Prefer thy follies to the woes of war."

Prologue to " Fashionable Friends."
—Mary Berry.

Women's Dress
1800–1810

" La Mode est un Tyrant dont rien ne nous delivre ;
A son bizarre gout il faut s' accommoder
Et, sous ses folles lois ètant forcè de vivre,
Le sage n' est jamais le premier à les suivre
Ni le dernier à les garder.''

—ÉTIENNE PAVILLON.

A T the beginning of the nineteenth century Fashion reigned supreme over all the civilized countries on both sides of the Atlantic, overcoming geographical and even political restrictions. Monthly magazines with coloured plates of the latest edicts of the invincible tyrant were published in London as well as in Paris,* and were sent regularly to America instead of the fashion dolls of the preceding century. One of the earliest of these fashion books was "The Ladies' European Magazine " edited by a coterie of women of fashion and first published in London in 1798. Another, " La Belle Assemblée," or " Bell's Court and Fashionable Magazine " was issued regularly in London from 1806 to 1832, when a new series was started of which the Hon. Mrs. Norton was editor and the name was changed to " The Court Magazine and Monthly Critic." In addition to the

* " Magazin des Modes" was published in Paris as early as 1785, and "Galleries des Modes " a year or two later.

fashions, it contained serial stories, literary reviews, and original poetry contributed by the distinguished editor. This periodical was quite as popular in the United States as in England and, judging from the mutilated plates in the copies I have seen, probably furnished several generations of American children with fascinating paper dolls. A letter from Paris every month kept its readers in touch with the court of the "Great Mogul," as Walpole called fashion, and the Calendar of the English Court, which formed the supplement of the second series, was evidently read with great interest on both sides of the ocean.

Ackermann's "Repository," published in London in 1809, was another popular periodical which contained especially tasteful plates of the latest modes. In Philadelphia Mr. Dennie's "Port Folio," which appeared with the first year of the century and had great local celebrity from 1801 to 1805, gave a column or more of its racy pages to the novelties in dress. Under the heading "Festoon of Fashion" a brief review of the modes in France and England was given, but "Mr. Oldschool"* indulged only in pen portraits of the costumes. All these magazines have been long out of print, but odd volumes of them may be found in many of our libraries; unlike their successors of the present day, they are good reading. Moreover, they are faithful records of the social life of their time.

During the first Consulate and the Empire, France was possessed with a pseudo-classic mania in women's dress. This revival of classicism is attributed by Ashton in his "Dawn of the Nineteenth Century" to the influence of the painter David. Clinging draperies and Greek and Roman hair-dressing were carried to an extreme which was not noticeable in England or America, although followed in both countries to some extent. The simple domestic tastes of George III and

* Pen name of the editor.

Queen Charlotte set an example both in dress and social gayeties which was notably free from extravagance. The English princesses, so loved by Miss Burney, spent much of their time embroidering their own dresses for state functions ; while in our own country, President Adams and his wife were living very quietly and, according to the graphic letters of the latter, most uncomfortably in the new home of the government in Washington, indulging in but few entertainments, and going to Philadelphia for most of their shopping. When Madame Recamier visited London in 1802 her "costume à l'antique" caused much comment. She appeared it seems one day in Kensington Gardens, "in a thin muslin dress clinging to her figure like the folds of drapery in a statue, her hair in a coil of braids at the back and arranged in short ringlets round her face ; a large veil thrown over her head completed an attire which not unnaturally caused her to be followed and stared at." As early as 1801 Paris fashions had evidently made their way to America, for Mrs. Samuel Harrison Smith writing from the capital in that year observes, "There was a lady here who afforded us great amusement. I titled her Madame Eve and called her dress the fig leaf." *

Letters of the day give us much information on the subject of the prevailing fashions, but the most valuable sources of the history of dress in the nineteenth century are the actual garments which in many cases have been handed down to posterity unaltered, and afford a subtle insight into the character and taste of the wearers. An old writer says, "As the index tells us the contents of stories and directs to the particular chapter, even so does the external habit and superficial order of garments (in men and women) give us a taste of the internal quality of the soul."

* First Forty Years of Washington Society.

The numerous portraits of the day record fashionable costumes and illustrate the customary accessories and styles of hair-dressing. In England, Lawrence, Beechey, Hoppner and Russell achieved some of their best work in the early years of the nineteenth century. Raeburn, Hayter, Chalons and Winterhalter followed in their illustrious footsteps. David, Vernet, Ingres, Le Brun, Manet and Fontan-Latour were the great portrait painters of France between 1800 and 1870; while, in our own country, Stuart, Sully, St. Memin, Inman and Healey have also left immortal canvasses which bear abundant evidence of the transatlantic sovereignty of Fashion.

> " Fashion come, on me a while
> Deign, fantastic nymph, to smile."

Looking through the old magazines of 1800–1810, "Sacred to Dress and Beauty's pleasing cares," we see that the short waists which came into vogue at the close of the eighteenth century were worn for at least ten years of the nineteenth century. Skirts were very narrow and the ultra-fashionable wore them of very soft, sheer, clinging materials. These gowns were the subject of many a satire. We read of one critic " fond of statistics who calculated that in one year eighteen ladies caught fire and eighteen thousand caught cold." Another wit of the day remarked, " The change in the female dress of late must contribute very much to domestic bliss; no man can surely now complain of petticoat government." In winter, to be sure, warm cloaks which completely covered the gowns were worn out-of-doors (Figures 42, 59, 96, 98, 102), but slippers or half-shoes with the thinnest of soles were worn even for walking and must have prevented the " wrapping cloaks " and big muffs (Figures 11, 102) from keeping the wearer's body at a comfortable degree of warmth.

Perhaps the pursuit of fashion is in itself so stimulating an exercise that it acts as a preventive and keeps off the dangers apparently courted by her votaries.

Bodices were exceedingly short in the early years of the nineteenth century. The waist line was entirely obscured (Figures 5, 9, 13, 51, 53, 54, 56, 58, 243). A satirical couplet of the day runs :

> " Shepherds, I have lost my waist
> Have you seen my body ? "

We are all familiar with the portrait of Madame Recamier on an Empire sofa, her Grecian drapery falling around her in graceful lines which could not possibly have been maintained if she stood up, or tried to walk. The mystery of the possibility of this fashion is explained (Figures 3–6) by the famous caricaturist Gillray whose pictures " give us a glimpse," as Ashton says, " of the mysteries of the toilet such as might be sought in vain elsewhere ; and are particularly valuable as they are in no way exaggerated and supply details otherwise unprocurable."

The long and close-fitting stays, though not as stiff and unyielding as their predecessors of the eighteenth century, prevented the untidy negligee appearance the high-waisted gowns would have had without them. As the bodices grew longer, the stays grew shorter until 1819 or 20 when the first French corset in two pieces and laced up the back came into fashion and has retained its popularity ever since. A pair of short stays worn about 1820 may be seen in the Rhode Island Historical Society's rooms at Newport.

In many old portraits we may notice wigs of short, close curls which were in the height of fashion in the year 1800 (Figures 7, 22), and in a letter of that date, written in Boston by Elizabeth Southgate to her mother, we find that five dollars would buy one of these coveted articles.

1800-1807

FIGURE 2.—1801—A Turkish vest of black velvet. Turban of muslin with a falling end fringed with gold and a bird of paradise feather. Necklace of coral and gold beads.

FIGURES 3, 4, 5, 6.—1800—Progress of the toilet, showing long stays, laced up the back, the dress worn over them, and the maid's costume of the same date.

FIGURE 7.—1801—Afternoon head-dresses.

FIGURE 8.—1801—Gypsy hat, worn from 1800 to 1810.

FIGURE 9.—1800—Cap trimmed with Amaranthus crêpe, locket watch.

FIGURE 10.—1801—A velvet turban with a "banditti" plume and a veil hanging to the shoulders.

FIGURE 11.—1801—Silk bonnet with lace frills, silk spencer with short sleeves and long ends trimmed with lace, large muff and fur.

FIGURE 12.—1801—Morning dress of spotted muslin, cap and neck-frill trimmed with lace.

FIGURE 13.—1807—Summer walking costume, pelisse and dress of Jaconet muslin and a Lavinia hat of straw.

FIGURE 14.—1806—Dress of muslin with a pleated shoulder-cape, straw bonnet with a silk crown to be worn over a cap.

"Now Mamma, what do you think I am going to ask for?— a wig. Eleanor has got a new one just like my hair and only five dollars, Mrs. Mayo one just like it. I must either cut my hair or have one, I cannot dress it at all stylish. Mrs. Coffin bought Eleanor's and says that she will write to Mrs. Sumner to get me one just like it; how much time it will save—in one year we could save it in pins and paper, besides the trouble. At the Assembly I was quite ashamed of my head, for nobody has long hair. If you will consent to my having one do send me over a five dollar bill by the post immediately after you receive this, for I am in hopes to have it for the next Assembly—do send me word immediately if you can let me have one.

" ELIZA." *

They were still in fashion in 1802, for Martha Jefferson Randolph wrote the following letter to her father just before his inauguration as third President of the United States :

" Oct. 29, 1802.

" DEAR PAPA,—We received your letter, and are prepared with all speed to obey its summons. By next Friday I hope we shall be able to fix a day ; and probably the shortest time in which the horses can be sent after receiving our letter will determine it, though as yet it is not certain that we can get off so soon.

" Will you be so good as to send orders to the milliner— Madame Peck, I believe her name is, through Mrs. Madison, who very obligingly offered to execute any little commission for us in Philadelphia, for two wigs of the colour of the hair enclosed, and of the most fashionable shapes (Figures 5, 7 and 22), that they may be in Washington when we arrive? They are universally worn, and will relieve us as to the necessity of dressing our own hair, a business in which neither of us are adepts.

* A Girl's Life Eighty Years Ago.

"I believe Madame Peck is in the habit of doing these things, and they can be procured in a short time from Philadelphia, where she corresponds, much handsomer than elsewhere.

"Adieu, dearest Father."

A rhyme current in the early part of the nineteenth century emphasizes the annoyance of finding a wig necessary in full dress :

> " There was an old woman of Gosport
> And she was one of the cross sort,
> When she dressed for the ball
> Her wig was too small,
> Which enraged this old woman of Gosport."

Miss Southgate was born in Scarborough, Maine, but spent much of her time in Boston, writing to her mother from there delightfully intimate and chatty letters, which give a charming picture of the social life of the time. The dances, the sleighing parties, etc., are all vividly described, and her remarks about dress are a valuable contribution to our subject.

" *July 17, 1800.*

" I must again trouble my Dear Mother by requesting her to send on my spotted muslin (Figures 12 and 58). A week from next Saturday I set out for Wiscassett, in company with Uncle William and Aunt Porter. Uncle will fetch Ann to meet us there, and as she has some acquaintance there, we shall stay some time and Aunt will leave us and return to Topsham ; so long a visit in Wiscassett will oblige me to muster all my muslins, for I am informed they are so monstrous smart as to take no notice of any lady that can condescend to wear a calico gown. Therefore, Dear Mother, to ensure me a favourable reception, pray send my spotted muslin by the next mail after you receive this, or I shall be on my way to Wiscassett. I shall go on horseback. How I want my habit, I wish it had not been so warm when I left home and I should have worn it (Figure 105). I am in hopes you will find an opportunity to send it by a private conveyance before I go, but my muslin you must certainly send by the mail." *

The sketch of a riding habit of the period is given in Figure 105. The jacket and skirt should be of blue cloth with black velvet collar and double rows of gilt buttons called " Nelson's balls." A close cap of beaver with a gold braid around the crown and a feather in front. Gloves of fine tan leather and half-boots of black Spanish leather.

Another riding dress given in Figure 106 shows the front view of a habit of 1801. It is made of dark blue kersemere and trimmed with three rows of small blue buttons crossed with three rows of blue silk cord. Collar of blue velvet. A white beaver hat with a very narrow brim and two short white feathers.

In a letter from Paris during the First Consulate, Miss Berry, in her " Diary and Letters," describes an assembly at which she was present when Bonaparte addressed each lady with the question : " Do you ride on horseback ? " Evidently it was the correct thing for a lady to do in France as well as in England and America.

Miss Austen mentions the fashionable muslins too. Writing to her sister in 1801, she says :

" . . . I shall want two new coloured gowns for the summer, for my pink one will not do more than clear me from Steventon. I shall not trouble you, however, to get more than one of them, and that is to be a plain brown cambric muslin, for morning wear; the other, which is to be a very pretty yellow and white cloud, I mean to buy in Bath. Buy two brown

* A Girl's Life Eighty Years Ago.

ones, if you please, not both of a length, but one longer than the other; it is for a tall woman. Seven yards for my mother, seven yards and a half for me; a dark brown, but the kind of brown is left to your own choice, and I had rather they were different, as it will be always something to dispute about which is the prettiest. They must be cambric muslin." *

In another letter written in the same year we read of a new wrap:

" . . . My cloak came on Tuesday, and though I expected a good deal, the beauty of the lace astonished me. It is too handsome to be worn, almost too handsome to be looked at." †

A wrap trimmed with lace is given in Figure 11, from a plate of 1801.

Mrs. Ravenel in her delightful book, " Charleston, the Place and the People," gives us the following description of the ball dresses worn in that picturesque city of the South during the first quarter of the nineteenth century.

" No more the rich brocades and damasks, the plumes and powder; instead the scantiest and shortest of gowns, bodices at most eight inches long and skirts of two or three breadths, according to width of stuff and size of wearer, coming barely to the ankles. The stuff was the softest of satin, India silk, or muslin that could be found; the feet clad in heelless slippers tied with ribbons that crossed about the instep. The hair, descended from the high estate given it by the last and fairest of French queens, hung in loose waves upon the neck until the awful fashion of wigs came in. When that strange mania prevailed, it was hardly thought decent to wear one's own hair. No matter how long, how thick, how beautiful, the ruthless scissors must clip it close and a horrible construction by a hair-

* Letters of Jane Austen.   Edited by Lord Brabourne.   † Ibid.

dresser take its place. The wig fashion did not last long, only a year or two, then came the Grecian bands and plaits with short curls on the forehead, and next turbans."

Turbans, capotes and head-dresses of every possible material were in the height of fashion in the early years of the century. All the young ladies of that time were on the alert to get the newest designs and the following extract from an unpublished letter written by a Miss Smith in Philadelphia to a Miss Yeates of Lancaster, dated September 14, 1800, proves that it was fashionable to decorate turbans with hand painting.

"In the pacquet you will find three °painted Tiffany Turbans, of which I beg your acceptance of one, & Betsy & Kitty of the others. They are not as well done as I could wish, but they are as well done as I who never learnt to draw could do them." *

In Figures 2 and 7 specimens of fashionable head-dresses are given taken from the " Ladies' Monthly Museum " for January and March, 1801, which show that feathers and turbans were both worn with short hair.

In the " Festoon of Fashion " for October, 1801, is the following entry :

" A round dress of thick white muslin (Figure 13) ; a pelisse of cambric muslin, trimmed all round ; long sleeves. A bonnet of buff silk, trimmed with purple ribbon.

" A round dress of white muslin, drawn close round the throat with a double frill (Figure 12) ; long sleeves. A green handkerchief tied carelessly round the neck. A straw hat, turned up in front, and trimmed with green ribbons (Figures 27 and 31).

" A black silk hat, turned up in front, with a full crown, and ornamented with black feathers. A white muslin bonnet,

* Extract from letter to Miss M. Yeates, Lancaster.

trimmed and tied under the chin with white ribbon (Figure 23).

"A straw hat, turned up before, and lined with blue; blue ostrich feathers in front.

"A bonnet of dark green silk, two ostrich feathers of the same colour, placed in front, to fall contrary ways, a bow of green, edged with white, on the left side.

"A bonnet of pea-green, or other coloured silk, tied under the chin, and ornamented with white feathers.

"A cap of white and lilac muslin.

"A wreath of oak or laurel through the hair."

We are further informed : "The most fashionable colours are buff, scarlet, and blue for flowers and feathers, but white dresses are the most prevalent."

Two morning costumes of that year are copied from the "Ladies' Monthly Museum" for March, 1801 (Figures 11 and 12).

Bonnets were small and close-fitting and evidently of a variety of materials. We read in this same Philadelphia publication for 1802 of "a bonnet of black velvet trimmed with a deep black lace round the front. A close bonnet of purple, or other coloured silk, trimmed with ribbon of the same colour and ornamented with a flower in front. A bonnet of black velvet, turned up in front, and lined and trimmed with scarlet, a scarlet feather in front. A domestic or undress cap of fine muslin (Figure 12). A bonnet of pink silk, trimmed with black ribbon and a black feather; black lace round the front. A dress hat of white satin, turned up in front, and trimmed with purple velvet. A hat of brown velvet, turned up in front, and trimmed with pink ; bows before and behind."

As shown in Figures 24, 27 and 31, hats were small in the first years of the nineteenth century, but the following extract from "Lady Brownlow's Reminiscences" suggests that it was not the fashion to wear anything on the head in Paris in 1802.

"It was the month of November and cold weather and therefore the walking dress of the majority of the women surprised us not a little. It consisted of a gown *très décolleteé*, and extremely short-waisted, with apparently only one garment under it; this gown they held up so as to discover one *jambe*, a shawl hung over the shoulders, the feet *chaussées* in their slippers, no bonnet, or cap, and the curls on each side of the face greasy with *huile antique*." This description recalls the remark of Madame Jerome Bonaparte that dress at that time was chiefly an aid to setting off beauty to advantage; and her own famous wedding-gown of India muslin and old lace, which one of the guests declared he could have easily put into his pocket. But the fact that this airy costume excited so much comment at the time it was worn proves that it was very unusual even in those days of scanty drapery. It was a caprice of fashion impossible for ordinary mortals to follow.

In February, 1802, a striking walking costume is described: "Round dress of white muslin, under a Hungarian cloak made of scarlet silk trimmed all round with black lace. A bonnet of the same colour as the cloak, trimmed with black lace and ornamented with flowers of the same colour."

Then comes the description of a ball dress: "A short robe of fine muslin with a train of the same: the robe made plain over the bosom, with additional fronts, to fly open from the shoulders. The whole bound with scarlet ribbon, the sleeves and the robe from the shoulders to the bottom ornamented with scarlet ribbon. The bosom trimmed round with deep white lace. A hat of white silk, turned up in front, and lined with scarlet; a feather of the same colour fixed in front, to fall over the crown."

1800–1810

FIGURE 15.—1807—Fashionable hair arrangement. From a portrait by Hopner.

FIGURE 16.—1808—Evening head-dress. From a contemporary portrait.

FIGURE 17.—1806—A scarf of India muslin worn like a turban. From a portrait of the Princess Amelia.

FIGURE 18.—1810—Muslin turban, with the front hair arranged in bow-knot. From a portrait of the Princess Mary.

FIGURE 19.—1806—Head-dress of India muslin. From a portrait by Lawrence.

FIGURE 20.—1805—Head-dress of white mull. From a portrait by St. Memin.

FIGURE 21.—1800—Arrangement of short hair fashionable in the early years of the century. From a contemporary portrait.

FIGURE 22.—1810—Simple arrangement of hair, fashionable at the period. From a contemporary miniature.

A letter on London Fashions for the winter season of 1802 also describes evening dresses worn with hats:

"A dancing frock of white muslin; the train very long, and trimmed round the bottom with black and yellow trimming; over the train a plain drapery trimmed all round to match the train; the back plain, and ornamented with alternate bows of black and yellow; full sleeves of lace and muslin. Small hat of white satin, turned up in front, and ornamented with black and yellow ostrich feathers.

"An opera dress, made of white satin, and trimmed with swansdown. A mantle of the same, trimmed also with swansdown. A hat of black velvet, ornamented with one large ostrich feather." *

During a visit to Paris in 1802 Miss Berry describes a costume of Madame Napoleon Bonaparte: "A smart *demi-parure*, a pink slight silk gown with a pink velvet spot upon it, a small white satin hat with two small feathers, tied under the chin." †
And in England we find fanciful caps were as important an accessory of evening dress as they had been in the time of George I and George II. Some of the descriptions sound very attractive; for instance: "A cap of white lace with a deep lace border; bows of white ribbon on the front and left side. A cap of fine muslin, the front finished with white ribbon; the crown full, and finished on the left side with a long end. A cap of lace, made open behind to show the hair, and ornamented with an ostrich feather. A cap of white satin, ornamented with a small wreath of flowers. A close cap of white satin, trimmed round the front with fancy trimming, and ornamented with flowers. A Parisian cap, made of worked muslin, lined with pink silk; a deep lace border round the front. A cap of lace, drawn up close behind, and finished with

* Port Folio, 1802, Festoon of Fashion.   † Diary and Letters of Miss Berry.

a lace frill; a coquelicot feather (Figure 10) or flower in front"
(Figure 9).

A novelty of the spring of 1802 was the Bonapartian hat.
We read of one made of "salmon-coloured satin, in the form of
a helmet, surrounded with a wreath of laurel," and in Figure
243 a picture of one is given made of white gauze.

Plain white chip hats in the Gipsy style, without
any ornament whatever, tied carelessly under the chin
with coloured ribbon "were popular for a number of years"
(Figure 8).

Among the London modes we find described the "Archer
dress, a petticoat without any train, with a border of green or
blue; a blue or green sarsnet bodice, vandyked at bottom;
loose chemise sleeves, and no handkerchief. The head-dress, a
small white or blue satin hat, turned up in front." We also
learn that "brown, grey, or olive silk stockings, with yellow
or orange cloaks, are worn by the ladies"; that "feathers and
flowers continue to be much worn, and wreaths of roses
on the hair for full dress, in preference to more cumbrous ornaments" (Figure 160); and that small watches "are worn,
by a few dashing belles, on their bosoms, not bigger than the
round of an half guinea."

These were called locket watches and were suspended by a
gold chain from the neck (Figure 9).

Short pelisses (Figure 27) of black lace or of black silk
lined with scarlet or purple, and trimmed all round with fur or
lace, were very much worn (Figure 11).

A note on Parisian Fashions for the same winter (1802)
gives the information that "buff colour satin hats, with
amaranthus colour drapery, are very fashionable;" as are also
"apricot velvet hats, trimmed with amaranthus colour ribbons
with gold stripes, and feathers of the same colour;" and those

of "capucine colour velvet, with ribbons of the same colour, and some of pale blue velvet with blue feathers."

"The head-dresses in hair (Figure 18), which were entirely out of fashion, are again in favour; some ornamented with a polished steel diadem. The caps worn under turbans are generally made of black velvet instead of poppy-colour.

"Morning caps are of white crape and have bands of Chinese ribbon across them. The ends of the ribbons are left very long, and cut in the form of horns." For illustrations of caps see Figures 16, 18, 20, 21, 34, 35, 36, 37, and 38.

From Paris we hear that "silk stuffs are adopted for full dress for the winter, and muslins for undress. The *robes de bals à la Clotilde, à la Hebe, à la Syrène*, the Swiss, Italian and Spanish dresses are all made of these materials." We also learn of an alluring invention in cloaks called *belles douillettes à la Russiene.*

"These cloaks are of three cuts, and three different sorts of wadding according to the needs of the wearer. They are also adapted to different figures, some for slender persons, some for *en bonpoint*, and some for those who are much encumbered with flesh. They are extremely convenient, and find a ready admittance into fashionable society." Apparently nobody of any size could object to them.

Short pelisses and spencers, garments resembling jackets with the skirt cut off, were very popular in all materials and colours from 1800 to 1820 (Figures 11, 27).

"Nine heads" are described in the "Port Folio" for 1802:

1. "A bonnet of blue satin, trimmed round the front with deep black lace, and ornamented with black feathers.

2. "A bonnet of white satin, made open at top to admit the hair, and trimmed all round with chenille trimming; two white feathers in front.

3. " A hat of brown velvet, turned up in front, and lined with yellow ; brown and yellow feathers in front.

4. " A cap of white velvet, spotted with gold, and with gold trimmings.

5. " A bonnet of white satin, and yellow crape, ornamented with a white flower, and with yellow and white ribbons.

6. " A cap of white muslin, trimmed with gold trimming, three white ostrich feathers fixed on the right side to hang in front.

7. " The hair dressed in the present fashion, and banded with gold.

8. " Round bonnet of velvet and trimmed with steel beads, purple feather in front.

9. " Turban of white satin, with a band of muslin round the front, fastened on the left side with a gold loop; gold flower in front."

In the same year (1802) mention is made of two very pretty costumes worn by American ladies at the court of St. James.

" In the beginning of April last, at the queen's drawing-room, Mrs. Derby, of Boston, was presented by Mrs. King, and was much admired for her beauty, and the simplicity of her dress, which was of white crape, and tastefully arranged with wreaths of white flowers and beads.

" Miss Bingham, who was likewise presented by Mrs. King, wore a black crape petticoat richly embroidered with black bugles and beads, bodice and train to correspond. Head-dress, tiara of bugles with diamonds and feathers."

Among the London Fashions a quaint walking dress is described : " A dress of white cambric, made close round the neck with a collar. A spencer of lilac silk, trimmed with lace. Large straw hat, looped up in front with a straw button and tied under the chin with ribbon." Also: " A round dress of sprigged muslin, long cloak of cambric muslin, trimmed all round with lace ; close bonnet, trimmed and ornamented with lilac."

Reticules were so universally carried during the first part of the nineteenth century that they were popularly called " Indispensables," and a few years later ridicules. Miss Southgate describes one in a letter in 1802 : *

" Martha sent me a most elegant Indispensable, white lutestring spangled with silver, and a beautiful bracelet for the arm made of her hair ; she is too good to love me, as she says, more than ever."

Under date of June 18, 1803, the writer speaks of half handkerchiefs as a new fashion :

" I am just going to set off for Long Island and therefore promise but a short letter. I have a mantua maker here making you a gown which I hope to have finished to send by Mrs. Rodman. The fashions are remarkably plain, sleeves much longer than ours and half handkerchiefs are universally worn. At Mrs. Henderson's party there was but one lady except myself without a handkerchief, dressed as plain as possible, the most fashionable women the plainest. I have got you a pretty India spotted muslin, 'tis fashionable here." †

" Mr. Oldschool " is responsible for the following :

" RECEIPT TO MAKE A FASHIONABLE LADY

" Take about eight yards of gingham, or sprig muslin, that is seamed together in the form of a Churchman's pulpit robe. Slip on this easy frock, draw it across the shoulders, girt it round about, and across the middle ; and let the end of it sweep

* A Girl's Life Eighty Years Ago, by Eliza Southgate Bowne.
† *Ibid.*

at least a quarter on the ground. The flowing tresses, which Nature in her luxuriance designed to adorn and cover the shoulders, must be stuffed, powdered, knit at the end, and folded up under the turban *à la mode*, in the exact form of her refrigerating hand weapon. To the many other embellishments of the head-dress must be added a quarter and a half of black or green silk love crape, to defend from the insolence of the sun-beams and render the inhabitant within mosquito proof. Place this figure in a pair of red or blue Morocco slippers, and set her a-walking on the pavement, Phaon by her side, and the work is complete.

" N. B. To make her irresistible she must, at every other step, give her head a toss, smack her lips and turn up her eyes to her beloved country the Moon : making it evident, that she is none of the mean-spirited beings that delight in things below."

The following parody is also from the caustic pen of the editor of the " Port Folio " :

" An Exercise of the Lips
" Moisten your lips
Bite your lips
Open your lips
Close your lips
Pout your lips
Rest your lips."

From the advertisements of that time one gleans many amusing notes. The following is a Philadelphia hair-dresser's announcement for 1802 :

" Ross respectfully informs the ladies that he has on exhibition a most elegant and whimsical head-dress, calculated either for mask balls, full dress, or undress, and may be worn instead of a veil, having the peculiar quality of changing its shape, occasionally covering the whole face, yet capable of being disposed into wandering ringlets; as a mask the disguise is complete without oppression; as a veil it protects without the dull uniformity of drapery, and may be scented to the perfume of any flower; for beauty it cannot be surpassed, and for simplicity it stands unrivalled. The patent was granted by the Goddess of taste, inspired by the spirit of fancy, secured from imitation by the genius of merit, patronized by the votaries of elegance, and exhibited in the temple of fashion."

And this device of a London hair-dresser reminds one very much of the transformation arrangements of the present day:

"Mr. T. Bowman of London, peruke maker, etc., gives a noble specimen of a disinterested spirit, when he tells the ladies that his 'Full dress patent head-dresses are beautifully simple when folded up and fastened with a bodkin; are easily dressed in any style the best head of hair is capable of, and much *superior in beauty.*' Price 6, 8, 10, 12, 15 and *twenty guineas!*"

While on the subject of hair-dressing, it may be well to quote another London advertisement which assuredly promises a great deal:

"To those who are ashamed of red hair, which the Romans thought a beauty, and to those who are ashamed of grey hair, which many think looks venerable, we must recommend the following suggestions by the ingenious Mr. Overton, who seems to contradict the Scripture assertion, 'Thou canst not make one hair white or black':

"To the nobility, gentry, etc. . . . No. 47, New Bond Street, Mr. Overton's, where may be seen specimens of red or grey hair changed to various beautiful and natural shades of flaxen, brown, or black. As many ladies are compelled from their hair changing grey, at a very early period, to adopt the use of wigs, such ladies are respectfully informed that their own

1806-1812

FIGURE 23.—1808—Dress, mantle and gloves from original costume. Bonnet of white straw with full crown of silk and bows of taffeta ribbon.

FIGURE 24.—1806—Hat of fancy straw, with veil.

FIGURE 25.—1806—Turban and earrings.

FIGURE 26.—1808—Sketch of an original gown made of white muslin, embroidered with "Smyrna work" in red and green. Head with muslin turban.

FIGURE 27.—1802—Spencer of black lace. Hat turned up in front and tied under the chin.

FIGURE 28.—1808—Gown of India muslin, embroidered with silver. Head from a portrait.

FIGURE 29.—1812—Back of sage-green pelisse. Hat with feather.

FIGURE 30.—1808—Back view of white satin gown in Figure 56. Head from a portrait.

FIGURE 31.—1805—Hat of fancy straw, turned up in front.

FIGURE 32.—1808—Evening hat.

FIGURE 33.—1808—Gown of white India muslin with stripes of fine drawn-work. The hair curled under a "half-turban" of white mull trimmed with lace, is from a contemporary portrait.

hair may be changed to any shade they choose, in the course of a few hours, by the use of the never-failing tricosian fluid, and such is its permanency, that neither the application of powder, pomatum, or even washing, will in the least alter the colour. It is easy in application, and may be used at any season of the year, without danger of taking cold, being a composition of the richest aromatics, and highly beneficial in nervous headaches, or weakness of the eyes. To convince the nobility, etc., any lady sending a lock of her hair, post paid (sealed with her arms so as to prevent deception), shall have it returned the next day, changed to any colour shown at the places of sale. Sold in bottles at one pound one shilling by Mr. Golding, perfumer to her majesty, Cornhill; Mr. Overton, No. 47, New Bond Street; Mr. Wright, Wade's Passage, Bath, and nowhere else in the kingdom." *

The following squib on the subject of the scanty draperies worn by the most ardent votaries of Fashion, is taken from a Paris journal:

" THE PIN

" Our neighbours, the English, if we may judge from their marriage contracts, are, or at least were, the greatest consumers of pins in the world. Nothing is more usual than for a lady of fashion to be allowed a thousand pounds sterling a year for the single article of pins. Historians relate that in those days when pin-money was first introduced the English ladies consumed a vast number of pins to fasten their clothes. In process of time, however, the consumption of pins has decreased, and in exact proportion with the diminution of drapery. At Paris, God knows, a husband will not be ruined by the expense of pins. Now-a-days, an *elegante* makes almost as little use of a pin as of a needle." †

* Port Folio, July 3, 1802, Festoon of Fashion.   † *Ibid.*

Although bodices were cut very low and displayed a great deal of neck, tuckers or frills of lace were generally worn as we may notice in contemporary portraits, always more reliable sources of the history of dress than the fashion plates. Fans were small at this period (Figure 56). In the " Port Folio " for 1802 appeared this anecdote :

" A finished coquette at a ball asked a gentleman near her while she adjusted her tucker, whether he could flirt a fan which she held in her hand. ' No, Madam,' answered he, proceeding to use it, ' but I can fan a flirt.' "

As will be seen in the illustrations given, there were not any marked changes in the shape and cut of gowns or wraps during the first decade of the nineteenth century, but on the other hand an endless variety of head-dresses, trimmings and accessories followed with bewildering rapidity, and the names it was the fashion to give each innovation would fill a dictionary.

> " Variety is the very spice of life
> And lends it half its charm."

These names are worthy of mention, however, as by means of them the current historical events can be traced even in the pages of a " Magazin des Modes." It was an age of sentiment as well as of variety. Young ladies took great delight in the most romantic and fanciful nicknames. A couplet by Coleridge published in a periodical of 1803 runs :

> " I asked my fair one happy day,
>   What I should call her in my lay ;
>   By what sweet name from Rome or Greece ;
>   Lalage, Neaera, Chloris,
>   Sappho, Lesbia or Doris,
>   Arethusa or Lucrece ?

" ' Ah,' replied my gentle fair,
    'Beloved, what are names but air ?
        Choose thou whatever suits the line ;
    Call me Sappho, call me Chloris,
    Call me Lalage or Doris,
        Only, only call me thine.' "

Trains and round skirts were both worn, but all the gowns were very scanty, the latter measuring scarcely more than two yards at the bottom. (See Figures 5, 12, 51, 53, 54, 56 and 58.) The waists were made with a little fullness in front and cut very low about the shoulders. Guimpes of muslin with or without sleeves were worn on ordinary occasions (Figure 54), also low-necked dresses with long sleeves which could easily be removed, leaving the little puffs or short sleeves on the shoulders. Pin tucks and heavy cords were very much used for trimming. (See Figures 53 and 54.)

The costume of a French " milliner's assistant " given in the initial at the head of this chapter, is taken from an old print of 1804, and shows a bonnet with a high crown tied at one side of the chin, a kerchief knotted round the throat, a low-necked dress with short sleeves, and a very long apron. An English or an American girl of the same class would probably have worn a cape or a spencer covering the arms and shoulders.

Fur was worn too as trimming, and large muffs (Figure 11) of it were carried, not only in winter when they were needed, but they are often seen in many of the early fashion plates from 1800 to 1810 with straw hats and muslin costumes. In the " Port Folio " for 1803 we read :

" The contest between muffs and muslins is at present very severe among the ladies, most of whom condescend to keep their hands warm, though the cold and thin clothing should dye parts of their sweet persons an imperial purple."

Slippers with astonishingly thin soles and no heels (see Figures 3, 11, 26 and 54) were worn to match or contrast with the dress, and the long gloves as shown in Figures 5, 14, 28 and 51 were made of lace, linen, or kid. Veils were long and usually of very delicate lace. Muffs were large and made of beaver, chinchilla and swansdown. Chintz, lace, cambric, tissue, gauze, silk, satin and brocade were alike fashionable and worn as occasion required.

> " If on her we see display'd
> Pendant gems and rich brocade,
> If her chintz with less expense
> Flows in easy negligence."

It is said that " to encourage commerce, Napoleon bade his wife entertain as much as possible, thus setting an example to all those whose means permitted display. Josephine, who delighted in dress as much as ever, although her charms were somewhat dimmed, was only too glad of any pretext for devising new costumes, upon which she spent much time, and no less than a million francs per year. Her budget of expenses, which is not without interest, included in one year three thousand francs' worth of rouge. She paid her hair-dresser a salary of six thousand francs, and ordered in one year two hundred white muslin dresses costing from five hundred to two thousand francs apiece, five hundred and fifty-eight pairs of white silk stockings, five hundred and twenty pairs of dainty shoes, five hundred lace-trimmed chemises at three hundred francs each, two hundred and fifty-two hats, and, after shawls came into fashion, no less than sixty, which cost from eight to ten thousand francs apiece. Strange to relate, however, her wardrobe included but two flannel petticoats, and two pairs of tights for riding. Warmth was supplied by cloth or velvet gowns, which,

as they were low-necked and short-sleeved, were often supplemented by redingotes lined with fur or silk. The fit of gowns
in her day precluded the use of many underclothes, and, aside
from a chemise and corset, Josephine wore nothing but a slip,
even when her upper garment was one of her favourite white
muslins. The shoes and slippers made to match her gowns,
were for ornament more than use, for it is said that when she
once showed her shoemaker some footgear which revealed holes
after one day's wear, he gravely examined them, and justified
himself by exclaiming : 'Ah ! I see what it is. Madame, you
have walked in them !' Josephine also delighted in dainty
wrappers, nightgowns, and caps and her husband once declared
that her night toilet was as elegant as that used by day, and
that she was graceful even in bed."*

The Empire dress was a great favourite in Court circles, not
only in France, but in England, where Napoleon was more
feared than loved. Some very beautiful specimens of this style
may be seen in the South Kensington Museum in London, and
one of blue satin richly embroidered in coloured silks and
crape is on view in Memorial Hall, Philadelphia, which
through the courtesy of Mrs. Harrison we have been permitted
to reproduce in the frontispiece of this volume. The long
heavy trains of this mode were usually of some thick material,
velvet, satin or brocade, while the under-dress was of filmy embroidered gauze, India muslin, or soft finished satin.

The hair was worn in short ringlets over the forehead and
generally parted in the middle and coiled at the back. Although it did not require a great deal of hair for this
arrangement, wigs still continued in favour, to the evident
displeasure of a contributor to the " Evening Fireside," edited
in 1804.

* Empress of France, by H. A. Guerber.

"On Seeing S. L. Dressed in a Fashionable Wig

"As Nature to preserve an equipoise,
Redundant pow'r of principles destroys,
Blending attractive and repulsive might,
And mingling shade (to save our eyes) with light,
So modish dames repell us from the gaze,
And kindly deaden beauty's ardent blaze,
When o'er their charms, contrived in pireous gig,
They spread that monstrous veil y-clep'd a wig—
Had those famed Syrens whose allurments bland
Attracted heroes to the fatal strand,
Had they worn wigs, by modern artists shap'd,
Others besides Ulysses had escap'd . . .
Or when in Eden beauty held the bait
And tempted Adam from his blissful state,
Had round Eve's brows a shaggy wig been curl'd,
Her charms less potent had not lost the world."

Mrs. Smith, formerly Miss Bayard of Philadelphia, writing to her sister Mrs. Kirkpatrick, has given us graphic pictures of society in the United States. In January, 1804, she says:

"Since my last letters, we have been at a large and splendid ball at Mrs. Robert Smith's, a dancing party at Mdm. Pichon's, a card party at Mrs. Galatin's, at Mr. Beckley's and at Mr. Von Ness's, and at the City Assembly. Mrs. R. Smith's was by far the most agreeable. Mrs. Merry (wife of the British Minister) was there and her dress attracted great attention; it was brilliant and fantastic, white satin with a long train, dark blue crape of the same length over it, and white crape drapery down to her knees and open at one side, so thickly covered with silver spangles that it appeared to be a brilliant silver tissue; a breadth of blue crape about four yards long and in other words, a long shawl, put over her head instead of over her shoulders and hanging down to the floor, her hair bound tight to her head with a diamond crescent before and a diamond comb behind, diamond earrings and necklace displayed on her bare bosom.

"I am half tempted to enter into details of our city affairs and personages, but really I shall have to be so scandalous that I am afraid of amusing you at such a risk. But certainly there is no place in the United States where one hears and sees so many strange things, or where so many odd characters are to be met with. But of Madam —— I think it is no harm to speak the truth. She has made a great noise here and mobs of boys have crowded round her splendid equipage to see what I hope will not often be seen in this country, an almost naked woman. An elegant and select party was given to her by Mrs. Robert Smith; her appearance was such that it threw all the company into confusion, and no one dared to look at her but by stealth; the window shutters being open a crowd assembled round the windows to get a look at this beautiful little creature, for every one allows that she is extremely beautiful. Her dress was the thinnest sarsnet and white crape without the least stiffening in it, made without a single plait in the skirt, the width at the bottom being made of gores; there was scarcely any waist and her arms were uncovered and the rest of her form visible. She was engaged the next evening at Madam P.'s. Mrs. R. Smith and several other ladies sent her word if she wished to meet them there, she must promise to have more clothes on. I was highly pleased with this becoming spirit in our ladies."

We suspect that the heroine of this scandal was Madame Jerome Bonaparte, whose scanty draperies are mentioned in many contemporary letters, and whose wedding costume has been already described.

From a letter from Paris dated 1806 the following items are gleaned:

"Square shawls are more in favour than long ones. Few feathers or flowers are to be seen; they have almost entirely

1800–1812

given place to ribbands of various descriptions. Lavender is a new colour and much worn, dove, fawn, pale-pink and blue are the colours at present most admired."

The last mentioned, blue, appears to have been the most favoured colour of all ages. There is something blue in every list of costumes, calling to mind the popular old rhyme:

> " Green is forsaken
> And yellow forlorn
> But blue is the prettiest colour that's worn."

Thistleton Dyer, however, tells us that blue is considered unlucky for a wedding dress in some parts of England, proving that the time-honoured adage that no bride will be lucky who does not wear

> " Something old and something new,
> Something borrowed and something blue "

is not universal.

In the spring of 1806, " large shawls of silk or mohair were much worn, and of various shapes; some in the form of a long mantle, with a hood; others à la Turque; others again square. Loose spencers of pale blue or apple-blossom sarsnet, or of cambric muslin were popular. Pelisses were made of plain nankin and were very appropriate to the season. The most fashionable hats were of yellow straw, with a large rim à la Pamela, ornamented with very broad plain ribbon, or a flower; a sort of bonnet with a small brim of straw, and the crown of white silk, was worn with a riding habit. A lace frill was worn with this costume, round the neck, or a coloured hunting neck-handkerchief." The picture of a riding costume of 1806 is given in Figure 107. It is intended to be made of fine broadcloth, the colour a dark lavender blossom; it has a high rolled collar, lapelled front, deep cape à la pelèrine, a broad belt secured in front with a double-clasp of steel, and a high ruff of double-plaited muslin sloped to a point at the bosom.   Hat of amber coloured velvet, band of same formed in leaves.   Hair in close curls.   Light tan gloves; half-shoes of lavender blossom kid.   Certainly a very dainty creation for the purpose.   Everybody rode on horseback in the first half of the nineteenth century, and every lady had a riding habit, more or less elaborate, as the illustrations in Figures 105–117 show.   They are all taken from contemporary prints.

Riding hats were often trimmed with fur, and in a fashion magazine for 1806 we read : " The latest style for these hats is quite novel; they are made of a fawn-colour, the brims are raised on each side to the height of the shape, and are cut round to resemble a fan."

Pelisses and robes of velvet, cloth and silk were still fashionable.   We read of a pelisse " of dove-coloured velvet, worn loose and open before, embroidered in silk of the same colour down the front, with a running foliage of *vine* or *olive* leaves."

Later in the season bonnets and hats were of straw of different shapes, gracefully turned up in front and lined with various coloured velvets and ornamented with artificial flowers.

Fancy-coloured silk, nankin, and jean shoes, and parasols of white cambric were very generally in use.

The following details are from Paris :

" Silk hats à la *Turban* are generally covered with leno, or fine embroidered muslin ; they are popular and have a neat unobtrusive effect.   The Gipsy hat and cloak is a most distinguished outdoor covering, but suits only women tall in stature and graceful in carriage.   We never recollect a greater variety of fancy cloaks than have been introduced this spring.   The Spanish cloak now gives place to the Grecian scarf, which is exceedingly elegant. Lace and work is introduced as much as ever round the bottom, on the sleeves and up the front of dresses." *

In an English magazine of 1806, a new hat is described as of " fancy straw without any trimming, turned up on the left side immediately over the edge, the rest of the rim slouched. A plain lace veil of the scarf form with a narrow border all around is fastened on the top of the crown with a small antique stud, and left open in front." A picture of this is given in Figure 24.

The ruffs which came into vogue at this time are carefully described in the following extract from a letter from Paris :

" Before I bid you good-night I will endeavour to give you a practical description of the new ruff, now almost indispensable in morning and outdoor costume. (And I beg you to remember, dear Julia, that nothing is considered so vulgar and indecorous as to exhibit the bosom, throat or arms with the above mentioned habiliments.) This ruff has about half an ell of broad lace, fulled into a band of narrow raised needlework, a little larger than the size of the throat. A band of muslin is gathered full on the other edge of the work, about an eighth in depth, and finished with a row of similar needlework at the bottom. The lace, which sits high and straight round the chin, is finely crimped ; and the full muslin, confined by the rows of work, sits in hollow gathers round the throat. When the habit shirt is made without a collar, or with the high morning dress, this elegant ruff is particularly convenient and becoming." (For illustrations of ruffs see Figures 7, 11, 29, 31, 41 and 54.)

" Veils are still very prevalent; as head-dresses they are worn either at the back of the head, or flowing on one side, shading the shoulders (Figure 28), which would be otherwise entirely exposed. The gowns are made high in the bosom, and

* La Belle Assemblée.

low in the back. No trains are to be seen with morning dresses. The bodice of coloured sarsnet, a sort of spencer without sleeves, formed like the plain waist of a gown, with plaited net all round, has a very pretty effect."

Among the variations of Fashion described in 1806 are: " A full-dress lace turban, ornamented with gold-spangled net, an aigrette in front, with a large bow of muslin confining the whole, and a row of gold, intermixed with spangled net, hanging tastefully on one side of the forehead.

" The Circassian straw hat, which has some resemblance to a Gipsy hat, but has a fanciful crown, and is ornamented with lilac, salmon, and other spring coloured ribbands. A half Gipsy straw hat, tied down with yellow or green ribbands, is fashionable. A straw hat for mourning wear in the turban style, embellished in front with primroses, or a bunch of mignonette and yellow roses, and a loose bow of white ribbands."

A simple but attractive walking dress is shown in Figure 14. It consists of " a plain muslin frock, walking length, the front of the bodice and the short sleeves made rather full, the latter gathered with a band and finished with a bow of ribbon. The bonnet is of the cottage shape, the front of straw or chip with a round crown of lavender-blossom silk. A handkerchief of the same silk crosses the crown and is tied in a bow under the chin. Under the bonnet a small round cap with a frill of lace is seen. A sash to match the bonnet trimming is tied in the back under the pelerine, which is made of three falls of finely crimped or plaited muslin. The scarf is of pale green with a narrow variegated border. The long gloves and the half-shoes are of buff kid." With this costume, which is taken from a plate in " La Belle Assemblée " for the summer of 1806, we read that amber earrings were worn. Two fashionable straw bonnets in the summer of 1806 were the conversation (Figure 27) and the cottage (Figure 23) bonnets.

A simple evening dress is described in an English paper: " A French jacket of coloured crape, ornamented with narrow lace, also a trimming of lace round the bottom of the dress; long sash of ribbon tied carelessly on one side, of a colour corresponding with the dress. Front made plain and very high over the bosom, trimmed round with plain double *tulle*. No neckerchief or tucker is necessary with this dress; white kid gloves and shoes." Also a popular walking dress: " A short round frock of nankeen, trimmed round the bottom with sapphire ribbon, binding of the same round the bosom; narrow sash of the same ribbon tied on one side; lace chemissette; nankeen boots or shoes, and a Gipsy hat of silk."

Another letter from Paris says: " Ball dresses, dear Julia, were never more attractive than this spring. Frocks of French net over white satin, painted in natural flowers. Dresses of white Imperial satin, with a silver brocade ribband at the bottom, and French aprons of net or lace, bordered all round, and ornamented at the pocket-holes with Chinese roses. Round train-dresses of Moravian muslin, let in all round with fine footing lace, and fastened up the side with clasps of embossed gold or steel. These dresses, amidst many others, are conspicuous for their taste and elegance. I no longer remark the long sleeve in full dress, except on women who have passed their maturity. I hope, dear Julia, you have never worn the backs of your dresses immoderately low; a correct taste must ever condemn a fashion so disgusting. I am happy to tell you that at the last Opera, and at the Marchioness of D——'s Assembly, the most elegant women wore the backs of their dresses much advanced, or shaded with soft folds of muslin or lace.

" . . . Mary's French coat rivals the primrose hue, while

my Curacoa cloak the violet's shade assumes. Our Gipsy hats, of chip, are decked with wreaths in imitation of these beauteous offspring of the season. We have also hats of satin-straw, for half-dress, with the high tiara front and globe crown, the most novel and elegant article of the kind I have witnessed for many months."

A magazine much used in America makes the announcement for 1806 that "white satin dresses will continue fashionable the whole of the season; ball dresses worked in gold and silver *lamè*, or crape embossed in white or coloured velvets. Silver *chambery* is extremely fashionable and elegant both for turbans and dresses. The most fashionable ornaments are amethyst tiaras and *bandeaux* of velvet. Dove brooches are worn in the front of dresses, with or without other ornaments, and are much admired. Silks of every colour, spotted with white, are prevalent; silk hats and bonnets to correspond are worn with them. An evening dress of *leno*, worked in the Etruscan pattern, is much approved of; the back of this dress is low, drawn full, and is finished with a loose bow of narrow ribband, high in front, and is ornamented with footing lace. Head-dress of white satin, ornamented with flowers. Lace caps are now more universally worn than ever by our most fashionable females; the mob (Figures 35 and 39) has not entirely disappeared, but the small round cap seems to be more admired " (Figure 38).

An English walking costume of 1807 is thus described : " A Polish robe of purple velvet, open in front, rounded gradually from the bottom towards the lappels, which are continued across the shoulder, and finished in regular points on the back. A yoke of the same, with high fur collar; the whole trimmed all around with red fox, mole, leopard-spot or grey squirrel. A rich cord and tassel is attached to the centre of the back, and fastened at the waist in front. The bodice and skirt cut in one and the sleeve fitting close to the arm. Polish cap of the same material, trimmed round the edge and across the crown with fur, a cord and tassels hanging from the right side of the crown. York tan gloves and primrose shoes."

A trimming of spangled velvet is mentioned in the same magazine. "A ball dress of plain crape, over a white satin slip, made dancing length; plain back and sleeves, with quartered front, trimmed round the bottom, on the waist and on the sleeves with a white velvet ribband thickly spangled with gold or lace." In the words of a contemporary authority, "the chemissette, so long and so justly esteemed for its delicacy and utility, is now worn with a double plaiting of Vandyked muslin, forming a very high and stiff frill, which sits close round the throat, and is sloped to a point at the chin;" and the winged ruff is described as "a dignified and fashionable appendage to the evening dress." For short sleeves we learn a Vandyke trimming was preferred, but the crescent sleeve and the full puffed sleeve, formed in three divisions, with bands of lace, needlework, silver, or gold, were alike fashionable.

"The fronts of dresses are generally cut to fit the form," Mrs. Bell, the famous English authority, remarks, "and where the bust is finely turned, we know not of any fashion that can be more advantageous; but to a spare figure we recommend a little more embellishment." Specimens of this style are given in Figures 13, 21, 53, and 54. Round gowns were in 1807 arranged with French gores, so as to have no gathers at the bottom of the waist in front.

Veils, both as head-dresses and on bonnets, were much worn; a figure of one worn with full evening dress is given in Figure 28. The popularity of the veil is proclaimed in the following sonnet:

"THE VEIL*

"Though to hide a sweet face,
With a curtain of lace,
Makes oglers of fashion to rail;
Though our Fair would shine bright
Midst a full blaze of light,
My lines I'll devote to the veil.

"Master Cupid we know,
When he aims a sure blow,
With enchantment of face will assail;
Yet his Godship knows too,
How intense men pursue,
Ev'ry Venus that's deck'd with a veil.

"For the peace of mankind,
It is both right and kind,
Some fair ones their charms shou'd conceal;
Since a pair of bright eyes,
Will, in spite of disguise,
Inflict a deep wound through a veil.

"Now if one roguish beam,
From an eye can inflame,
And to do execution not fail;
What destruction of hearts,
Wou'd be found in all parts,
Did Beauty relinquish her veil!""

Pelisses, usually of cambric and opening down the front, were called "fugitive coats," a revival of the flying Josies popular for morning wear at the close of the eighteenth century. A sketch of one of these graceful garments is given in Figure 13, trimmed with Vandyke edging and embroidery, and worn with a Lavinia hat. The Lavinia hat is a variation of the Gipsy hat, which had been in favour for several years; and was probably named for the rustic heroine in Thomson's "Seasons," of whom the poet says:

* La Belle Assemblée, 1807.

> " He saw her charming, but he saw not half
> The charms her downcast modesty concealed."

The dress in the illustration is of Jaconet muslin made with a gored bodice finished with a tucker of fine embroidery. The cambric pelisse is made with long sleeves which fall over the hand ; the parasol is of silk to correspond with the hat trimmings and breast knot.

The following verses show that the use of rouge was neither universal nor unusual in 1807 :

THE FAIR EQUIVOQUE

> " As blooming Harriet moved along,
> The fairest of the beauteous throng ;
> We beaux gaz'd on with admiration
> Avow'd by many an exclamation.
> What form ! what naiveté ! what grace !
> What roses decked that Grecian face !
> ' Nay,' Dashwood cries, ' that bloom's not Harriet's ;
> 'Twas bought at Reynold's, Moore's, or Mariot's,
> And though you vow her face untainted,
> I swear by Heaven, your beauty's painted.'

> " A wager instantly was laid,
> And Ranger sought the lovely maid,
> The pending bet he soon reveal'd
> Nor e'en the impious oath conceal'd.
> Confused, her cheek bore witness true,
> By turns the roses came and flew.
> ' Your bet,' she said, ' you'll win I ween,
> For I am painted, Sir—*by Heaven.*' "

Although there were not any marked changes in the fashions of 1808, variations in trimmings were innumerable. Imported India muslins embroidered with silver and gold, and sometimes in small sprigs and figures, finished with a deep border of a very rich pattern, were in great favour for ball gowns. The dress in Figure 28 is a very beautiful specimen of silver embroidery on the sheerest mull and was worn over a slip of white satin. It belonged to Miss Lydia Leaming, whose wedding dress is given in Figure 56. The veil in our illustration is of thread-lace arranged after a contemporary print. The hair is parted on the left side and curls hang down over the left cheek. Drop earrings of Roman pearls finish this costume.

Another evening gown made for the same trousseau is pictured in Figure 26. The material is also India muslin, but in this costume the embroidery is of Smyrna work done with a fine chenille thread in green and red. A turban trimmed to correspond represents the popular head-dress as worn in 1808.

Much prettier, however, is the gown in Figure 23 embroidered by Miss Leaming herself. The material is also India muslin, probably imported, and the gloves which are hand-made of white linen must have been a comfortable fashion for a hot summer outing. The bonnet is copied from a print of 1808. It is of straw with a soft crown of white silk and is trimmed with satin ribbon.

The dainty gown in Figure 33 belonged to the same outfit of 1808. The trimming consists of stripes of drawn-work resembling innumerable rows of hemstitching with embroidered edges. The head is copied from a contemporary portrait, the loose, soft curls confined by a half-turban of thin muslin, the ends of which are trimmed with lace, and tied in a becoming knot. This was a favourite head-dress from 1800 to 1810 and may be noticed in many of the portraits by Russell and Sully (Figure 17). In Figure 30 the back view of Figure 56 is given. The head-dress is of blue velvet embroidered with seed pearls, and is taken from a print of 1808.

Little French caps were worn with morning dress (Figures 18, 19 and 20), shading the ears and covering the hair at the back. Bonnets followed the same lines and were trimmed with puffings of either lace or ribbon. (See Figures 23 and 32.) Long sleeves set in at the shoulder were first worn in 1808; also ruffs of scalloped lace with gowns cut high in the back. (See Figure 17.)

"La Belle Assemblée" for November, 1808, gives the following fashions :

"Walking Dress. A round cambric gown, with high fan ruff; a Polish coat with Carmelite mantle, of bright grass-green, or royal purple velvet, trimmed entirely round with ermine, and clasped up the side of the figure with steel or silver. A Shepherdess hat of green velvet, or moss straw, with variegated green feather, and a Chinese tassel. Shoes of black Spanish silk, or pale amber velvet, and gloves of York tan."

"Walking Dress. A round robe of muslin in white or colours. A plain French coat (Figure 59) of merino cloth, or shot sarsnet, the colour bright morone, or crimson, trimmed all round with chenille or fur. A three-quartered Opera tippet of the same. A Village bonnet (Figure 59) of sarsnet or satin, formed in French flutings in front, ornamented with a full bow of appropriate ribband in the centre and tied under the chin with the same. Shoes of grass-green, or morone velvet ; and gloves of grey Limerick."

"The cardinal, or rustic mantle, recommends itself also from its convenience and warmth, and from the graceful negligence of its folds, when wrapt round the figure."

A riding habit for 1808 is described as follows in the same periodical :

"A Spanish Habit or Polish Riding Dress, with the Patriotic helmet; formed of superfine Georgian cloth, or thin kerseymere. Gold buttons and trimmings to correspond. Small French watch, worn on the outside. Plain high cravat of French cambric; collar of the habit sitting close round the throat. Hair in irregular ringlets. Gloves and shoes of lemon-coloured kid." (See Figure 108.)

Miss Austen, writing to her sister in 1808 on the subject of the mourning considered appropriate on the death of a sister-in-law, says: " . . . I am to be in bombazeen and crape, according to what we were told is universal here, and which agrees with Martha's previous observation. My mourning, however, will not impoverish me, for by having my velvet pelisse fresh lined and made up, I am sure I shall have no occasion this winter for anything new of that sort. I take my cloak for the lining, and shall send yours on the chance of its doing something of the same for you, though I believe your pelisse is in better repair than mine. One Miss Baker makes my gown and the other my bonnet, which is to be silk covered with crape." *

Mourning dress at this time was very elaborate and certain rules of etiquette were observed strictly, with subtle distinctions between half and full mourning as well as between full and demi-toilette (see Figures 79 and 80), which must have been an occupation more or less diverting, and, where the grief was not of the heart, probably worked its own cure. Richter's adage, " the only medicine which does women more good than harm is dress," seems especially applicable to the intricacies of the fashionable mourning in the first half of the nineteenth century. Solace might also have been found in the general becomingness of sombre tints. Johnson described Stella's beauty:

> " But brightened by the sable dress
> As virtue rises in distress."

Bombazine is generally associated with crape and very deep mourning, but it appears to have been popular in colours at this

* Letters of Jane Austen.

time, as we often find mention of dresses of white, blue and red bombazine. According to Pope : " A saint in crape is twice a saint in lawn." It must have required considerable self-restraint to be a saint in bombazine of any colour, so irritating to the touch is the surface of that old-fashioned material. Gossamer satin sounds much more soothing and possibly was worn by Serena when she inspired the following verse :

" SERENA, IN A MOURNING DRESS
" So have I seen behind some sable cloud
(Its skirts just tinted with a silver hue)
The queen of planets veiled in lovely gloom,
Such gloom as o'er the saddening landscape sheds
The soft and soothing spirit of the sigh,
Such as the poet courts when fancy's pow'r
Wakes the loved shade of some departed hour,
Breathes in regret's dull ear a soothing strain,
And almost bids past joy be joy again."

Although convention required that only certain materials should be worn in mourning, it was not customary for mourners to seclude themselves, or refrain from social gayeties, for in all the fashion books of the first half of the nineteenth century, plates and descriptions of full dress as well as demi-dress, both in deep mourning and light mourning, are given. From a letter published in an English periodical of 1808, we quote the following elaborate description :

" Amidst the brilliant throng assembled this evening, I was much struck with the beauty and singular appearance of two young women dressed in slight mourning; and who I afterwards found to be the two Misses J——s, who were the reigning belles at Cheltenham and Worthing during the season. Their attire this evening consisted of a round train dress of black gossamer satin, rising to the edge of the throat, where it finished in a kind of neck-band of three rows of fine pearls. A fine silver filagree net extended over the bust in front, somewhat like the bibs worn by the ancients and it was terminated at the bottom of the waist with an elastic band, and large acorn tassels of silver. To these dresses were attached the long bishop sleeves like those already described as chosen by Mary, except that these were of plain French lawn, clearer than any I have ever before seen, and plaited with the utmost delicacy. On their heads they wore turbans of grey *chambery*, thickly frosted with silver; these were fancifully disposed, yet much in the Indian style. But the most attractive part of this interesting costume was a Jerusalem rosary, formed of the beads called Virgin's tears."

The following advertisement appeared in 1808 :

" INVISIBLE DRESSES.—Drawers, Petticoats and Waistcoats made of real Spanish Lamb's Wool.

"Mrs. Morris, late Mrs. Robert Shaw, informs Ladies she has now ready for their inspection an entire fresh and extensive Assortment of her patent elastic Spanish Lamb's Wool Petticoats, Drawers and Waistcoats, all in one, and separate. Articles much approved of for their pleasant elasticity, warmth and delicate colour, will add less to size than a cambric muslin, and warranted never to shrink in the wash. Children's of every size, and made to pattern, at the Original Hosiery, Glove and Welch Flannel Warehouses, No. 400 Oxford Street."

Reading this advertisement now, a hundred years after it appeared, we find a possible explanation of the most perplexing problem of the history of dress. The lamb's wool underwear, like the union suits so universally worn in our day, were invented for warmth, and yet were so close-fitting in shape that they did not interfere with the slim effect of the scanty gowns of sheer muslin and transparent gauze or silk tissue then in vogue.

FIGURE 51.—1800—A wedding gown of sheer India muslin embroidered with silver thread in diagonal stripes. It is very scanty, barely two yards in width and very high in the waist. This dainty little dress was worn by a bride of sixteen, Miss Charlotte J. Rumsey, of Cecil County, Maryland, who married Dr. John Bullus of the United States Navy, in 1800. The head in our picture is copied from a contemporary miniature.

FIGURE 52.—1803—Dress suit. From a contemporary plate.

FIGURE 53.—1804—An afternoon dress of Jaconet muslin. The long sleeves are finished with a puff at the top drawn up by a narrow tape in a casing. The narrow skirt is trimmed with many rows of corded tucks and hemmed in scallops. This very attractive gown was worn in Philadelphia about 1804, but the fashion prevailed for some years. The head is taken from a miniature of the day.

FIGURE 54.—1805—A gown of sage-green China crêpe worn in Philadelphia about 1805. It is brocaded in stripes and has a wide border of the same design on the hem, above which is a group of fine tucks. The head and hat are taken from a print of the same year.

FIGURE 55.—1806—Man in walking dress of 1806. Top-coat of green cloth, showing striped waistcoat, ruffled shirt, folded stock and high collar. A beaver hat with rolling brim, gloves of tan kid and high boots of soft leather complete the costume, which is copied from a contemporary plate.

FIGURE 56.—1808—Taken from an original wedding costume of white satin worn in Philadelphia in 1808. The only trimming is a row of lacing up the front of the bodice, but the dress fastens under the right arm. The reticule is of spangled gauze. The arrangement of the hair is copied from a miniature, being braided and carried in two bandeaux across the head. A photograph of the veil is given in Figure 223, showing the beauty of the lace. The bride was Miss Lydia Leaming, who married Mr. James Smith of Philadelphia.

FIGURE 57.—1808—Dress suit of a gentleman of the period. The blue cloth coat is cut very high at the back. The high rolling collar of the same cloth allows a fine cambric stock and ruffled shirt-front to show above a white satin waistcoat. The short trousers are of buff kerseymere, fastened at one side of the knee with small bows of the same. The stockings are of white silk. The low slippers are of black leather. The hat has a rather wide brim and the gloves are of yellow kid. This costume is taken from a portrait by Sully.

FIGURE 58.—1808—A gown of yellow gauze with a raised spot of velvet which was part of the outfit of Miss Lydia Leaming. The lace scarf, a photograph of which is given in Figure 224, belonged to the same lady. The head is copied from a portrait of 1808.

FIGURE 59.—1805—Back view of a pelisse worn in Philadelphia about 1805. It is of green China silk and lined with pink cambric. The beehive or cottage bonnet is copied from a plate of that year, but was a popular fashion from 1800 to 1812.

1800-51   1803-52   1804-53   1806-54

1806-55   1807-56   1807-57   1807-58   1806-59

We do not read, however, of any similar invention to protect the feet, which it was still the fashion to dress in very thin-soled slippers even for the street. As the season advanced, the ingenious Mrs. Robert Shaw offered another novelty for the requirements of spring, union suits much like those in the advertisements of to-day :

"Invisible India Cotton Petticoats, Drawers, Waistcoats and Dresses all in one.

"Mrs. Robert Shaw respectfully informs those Ladies she had the honour to serve for several years, and Ladies in general, that she has manufactured for the Spring a fresh and extensive assortment of the above articles of real India Cotton ; which articles Ladies will find well worthy their notice ; being of a soft, thin, delicate and elastic texture, will add less to size than a cambric muslin, and warranted never to shrink the least in the wash. Children's of every size and made to pattern, at her Hosiery, Glove and Flannel Warehouse, No. 400 Oxford Street."

A quaint ball dress is given in a Philadelphia magazine for 1808 : " A round robe of India muslin, worn over a white sarsnet slip ; tamboured in a small stripe either in white or colours. The dress formed on the most simple construction, plain back and wrap front, sitting close to the figure ; a plain frock sleeve edged with the antique scollop ; a short train, finished round the bottom in a similar style. Hair brought tight from the roots behind, and twisted in a cable knot on one side, the ends formed in falling ringlets on the other ; with full irregular curls. A full red and white rose, or ranunculus placed on the crown of the head towards one side. Emerald necklace linked with dead gold. Earrings and bracelets to correspond. French kid gloves above the elbow. Pea-green slippers of fancy kid."

We read in the same periodical that "no lady of fashion

now appears in public without a ridicule—which contains her handkerchief, fan, card-money and essence-bottle. They are at this season usually made of rich figured sarsnet, plain satin or silver tissue, with strings and tassels, their colours appropriate to the robes with which they are worn." (See Figures 48 and 56.)

"La Belle Assemblée" for August, 1808, describes the following costumes : "A round robe of white or jonquille muslin made a walking length, with spencer waist, and deep falling lappels, trimmed with lace and edged at the wrist to correspond. A bonnet of celestial blue crape, with jockey or antique front, edged and ornamented with the shell or honey-comb trimming, formed of the same material. Gloves and shoes of pale blue or lemon-coloured kid. Necklace and bracelets of the composition pebble, and earrings of silver filagree of the hoop form. Hair in full irregular curls. Quilted parasol of shaded silk, lined with white satin."

" A round dress of pea-green or lilac muslin, over a white cambric slip ; a short cottage sleeve, plain back and handkerchief front, fastened in a small tufted bow and ends at the centre of the bosom. Provincial bonnet of fine split straw, or moss straw, with band and full bow of folded sarsnet the colour of the dress, terminating in a pendant end on the left side, and finished with a corresponding tassel. A Sardinian mantle, of French net, muslin, or spotted leno, the corners terminating in a full knot. A double high frill around the throat, edged with scolloped lace, tied in front with a ribband."

The following concoctions for the complexion are taken from a periodical of 1808 :

"Saccharine Alum.—Boil white of eggs and alum in rosewater ; make into a paste and mould into the form of small sugar loaves. The ladies use this paste to give greater firmness to the skin."

" Eau de Veau.—Take a calf's foot and boil it in four quarts of river water till it is reduced to half the quantity. Add half a pound of rice, and boil it with crumbs of white bread, steeped in milk, a pound of fresh butter and the whites of five fresh eggs, with their shells and membranes. Mix with them a small quantity of camphor and alum and distil the whole. This cosmetic is one that may be strongly recommended."

So accustomed are we to the advertisements of Pear's soap in all the magazines of our day that it is indeed surprising to read it in a periodical of a hundred years ago. It was introduced as a novelty, and made its first appearance in print, in October, 1808. We quote from " La Belle Assemblée ":

" PEAR'S CELEBRATED SOAP. The Proprietor of this excellent composition is proud to offer it to the notice of the Nobility, Gentry and the Public at large. The virtues of this Soap are almost too many to enumerate; while it possesses the cleansing and purifying properties of other Soap, it is free from those noxious ingredients which are so prejudicial; on the contrary, while it cleanses the skin, it adds a delicacy and beauty indescribable to the face and hands. The Ladies will find it a most agreeable appendage to the Toilette, and in using they will be convinced that it will render the arms inimitably white, equal, if not superior, to the most celebrated cosmetic. One trial is sufficient to evince its agreeable and salutory effects. Sold in Pots at 3 s."

In 1809 women began to wear their bodices longer. Miss Austen in a letter of that year says: " . . . I can easily suppose that your six weeks here will be fully occupied, were it only in lengthening the waists of your gowns." (See Figure 30.)

The editor of an old fashion magazine, referring to the red cloaks or Cardinals which came into vogue before the American Revolution and were popular in the early years of the nine-

teenth century, remarks : " Red cloaks are at length completely abandoned, and we congratulate our lovely readers on
their emancipation from the most despotic dress that ever was
introduced by the whimsical and arbitrary goddess of fashion.
The writer of this article predicted, on their first appearance,
that a colour so disadvantageous to beauty could never become
prevalent."

In the styles of hats and bonnets for 1809 there were a few
changes. Among them we read in " La Belle Assemblée " of
" the Spanish hat in split straw, with the long white drooping
ostrich feather," and of " the Flushing hat; it is of the Gipsy
form, in white chip, with a double or second crown supplying
the place of a cap. This is at once novel, elegant, and
convenient; it is usually worn with a wreath of puffed ribbands
or wild flowers. The Cottage bonnet is still seen, made of
satin, with the crown a little raised and called by some
ingenious milliners the Parisian bonnet. Caps with veils,
ornamented with artificial flowers, are in great favour in morning and evening dress, varying, however, slightly in their form
and texture. Our most matronly belles seem indeed (and we
think very judiciously) to reject the straw bonnet altogether.
Lace and finely embroidered muslin with an intermixture of
satin are unrivalled in the construction of caps, which continue
still to be made close to the head, raised rather more behind
than before."

Among the novelties introduced in 1809 was the Hungarian
wrap. A contemporary description reads: " This graceful garment is usually made of velvet, or brocaded sarsnet, generally
wadded and lined throughout with a corresponding silk ; it has
large loose sleeves ; it hangs loose from the back and shoulders
and is wrapped in folds round the figure."

Long mantles of Devonshire or reddish-brown velvet,

trimmed round with broad leopard skin or chinchilla, and worn with bonnets of the same, were also very fashionable. Sable caps and furs of various qualities are often mentioned ; indeed, skins of every kind were much in request.

Another invention of this period was, " the Grecian sandal in the form of a half-boot, cut out on each side of the lace holes, showing the stocking, made of white kid, bound, laced and embroidered in silver."

In a letter from Paris written in October, 1809, we read : " The newest materials are the striped sarsnets, but imperial bombazines, gossamer gauzes, Italian tiffanies, spotted cambrics and fine embroidered muslins are still much worn in full dress. Shot and figured twill sarsnets remain high in fashionable favour. Scarfs are still popular ; we have noticed several in bright jonquil. The simple pelerine in white tiffany lined with satin and trimmed with swansdown is truly elegant. The round tippet in pink or white satin with handkerchief ends edged with lace or swansdown, crossed over the bosom and tied behind with a bow of ribband, is also very genteel. Mantles of every possible form are still to be seen; the prettiest we have observed has a wrap front attached to the shoulder, and is confined to the figure by a sash passed round the back and brought to tie in a bow before. Morning and walking dresses are still made high in the neck, but with collars of lace meeting in front and trimmed round the throat and wrists with a double row of shell lace. In full or evening dress the backs of gowns are made square and rather high, without lining, let in on the bottom of the waist with an easy fullness ; the bosoms are worn low and shoulders much exposed, the sleeves long and mostly of lace ; trains are still moderate in length ; the favourite sash is of ribband tied on the left side with small bows and long ends.

" Lace caps or combinations of lace and satin have taken the place of straw bonnets." A very striking cap is described in the same letter. " It is of oriental silk fastened under the chin by a Turkish handkerchief caught in a rosette at the right side, ornamented with a demi-tiara of Indian feathers." Another creation is described of " pink satin and lace with a cone-shaped crown, the front of alternate stripes of lace and ribband. It is tied in a careless bow on the right, and a small full wreath of heath is placed under the brim in front."

Another invention in shoes, and a rival to the Grecian sandal, was the " high shoe " in white kid bound and laced with a coloured ribbon. Gloves were made in straw, stone colour, and bloom-pink as well as in white. Necklaces in amber, sapphire, topaz, pearl and gold, with drop earrings to correspond were much worn.

The foreign names which it was the popular fancy to give to each article of apparel as it appeared, were carried to excess about 1809, and in an old paper of that year, we find the following satirical comment :

" Mr. Adair's treaty with the Sublime Port will doubtless introduce amongst our spring fashions a profusion of Turkish turbans, Janizary jackets, mosque slippers, and a thousand similar whimsicalities; all of which (provided a northern coalition be accomplished) must speedily give way to Russian cloaks, Hussar caps, Cossack mantles, Danish robes, etc., etc., so that by the setting in of the dog-days our ladies will stand a chance of being arrayed in the complete costume of all the shivering nations of the north. Such is the capricious system introduced and acted upon in the empire of the despotic Goddess of Fashion."

Women's Dress

1810–1820

"My love in her attire doth shew her wit,
    It doth so well become her,
    For every season she has dressings fit,
    For Winter, Spring and Summer."
                                        —ANONYMOUS.

N 1810 we remark a few noticeable changes. According to "La Belle Assemblée," "the dresses of all descriptions are made fuller, which is undoubtedly a great improvement, it gives ease and play to the figure. Coloured muslin pelisses of a very transparent texture are very fashionable, the colours of every kind of dress are of pale and undecided hues, gay colours at this season would appear gaudy. A new kind of hat has just appeared, made in white whalebone, which has all the delicacy of chip and from its transparent quality, has the appearance of being lighter; we have observed several coloured chips and straws, and have also remarked that they are very unbecoming, as well as inconvenient, being difficult to adapt to every kind of dress; a mixture of ribband and straw is surely to be preferred " (Figure 48).

The following description of an evening full dress in 1810 is quoted from a popular authority : " A pale blue gossamer silk

87

60   G.W.T. 1907. After Pri.

61   G.W.T. 1907 After Print.

62   G.W.TROUT 1907

63   C.W. TROUT 1907

64   G.W.T 1907 After Print.

65   S.B. STEEL. 06 after a print.

dress, worn over a white satin slip, made with short train, opening up the front and tied with small bows of white satin ribband; long sleeves of pale blue gossamer net, and the same
shade as the gown, caught down on the outside of the arm with
small pearl brooches, the tops of the sleeves and bosom of the
dress bound with silver edging, and trimmed with Valenciennes
lace; the bottom of the skirt and train are trimmed with a silver edging, a little above which is laid a rich Valenciennes lace,
on the head is worn a bandeau of pearls, fastened in a knot on
the right side, with a Bird of Paradise plume. The hair in
rather short full curls over the forehead, and curled in light
ringlets on the right side of the neck. A scarf of pale buff silk
(ornamented at the ends with white silk tassels) is worn fancifully over the figure and confined in a pearl ring. Pearl earrings, shoes of pale buff satin, yellow kid gloves."

The English fashion books for August, 1810, record the following attractive costumes : " A lemon-coloured sarsnet dress,
trimmed with an embroidery of roses: a white lace drapery
with train, fastened down the front with topaz snaps ; a richly
embroidered scarf is thrown carelessly across the shoulders.
Topaz necklace and earrings. The hair in loose ringlet curls,
divided by an ornamental comb. Gloves and shoes of white or
lemon-coloured kid. A bouquet of natural flowers."

" Promenade Walking Dress.—A plain cambric morning
dress, made high in the neck, with short train, let in round
the bottom with two rows of worked trimming. A pelisse of
green sarsnet, made to fit the shape, trimmed round with a narrow fancy trimming fastened with a gold brooch, and confined
round the waist with a girdle of the sarsnet with a gold clasp.
A Lavinia unbleached chip hat, tied down with a broad white
sarsnet ribband, a small white satin cap is worn underneath,
with an artificial rose in front. The hair is dressed in full

curls. A plaid parasol, with York tan gloves, green silk sandals." A picture of the Lavinia hat is given in Figure 13.

A new fashion in 1810 was the walking shoe of brocaded silk, or embroidered satin. A pair of the latter may be seen in the South Kensington Museum (London) of black satin embroidered in coloured flowers, laced up the front. They have leather soles and no heels. Walking shoes of nankeen and sandals of jean bound with coloured ribbon were popular, while the newest slippers for evening wear were of white satin trimmed with silver or made of silver brocade. Light delicate colours were especially fashionable at that time, the favourites being pale blue, pink, buff, lavender, straw, lilac and yellow. White satin tippets interlined with wadding and edged all round with white swansdown, were popular for chilly days. Later in the season a mantle of white bombazine lined and bound with pale green is mentioned as a novelty, and white satin caps turned up in front with two small ostrich feathers, also lace hoods trimmed with small bunches of flowers and fastened under the chin, were introduced in the autumn of 1810.

In the same year we read of a variation in gowns which sounds very much like the Princess dress so fashionable a year or two ago. "Dresses are made tight to fit the shape without a band, buttoned from the neck to the feet with small raised buttons." A few illustrations may be seen in the fashion plates of that year, and there is a well-known portrait of Marie-Louise arriving at Compèigne in a similar costume, but it does not appear to have been a very popular fashion.

We read with pleasure that " skirts are increased in width ; they must no longer cling but hang lightly on the figure." Morning dresses were made high in the neck and finished with a standing ruffle and with long sleeves. Dinner gowns were worn both high and low according to the taste of the wearer and were usually made with moderate trains.   Dancing frocks were invariably short and on entering a ballroom one could tell at a glance which ladies expected to dance that evening.

During Jefferson's two administrations, 1801–1809, life at the capital was marked by a modest simplicity.   Under the genial sway of the wife of Mr. Madison, who took up her abode at the White House in March, 1809, her biographer, Mrs. Goodwin, says: "Dress grew gayer, entertainments more elaborate, and when the President's wife took the air it was in a chariot built by Fielding of Philadelphia at a cost of fifteen hundred dollars."   In her daily home life, however, we read that this lady wore a "stuff dress protected by a large housewifely apron with a linen kerchief pinned about the neck."   At that period ladies of fashion everywhere made use of rouge and pearl powder. Speaking of this practice a contemporary letter mentions: "Mrs. Madison is said to rouge, but it is not evident to my eyes, and I do not think it is true, as I am well assured I saw her colour come and go at the Naval Ball when the Macedonian flag was presented to her by young Hamilton."   There are several portraits of Mrs. Madison from which we can judge for ourselves of her style of dress.   The most familiar is probably the half length painting by Wood in a turban (Figure 41).   Almost equally well known is another, in a simple white muslin gown, with low neck and short sleeves, the hair simply parted and curled on the temples.   A very attractive miniature by Peale taken before her marriage to Mr. Madison, is reproduced in Miss Wharton's "Social Life in the Early Republic."   The quaint cap with high puffed crown in the portrait is very becoming.

On the occasion of one of the state balls in Washington Mrs. Madison is described as wearing a stately gown with a long train of buff velvet, and a turban of the same colour ornamented with a Bird of Paradise.

The period known as the "Regency" in English history, covered the years from 1810–1819 and was distinguished from the first decade of the century by an almost lavish extravagance in social life and costume. Brighton was the centre of gayety and the famous dinners and suppers of the Prince Regent were notoriously expensive. There are many portraits of the beautiful Mrs. Fitzherbert, who for a time set the fashions for the London world.

The most noticeable changes in 1811 were in the bonnets and hats which were worn much larger than before, the brims being lined with a bright colour to correspond with the trimming. Full frills of lace were worn on the edge of some of the most fashionable bonnets and hung down over the forehead (Figure 75). Lace was used in great profusion at that period and several different kinds of this beautiful trimming were worn on one costume. Mechlin lace was perhaps the favourite, but Brussels, English Point and Valenciennes were all popular. There were many varieties of pelisses in fashion, but the close wrapping kind "was universally adopted for cold weather." They were wadded throughout and lined with a contrasting colour of soft cambric for in the "good old days" silk linings were not considered essential (Figures 96 and 98). Frogs of sewing silk called Brandenburghs were used to fasten the pelisses down the front, and they were very often trimmed with fur. Shoes of white Morocco are mentioned among the novelties of 1811, also Kemble slippers. Roman sandals vied in popularity with the Grecian sandals of the preceding year, but the exact point of difference is hard to discover. Nets, muslins, gauzes, and crapes were still the favourite materials for gowns, but we read also of evening dresses of satin and velvet. Jonquille and amber were the most fashionable colours. Many new hats are mentioned in the magazines of

London and Paris, among them the Comet hat which we are told was considered very stylish for carriage wear. In Figure 47 a sketch is given of a Spanish hat of purple velvet with a white ostrich plume and an ermine tippet, taken from a contemporary print. The Buonapartian hat of gauze trimmed with a wreath of laurel in Figure 243 is from a plate of 1811. The Cavalier's hat trimmed in front with a large ostrich feather and the Pilgrim's hat of Carmelite brown cloth or velvet with an ornament in the shape of a cockle-shell. Dress-caps made of lace or silk and lace combined were worn by young and old with evening dress. A new creation was the Devonshire mob with a point on the forehead and usually made of fine Brussels lace. It was worn very much on one side with the hair in full curls on the exposed side. On ordinary occasions the hair was dressed with great simplicity, generally in soft curls held in place by a comb. For full dress, flowers, feathers, dress-caps and turbans, still in popular favour, were worn. In a September magazine of that year (1811) we read of a new bonnet made of India muslin with a cone-shaped crown and trimmed with a bow of lace on top, around the face a deep frill of Mechlin lace, and the bonnet lined throughout with a bright sea-green sarsnet (Figure 75); but the greatest innovations of fashion were the short kid gloves which suddenly superseded the long gloves so many years considered indispensable with short sleeves. Gowns made with close-fitting fronts were preferred and were cut rather higher in the back than the front. The very short Grecian waists of 1800–1802 were temporarily revived by the ultra-fashionable. The sleeves were usually short and the skirts a trifle wider at the bottom measuring about three yards. In some of the dresses of that date we find the front breadth slightly gored at the waist.

Gold chains were in great vogue and a number of rings and

bracelets in every possible device were worn. A single string of large pearls fastened with a diamond clasp was much admired, but emeralds and garnets were considered especially becoming to the complexion. Watches were still worn in locket fashion, but they were smaller than they had ever been.

"La Belle Assemblée" describes nankeen pelisses with an undervest of blue satin or sarsnet, to be worn at fêtes champêtres. Morning dresses, it seems, were made in the pelisse shape, buttoned down the front with small raised buttons, or with an apron front and stomacher let in and laced across like a peasant's bodice, with coloured ribbons, and others again with a short jacket trimmed with lace. Spencers and mantles edged with lace also and large squares of lace were worn over the shoulders. Dinner dresses were made low in front and high in the back, and in the following description of an evening gown in a London periodical we notice that long sleeves are mentioned: "A gown of plain white India muslin, made loose in the neck, with long sleeves, and short train trimmed with a fancy border of stamped leaves in satin. A white satin cap, ornamented with crimson or morone coloured floss silk trimming. A short Persian scarf of morone coloured silk, with rich border and tassels, is fancifully worn over the shoulders. Amber necklace and earrings. Hair in full curls, divided rather towards the left side. Gloves and shoes of white or morone kid." Another evening costume mentions slippers with very pointed toes and instead of the newest fashion of short gloves, long ones, "à la Mousquetaire, with many wrinkles."

"A gossamer satin robe of French grey or celestial blue, with a demi-train; stripes of white lace let in the cross way of the skirt, and relieved by a very narrow border of black velvet; a broad lace Vandyke pattern round the bottom; short sleeves fastened up in front by a row of pearls. A lace tippet, à la Duchesse d' Angoulême, edged with a border of Vandyke lace. The hair in soft curls next the face, à la Greque; head-dress composed of plaited braids of hair and pearls, surmounted with a large red cornelian ornament, set round with small pearls; the back hair arranged in a knot and surrounded with a row of pearls; necklace also of pearls in two rows. Drop earrings, each composed of one entire pearl, which should be large. A square cornelian brooch, set in gold, with a drop pendant of pearl to match the earrings. Long tippet of swansdown. White kid gloves, wrinkled so as to cover very little of the arm, below the elbow. Slippers of kid the colour of the gown, the toes more pointed than usual, with small pearl or white bugle rosettes."

A simple every-day costume of 1812 is given at the head of the chapter, taken from a gown of white corded muslin striped with yellow, which was worn in Philadelphia. The bodice and sleeves are cut on the bias of the material and the round skirt is trimmed with two bias ruffles.

In 1812 a Pamona hat of green satin is described as a novelty. It was turned up in front and drooped low on each side of the face, not unlike the hat in Figure 31, which was a shape popular for several years. A new morning dress came into great favour at this time. It is thus described by a contemporary authority: "The most fashionable dishabille is the York morning dress. It is made up to the throat; the body is composed of alternate stripes of muslin and lace, cut in a bias form; round the throat a rich lace ruff, and the sleeves edged with a very fine narrow lace; it is buttoned up the back and has a demi-train without any trimming." Another popular morning dress is announced in an English magazine: "The Russian wrapper, of twilled stuff, is a very neat morning dress, and begins to be a favourite; it is made quite tight to the

1810–1824

FIGURE 66.—1817—Fashionable carriage costume. From a portrait of Princess Charlotte, by Chalons.

FIGURE 67.—1810—Court dress. From a portrait of Mrs. John Quincy Adams, by Leslie.

FIGURE 68.—1820—Carriage costume. From a contemporary portrait.

FIGURE 69.—1818—Street dress. From a portrait of Queen Charlotte.

FIGURE 70.—1824—High comb and turn-over collar. From a miniature.

FIGURE 71.—1820—Street costume. From a portrait of Queen Charlotte.

67

68

66

70

71   69

shape and wraps over on one side very much; it is fastened down the front with small silk buttons to correspond with the dress; a trimming of swansdown goes round the throat, down the side which wraps over, and also round the bottom of the dress, which is made walking length; long sleeves edged also with swansdown."

Figure 111 shows a fashionable riding habit of 1812 of bright green cloth ornamented down the front and on the cuffs *à la Militaire* with black braid. The small riding hat is of black beaver trimmed with a gold cordon and tassels and a long green ostrich feather. The half-boots are black, laced and fringed with green, and the gloves are York tan. As this sketch is taken from the famous English magazine of fashion, it may have been followed by Lady Caroline Lamb, who we are told had just returned from her daily ride in the park, heated and dusty from exercise, when Lord Byron called upon her for the first time. She rushed to her room, "to clean herself" as she expressed it, and returned radiant in a fresh toilet.

The back view of another riding dress is given in Figure 109. It was made of the fashionable Georgian cloth (a light-weight broadcloth) and trimmed with frogs. A hat of green velvet and white fur, buff kid boots and gloves completed the costume.

A series of letters published in the " National Intelligencer " at Washington, during the administration of President Madison, puts us in touch with the fashionable life in America. Under the date, November 12, 1812, we read an enthusiastic description of the President's wife: " . . . I would describe the dignified appearance of Mrs. Madison, but I could not do her justice. 'Tis not her form, 'tis not her face, it is the woman altogether, whom I should wish you to see. She wears a crimson cap that almost hides her forehead, but which becomes her extremely, and reminds one of a crown from its brilliant appear-

ance contrasted with the white satin folds of her dress, and her
jet black curls ; but her demeanour is so far removed from the
hauteur generally attendant on royalty that your fancy can
carry the resemblance no further than the head-dress." *

This " crimson cap " was of the shape popularly called a
turban. A portrait of Mrs. Madison is given in Figure 41, in a
similar coiffure. One of these letters describes a dinner given
on board the " Constellation," that famous old war-ship which
is still preserved at the training station at Newport, and proves
that fashions have changed very much in ships as well as in dress
during the last hundred years : ". . . Some days ago in-
vitations were issued to two or three hundred ladies and gentlemen, to dine and spend the day with Colonel Wharton and
Captain Steward on board the ' Constellation,' an immense ship
of war. This, of all the sights I have ever witnessed, was the
most interesting. . . . On reaching the deck we were ushered
immediately under the awning composed of many flags, and
found ourselves in the presence of hundreds of ladies and gentlemen. The effect was astonishing : every colour of the rainbow,
every form and fashion, nature and art ransacked to furnish gay
and suitable habiliments for the belles, who with the beaux in
their court dresses, were gayly dancing to the inspiring strains of
a magnificent band. The ladies had assumed youth and beauty
in their persons, taste and splendour in their dress ; thousands
of dollars having been expended by dashing fair ones in preparation for this fête. . . . At the upper end of the quarter-
deck sat Mrs. Madison, to whom we paid our respects, and then
participated in the conversation and amusements with our
friends, among whom were Mrs. Munroe, Mrs. Gallatin, etc. I
did not dance (though 'twas not for want of asking) being
totally unacquainted with the present style of cotillions, which

* By Mrs. Seaton.

were danced in the interstices, that is, on a space four feet square. There was more opportunity to display agility than grace, as an iron ring, a coil of rope, or a gun-carriage would prostrate a beau or belle."

In another letter (January 2, 1813) Mrs. Seaton mentions the gay and youthful dressing of ladies who had reached the advanced age of fifty. Alack! History sometimes repeats itself!

"The assembly was more numerous at the Secretary of the Treasury's, more select, more elegant, than I have yet seen in the city. Ladies of fifty years of age were decked with lace and ribbons, wreaths of roses and gold leaves in their false hair, wreaths of jasmine across their bosom, and no kerchiefs! Indeed, dear mother, I cannot reconcile this fashion to myself, and though the splendid dress of these antiquated dames of the *beau monde* adds to the general grandeur, it certainly only tends to make the contrast still more striking between them and the young and beautiful. . . . Madame Bonaparte is a model of fashion, and many of our belles strive to imitate her ; . . . but without equal *éclat*, as Madame Bonaparte has certainly the most transcendently beautiful back and shoulders that ever were seen. . . . It is the fashion for most of the ladies a little advanced in age to rouge and pearl, which is spoken of with as much *sang froid* as putting on their bonnets."

In all the fashion books of that time we find frequent mention of the Regency wrapper, a morning dress which was long and close fitting, and laced up the front with a silk cord. It was richly trimmed with velvet or sealskin, and finished at the throat with a collar cut in points. The sleeves were long and tight and trimmed with epaulets. Another popular garment was the Regency mantle, which was generally of cloth with a small round cape and high collar trimmed with bias folds of velvet or satin edged with a narrow cord. One of these mantles is described in " La Belle Assemblée " (1813) of black cloth trimmed with apple green satin.

The costume in Figure 44 shows the popular Regency hat of velvet trimmed with sealskin. The high crown was large at the top and a long ostrich plume was fastened at the right side, brought across the crown and drooped over the left ear. A gold buckle ornaments the brim in front. Worn with this hat was the Regency jacket of cloth trimmed with narrow bias folds and edged with sealskin and the long sleeves with epaulets which were apparently the chief distinction in the Regency garments. Of course there was a Regency ball dress too. This was a frock of velvet, satin or satin-cloth trimmed around the bottom and up the fronts with a bias fold of satin or velvet edged with narrow silk fringe. Epaulets of satin and fringe were worn on the shoulders, and the long sleeves fastened in front of the arm with three small buttons.

A London correspondent for a contemporary magazine says : " Everything now takes its name from our beloved Regent ; hats, caps, dresses, mantles, in short all the paraphernalia of a well-dressed belle is distinguished by that appellation, and so various are the habiliments which have no other name, that we were not surprised at hearing a young lady from the country inquire the other day of a fashionable dressmaker at the west end of the town, who had been showing her a variety of head-dresses, ' Pray, after all, which of these is the real Regency cap ? ' "

We trust the picture in Figure 45, taken from an unimpeachable authority, may prove satisfactory to our readers : " A Regency cap of white lace, with a small front turned up all round, and what was formerly termed a beef-eater's crown of lace drawn very full ; three ostrich plumes are affixed to the right side of the crown, and a twisted rouleau of satin ornaments the front."

The unfortunate Princess Caroline also had a bonnet named for her. The description is most attractive : It was made of " white satin with a round crown, the front turned up a little on one side; at the other a small white lace cap was just visible. The edge of the front was finished with a rich silk trimming, of the palest pink and a very long pale pink feather fell over to the left side." A contemporary authority says, " Nothing can be more elegant than this bonnet, which is also the most generally becoming thing that we have seen."

The Cossack hat was also very fashionable ; it was made of white satin too, but the shape was a helmet crown and the front, which turned up all round, was sloped a little in the middle, and was edged with pearls ; it was finished with a small white feather, placed rather to the side.

For every-day wear cottage bonnets were still in favour, and riding hats which were of plain straw of the same shape as the gentlemen's, were adopted for walking dress also (Figure 113). They were sometimes trimmed with a figured ribband with a bow in front, while the cottage bonnets were appropriately trimmed with flowers. As we notice in the following description of a walking dress in "La Belle Assemblée" for June, 1813, bodices were again worn very low and full, and the skirts were again narrower, a revival of the fashion prevalent from 1800–1810.

" Short dress of jaconet muslin, made rather scantier in the skirt than they have been worn, and cut down as much as possible all round the bosom and back of the neck. The body full, but drawn in at the top of the back, which is ornamented with a white silk button and confined to the waist by a girdle of rich white figured ribband, a jacket of the same materials as the gown, fastened to the waist by a white silk button. Over this our fair pedestrians throw a sky-blue scarf, bonnet of white willow-shavings, ornamented with a flower and wreath of sky-blue, and tied under the chin with a ribband to correspond. Hair dressed in very loose curls on each side of the temple, and parted in front. Gloves and sandals of sky-blue," and to complete the colour scheme " a parasol also of sky-blue silk, trimmed with a deep fringe to match."

In the winter of 1813 we read of a "high dress for walking, of ruby merino cloth, made very tight to the shape and the waist rather longer than last season. Made up to the throat, without a collar: buttoned in front from the throat to the waist, and finished at the waist by a broad band of rich fancy ribband of a very dark bottle green shot with ruby; two rows of the same ribband go around the bottom of the dress, which is made walking length. A long sleeve, easy but not very wide, is finished by a cuff of the same ribband. The throat was also finished with a binding of ribband and displayed a rich lace shirt with a collar also of lace put on quite plain. White satin cap, with a rich broad lace quilling in front, and tied under the chin by a white lace handkerchief. A white lace veil reaching to the shoulders was thrown carelessly over the cap. With this costume were worn York tan gloves, and black kid half-boots."

Another striking garment was the Kutusoff mantle, made of pale pink or scarlet cloth, trimmed with a broad velvet ribband to correspond, a spencer of the same material, one sleeve of which was concealed by the folds of the mantle; the collar, which was high and puckered, fastened at the throat with a broach; and a long lappel, ending in a point fell over the left shoulder. A Kutusoff hat to match turned up in front, with a little corner to the right side, tied under the chin, and was finished with a pink or scarlet feather; a full puffing of lace or net was seen underneath * (Figure 81).

The Rutland poke was a popular variation in bonnets; of white satin, edged with swansdown, and wadded and lined with white sarsnet, the front was cut in points, and tied under the chin with a soft white ribband; an ostrich feather of a colour corresponding with the pelisse or mantle was placed very much on one side.

Miss Austen wrote from Bath in 1813, on the subject of caps, to her sister: ". . . Miss Hare had some pretty caps, and is to make me one like one of them, only *white* satin, instead of blue. It will be white satin and lace, and a little white flower perking out of the left ear, like Harriet Byron's feather. I have allowed her to go as far as £1 16 s. My gown is to be trimmed everywhere with white ribbon plaited on somehow or other. She says it will look well. I am not so sanguine. They trim with white very much." † And we read in one of the authorities of the day that "lace caps are universal for full dress, although turbans have not lost their popularity." Among other novelties the "Wellington hood" seems to have been a lace cap made full at the temples and ornamented with a sprig of geranium in front but suggests neither in style nor colour the name of the great warrior. Much more worthy of its name is the Wellington mantle, which is described as follows: "A piece of cloth about three yards in length, and one in breadth, entirely bias, which makes it hang very gracefully, and sloped at each end to a point; the cape is formed like a half handkerchief and the collar which is about an eighth of a yard deep falls a little over it. The mantle is drawn in with a slight fullness to the waist and forming a sort of jacket in the back; it is usually made of slate colour or brown cloth; and

* La Belle Assemblée.   † Letters of Jane Austen.

1832–1838

FIGURE 72.—1834—Wedding dress of white gauze over satin, worn by a Quaker bride in Philadelphia. Head from a portrait of the day.

FIGURE 73.—1832—Yellow brocade trimmed with folds of the same material, worn by Miss Mary Brinton, of Philadelphia. Head from a contemporary portrait.

FIGURE 74.—1838—Dress of pale pink satin, sleeves trimmed with blonde lace, part of the wedding outfit of Miss Mary Brinton, of Philadelphia. Head from portrait of the day.

FIGURE 75.—1833—Dress of blue-green taffeta, with puffed sleeves and cape trimmed with pipings of the silk. Head from a contemporary print.

its principal attraction is the trimming which is a very rich embroidery of laurel leaves in coloured silks ; the effect is really beautiful."

An attractive half-dress is given for February, 1813 :

" Plain frock of amber satin-cloth, shot with white, and ornamented round the bosom and the waist with a rich white silk trimming, called frost work ; it is the lightest and most elegant trimming we have seen for some time, and is universally worn ; a double row of this trimming crosses the breast. The back, which is plain and very broad, is ornamented with pearl buttons, or small silk ones to correspond with the trimming. White lace sleeves, made very full, fastened about the middle of the arm by a broad band of ' letting in ' lace [insertion] and drawn up by two buttons near the shoulder, while the fullness which falls near the bottom is confined by one; plain demi-train." *

In the year 1814, Napoleon having given up the fight for a time and retired to Elba, the English people of fashion hastened to Paris, and a wag of the day expressed his sentiments in this couplet :

" London now is out of town,
    Who in England tarries,
  Who can bear to linger there
    While all the world's in Paris ?
  Mrs. Brills is full of ills,
    Nothing can improve her,
  Unless she sees the Tooleries,
    Or waddles thro' the Louvre ! "

Later the Emperor of Russia went over to London with his sister the Duchess of Oldenburg who introduced a novelty in bonnets which was immediately named after her. This bonnet was long and narrow, projecting far over the face, and was ridiculed by a contemporary comic singer.

* La Belle Assemblée.

" Then the ladies their dresses are equally queer,
They wear such large bonnets their face can't appear,
It put me in mind, don't think I'm a joker,
Or a coal-scuttle stuck on the head of a poker."

The sketch of the Oldenburg bonnet given in Figure 43 is copied from a portrait of the Duchess at the time of her visit.

Dear Miss Austen gives us some interesting items of the fashions in England, in her letters of 1814. Of an alteration in the shape of stays she says : " I learnt from Mrs. Tickars's young lady, to my high amusement, that the stays now are not made to force the bosom up at all ; *that* was a very unbecoming, unnatural fashion. I was really glad to hear that they are not to be so much off the shoulders as they were."

The fashion of using ribbon for trimming, and the comfortable feeling of having a suitable dress, which has doubtless found an echo within many a pair of stays, are expressed in an extract from another letter of the same year : ". . . I have determined to trim my lilac sarsnet with black satin ribbon just as my China crape is, 6d. width at the bottom, 3d. or 4d. at top. Ribbon trimmings are all the fashion at Bath, and I dare say the fashions of the two places are alike enough in that point to content *me*. With this addition it will be a very useful gown, happy to go anywhere."

The following extract mentions a gown with long sleeves, about which Miss Austen expresses some doubt : ". . . I wear my gauze gown to-day, long sleeves and all. I shall see how they succeed, but as yet I have no reason to suppose long sleeves are allowable. I have lowered the bosom, especially at the corners, and plaited black satin ribbon round the top. . . . Mrs. Tilson had long sleeves too, and she assured me that they are worn in the evening by many. I was glad to hear this."

Mrs. Bell, the celebrated London modiste, made a happy hit when she invented an evening crush hat for ladies. It is eloquently announced in her magazine for January, 1814:

" A Lady's Chapeau Bras.—A most novel and ingenious Ladies' head-dress will make its appearance, *for the first time*, on Thursday, February 3d. It is a *Lady's Chapeau Bras*, an original and unrivalled head-dress of Millinery, and combines the following most important advantages :—*Elegance*, from the originality of its form, and the beauty of its materials. Secondly, *Convenience*, as it is adapted to be worn *over the head-dress of Ladies*, without the hair or any part of the dress being in the least deranged when the *Chapeau Bras* is removed from the head. Thirdly, it is made so that it may be taken off previous to entering a room, or public place of resort, and carried *in the hand* or *under the arm*, with as little inconvenience as a pocket-handkerchief; in truth, with no inconvenience whatever. It has also the additional advantage that a Lady *may walk full dressed along the streets without being conspicuous*. The idea suggested itself to the Inventress from the numberless inconveniences ladies are subjected to when full dressed from the want of a proper covering for the head-dress, in going to routs, operas, plays, etc., etc. By this original and elegant preserver of *Ladies' head-dresses*, the health will be preserved, and the dangerous effects of colds will be prevented. In short the *Ladies' Chapeau Bras* will be found a *desideratum* in Ladies' costumes, and requires only to be seen to be approved. Ladies in the country can be supplied with the *Chapeau Bras*, on commissioning a friend in London ; its form being generally adapted to all complexions and sizes."

This convenient head-covering was made like the calashes of the previous century, on wires run through cases.

The Oldenburg dinner dress, named by Mrs. Bell, in honour

of the distinguished visitor, was a " white satin slip, decorated round the bottom with a rich white lace, and headed with pearl trimming.   Over the slip is a short Russian robe of white crape open front, edged with a rich pearl trimming to correspond with the slip ; the wreaths which ornament the robe are formed of pearls also, to correspond.   The back is made full, and the waist very short.   Long sleeves of crape trimmed with pearl bands at regular distances.   Small lace cap, decorated with pearls, and finished with tassels to match ; a fancy flower is placed to the side."   " The form of this cap " we learn " is extremely elegant, exquisitely tasteful, and becoming."   Also that " a white satin *Chapeau Bras*, ornamented with a spread eagle on the crown, worked in chenille, is indispensable." With this costume the hair should be worn in loose ringlets in front, and twisted up *à la Greque* on the left side, and there fastened in a full knot.   Gloves and slippers of white kid are suggested and an ivory fan.*

Scotch plaid or tartan came into fashion again in 1814.   An adaptation of scarf and bonnet for walking costume is shown in Figure 49 called the Huntley costume.

In the pages of the " National Intelligencer," a letter of Mrs. Seaton, wife of the editor, is given describing the New Year's Reception at the White House, and the discomforts of the heat and crush :

" January 2, 1814.

"   .   .   .   Yesterday being New Year's day, everybody, affected or disaffected towards the government, attended to pay Mrs. Madison the compliments of the season.   Between one and two o'clock we drove to the President's where it was with much difficulty we made good our entrance, though all of our

* La Belle Assemblée, July, 1814.

acquaintances endeavoured with the utmost civility to compress themselves as small as they could for our accommodation. The marine band, stationed in the anteroom, continued playing in spite of the crowd pressing on their very heads. But if our pity was excited for these hapless musicians, what must we not have experienced for some members of our own sex, who, not foreseeing the excessive heat of the apartments, had more reason to apprehend the efforts of nature to relieve herself from the effects of the confined atmosphere. You perhaps will not understand that I allude to the rouge which some of our fashionables had unfortunately laid on with an unsparing hand, and which assimilating with the pearl-powder, dust and perspiration, made them altogether unlovely to soul and to eye."

Our ladies of fashion were following the example of their cousins across the sea even in those days. A London wit, parodying the " Maid of Athens," wrote to a suburban damsel :

> " Is thy blush, which roses mocks,
> Bought at three and six per box?
> And those lips I seem to taste,
> Are they pink with cherry paste?
> Gladly I'd the notion scout,
> Answer me, ' It is not so '
> Maid of Clapham, come, no larks,
> For thy shoulders leave white marks,
> Tell me, quickly tell to me,
> What is *really* real in thee?"

The President's wife, as we have already been told by a contemporary, did not use either rouge or pearl-powder, and without the aid of these artificial agents made a very imposing appearance on occasions of state. According to Mrs. Seaton, " Her majesty's appearance was truly regal, dressed in a robe of pink satin, trimmed elaborately with ermine, a white velvet and satin turban, with nodding ostrich plumes and a crescent in front, gold chain and clasps around the waist and wrists. 'Tis here the woman that adorns the dress and not the dress that beautifies the woman. I cannot conceive a female better calculated to dignify the station which she occupies in society than Mrs. Madison. Amiable in private life and affable in public, she is admired and esteemed by the rich and beloved by the poor. You are aware that she snuffs; but in her hands the snuff-box seems only a gracious implement with which to charm. Her frank cordiality to all guests is in contrast to the manner of the President, who is very formal, reserved and precise, yet not wanting in a certain dignity. Being so low of stature he was in imminent danger of being confounded with the plebeian crowd; and was pushed and jostled about like a common citizen, but not so with her ladyship! The towering feathers above the excessive throng distinctly pointed out her station wherever she moved."

Noticeable among the new modes of 1814 were the Cachemire shawls. They were very expensive and therefore very much admired, but a contemporary authority speaks of them as " most graceful and becoming."

Pelerines were still very popular, but they were made longer and fuller, the ends crossed over the bosom and held in by a sash at the waist and hanging down each side. They were especially pretty made of sheer muslin, trimmed with a frill of the same; and of China silk, finished with a puffing of ribbon.

The Bourbon hat and mantle were named to celebrate the return of the Royal family to Paris. The hat was a favourite of the Duchesse d'Angoulême, and was generally made of blue satin trimmed with fleurs-de-lis in pearls; an edging of floss silk and pearls finished the brim and a white ostrich feather was placed on one side. It was said of this hat in the advertisement, that not the least of its recommendations was that it could be "packed in a portmanteau in scarcely any space." Fleurs-de-lis trimmed both the Bourbon dress and mantle. The Angoulême spencer and the Angoulême hat also had temporary popularity. The back of the former was made full and was very becoming to the figure, the front was trimmed with fleurs-de-lis of chenille. This costume is illustrated in Figure 60 from a fashion plate of 1814.

Large Spanish hats and feathers were a pretty fashion which followed the Regency hats in favour, and small slouch hats and feathers are spoken of as "very becoming to a delicate face." Of veils we read : " Nun's veils are now worn as drapery in full dress, but the manner in which they are put on depends entirely on the taste of the wearer. Some ladies bring them round the neck, so as partly to shade it, and one side of the face also ; others have them fastened very far back on the head, and wrap them carelessly round one arm ; but in whatever way they are worn they can be becoming only to tall and graceful figures ; when adopted by undersized belles they are the very reverse of becoming."

The Princess Augusta poke bonnet, named for the king's daughter, was usually made to match the pelisse, both in material and colour.

In her entertaining book, " Social Life in the Early Republic," Miss Wharton says : " Washington was so gay during the winter of 1815 that it would have been difficult to believe it had so recently known war and devastation, had it not been for those silent witnesses, the ruined Capitol and White House, whose charred remains were blots upon the smiling plain." On their return to the capital after the conflagration, Mr. and Mrs. Madison took up their abode in the famous Octagon House, where in the following February the Treaty of Peace was signed.

76

77

78

80

79

81

In a delightful letter quoted in this book there is a note on costume during the escape from the burning city. "On leaving the city," says the writer, "I wore a bonnet that was considered just the style for a young lady of fifteen beginning to think her personal adornment of some importance; it was of white satin gayly trimmed with pink; also as was the fashion a large shell comb."

During the hundred days following Napoleon's dramatic return from Elba, political feelings were outwardly demonstrated in dress. Violets, the Emperor's favourite flower, became the badge of his adherents. After the twentieth of May, 1815, no "Imperialist lady" appeared in public without a large bunch of these flowers on her breast, while "Royalist ladies" wore white jaconet gowns with eighteen tucks in their skirts in honour of Louis XVIII.

Many varieties of Cornettes and Mob caps were worn. For morning dresses they were made of violet cambric trimmed with figured satin ribbon; for more dressy occasions, fine spotted India muslin was used, trimmed with lace and rose-coloured ribbon.

An unusually attractive riding habit appeared in an English fashion plate of 1815. It was the invention of the famous Mrs. Bell who had the happy faculty of adjusting the extravagant fancies of the Parisian modistes to suit English taste. A copy of the original print is given in Figure 112. This habit was made of "finest pelisse cloth, the body cut in a novel style, with front and cuffs tastefully embroidered. A lace ruff was worn around the neck. The hat was of moss silk and ornamented with feathers to correspond." In the words of the fashion editor of "La Belle Assemblée": "The *tout ensemble* of this dress is striking and tasteful beyond what our descriptive powers can portray, and we have no doubt that its striking utility as well as elegance will very soon render it a general

favourite ; at present it is adopted by some of the most distinguished fashionables of the *haut ton*."

In 1816 the new creations of fashion were named in honour
of the Princess Charlotte, and her marriage to Prince Leopold
of Saxe-Coburg; we hear of the "Coburg walking dress," a
round dress of fine cambric under a pelisse of amber shot sarsnet, trimmed with blue satin ribband. "Oatlands" hat to correspond with the pelisse, tied with a chequered ribband of blue
or white, and surmounted with a bunch of tuberoses or passion
flowers. Morocco shoes or half-boots of light blue the colour of
the pelisse trimming. Limerick gloves, and the hair dressed
forward in curls. The hat gets its name from the country seat
of the Duke of York where the Princess spent her honeymoon.

Feathers striped in two colours and called "Zebra feathers"
were a novelty in 1816, and a straw hat or bonnet lined with
lilac silk and trimmed with a Zebra plume of lilac and white
was a favourite combination. The "Sempstress cap" was of
muslin, "the crown drawn in with two rows of narrow pink
ribband next the head piece, and bound round with a pink brocaded satin band." An authority of the day says: "White
dresses are now becoming general, and several gowns have appeared made of superb India muslin of exquisite texture, with
half-sleeves, embroidered in colours, and the border of the robe
ornamented in the same manner." The newest wraps were
comfortable garments called "Carricks;" long double capes
of cloth lined with silk and fastened down the front with straps
which buttoned "like a Canadian hunter's coat." They were
worn by both men and women.

The Caledonian caps of black and crimson with a profusion of
black feathers, Neapolitan head-dresses made of blue and white
striped gauze and trimmed with silver ornaments, and theatre
head-dresses of tulle and satin "with a quilling of net next the

face and fastening tastefully under the left ear ; " Netherland
bonnets with crowns of carmine velvet and brims of white satin
edged with the velvet and finished with white plumes, are mentioned in " La Belle Assembleé " for the winter of 1816.   The
new colours were " Carmine, Burgundy, Nicolas blue, and
American or Forrester's green."

Among the novelties we notice : Mrs. Bell's " new invented
long corsets : ladies inclined to too much *embonpoint* will derive
singular advantage from them : they are equally free from hard
substances as the short ones, which for more slender ladies have
given such universal satisfaction."

In 1817 a contemporary fashion book describes a new and
very expensive wrap, the " Witzchoura."   The name suggests a
Russian or Polish origin.   It was lined throughout with fur
and finished with a high standing collar, to which sometimes
a pelerine was added, both of fur.

In the entertaining memoirs of the Comtesse de Boigne the
changes in customs of dress are amusingly described.   " Among
other changes, or among changes which I had forgotten during
my absence, was the style of ladies' dress in the country.   I
learnt this change to my cost.   I had been somewhat intimate
with Lady Liverpool in the days of our youth.   She invited me
to go to dinner some miles out of London where Lord Liverpool
had a house.   She asked me to come in good time, that she
might show me her garden and spend a pleasant day in the
country.   I arranged to go with my father, but he was detained
by business, and we did not arrive until half-past five.   Lady
Liverpool scolded us for our late arrival, and then took us
round her garden, her greenhouses, her kitchen garden, her
farmyard, her fowl-house, her pig-sty, all of which were in
somewhat poor repair.

" Lord Liverpool arrived from London ; we left him with

my father and went back towards the house. I remember that I was wearing a long coat of Tours silk, flounced all round ; I had a white straw hat with flowers, and thought myself very beautiful. When I came into the house Lady Liverpool said to me :

" ' Will you come into my room to take off your coat and hat ? Have you brought a maid, or would you like to have mine ? '

" I answered with some embarrassment that I had made no arrangements for changing my dress.

" ' Oh, it does not matter in the least,' she replied. ' Here is a book to look at while I am dressing.'

" I had hardly been alone for one moment when I heard a carriage arrive, and Lady Mulgrave soon entered, in a satin dress with jewels and flowers in her hair. Then Miss Jenkinson, a niece of the family, appeared in a white dress with white shoes and a garland of flowers. Then came Lady Liverpool herself : I forget how she was dressed, but she was wearing on her head a veil held back with a golden diadem encrusted with precious stones. I hardly knew where to hide my head. I thought that a magnificent diplomatic dinner was on foot, and that we were about to see the arrival of all the fashionable people in London.

" We sat down to dinner, eight in number, and of these five were members of the household. No other guests were expected. The custom, however, is to dress for a quiet dinner in the country as for a great public reception. Henceforward I have never set out for a pleasant day in the country earlier than half-past seven, and never in morning dress.

" While I am on the subject of dress I must speak of that in which I appeared at court. Possibly in twenty years it will be as ordinary as it seemed extraordinary to me when I wore it. Let us begin with the head.

"My head-dress was surmounted by the obligatory plume. With great trouble I had induced the fashionable plumier, Carberry, to make it only of seven enormous feathers, the smallest number allowed. Plumes of moderate size were composed of twelve or fifteen feathers, and in some cases of as many as twenty-five. Beneath the plume I wore a garland of white roses resting upon a circlet of pearls. The finishing touches were given by diamond buckles, a diamond comb, and tassels of white silk. This mixture of jewels, flowers, and feathers was highly repugnant to our taste, which had remained classical from the time of the Greek costumes.

"That, however, was a trifle. The body of my dress was arranged much as usual. When the bodice was put on, an enormous hooped skirt, three ells long, was laced to my waist. The skirt was made of waxed calico stretched upon whalebone, which made it very wide in front and behind, and very narrow at the sides. Over the satin skirt was placed a second skirt of tulle, ornamented with a large furbelow of silver lace. A third and shorter skirt, also of tulle with silver spangles, ornamented with a garland of flowers, was turned up as a drapery so that the garland surmounted the skirt crosswise. The openings of the tucks were ornamented with silver lace and surmounted with a large bouquet of flowers. I carried another bouquet in front of me, so that I seemed to be emerging from a basket of flowers. I also wore all the jewels for which room could be found upon my person. The bottom of my white satin dress with its silver embroidery was turned up in loops, and did not reach the bottom of the skirt, such being the fashionable etiquette. The Queen alone wore a train, while the skirts of the princesses were not turned up, but hardly touched the ground.

"When I had seen the immense preparations for this toilet,

I was doubtful whether to laugh at their absurdity, which seemed entirely comical, or to be vexed by the necessity of dressing in such ridiculous style. I must admit that when the process was complete I was well pleased, and thought that the costume suited me " * (See Figure 78).

Shoes lined with fur were introduced into England about this time, 1816. They were cut high and were finished with three bows of ribbon on the instep one above the other. They sound very comfortable for a cold winter, and were very picturesque when made of velvet either black, dark green, or mazarin blue.

Figured sarsnet of a white ground, with small sprigs of colour came into fashion at this time, also striped gauzes for ball-gowns.

A spring costume for 1817 is thus described. " Round dress of fine cambric, under a pelisse of emerald-green rep sarsnet, ornamented with flutings of green and white satin, elegantly finished by British silk trimming ; the waist girt by a rich silk cordon of the same manufacture with full tassels. Spring bonnet of green curled silk, the crown and ornaments of white satin and emerald-green, to correspond with the pelisse. Green satin half-boots and Limerick gloves. Berlin ridicule of green and white satin."

The very elaborate mourning of that period is illustrated in Figure 42. It consisted of a " round dress of fine black bombazeen, the trimming of crimped crape, formed into small roses. . . . Over this dress is worn a new and elegant wrapping cloak, made of grey mole skin or fine Bath coating ; it descends to the feet and is wide enough to protect the wearer from the inclemency of the weather ; it is cut out on the shoulders to fit the shape with large military cape and hood,

* Memoirs of the Comtesse de Boigne, 1815–1819, Vol. II.

which folds, being made like the ladies' *chapeau bras*, lined and bound with black sarsnet. Shade bonnet of fine black cane, embroidered with chenille and velvet flowers round the front; the crown, of black satin very full, and high in the back, is made of cane and chenille like the front. The crown is surrounded with a wreath of crape and satin flowers, and tied under the chin with a broad satin ribband. Beaver gloves and shoes."

An extract from the " Memoranda of a Residence at the Court of London " describes the Drawing-room held in celebration of Queen Charlotte's sixty-seventh birthday, and the Court costumes with the prescribed court hoops as they impressed the Envoy Extraordinary and Minister Plenipotentiary from the United States in 1818 : *

" February 27. Yesterday Her Majesty held a Drawing-room. It was in celebration of her birthday. My wife was presented to her, by Lady Castlereagh. Besides being a birthday celebration, it was the first drawing-room of the season and the first since the death of the Princess Charlotte.

" Foreigners agreed that the united capitals of Europe could not match the sight. The glitter of the carriages was heightened by the appearance of the numerous servants in glowing livery, there being generally two and often three footmen behind each carriage. The horses were all in the highest condition, and, under heavy emblazoned harness, seemed like war horses to move proudly. Trumpets were sounding and the Park and Tower guns firing. There were ranks of cavalry in scarlet, with their bright helmets and jet black horses, the same, we were informed, men and horses, that had been at Waterloo. Their appearance was in a high degree martial and splendid. The hands of the men grasped their swords in

* Richard Rush, Minister, 1817–1825.

82

83

84

85

86

87

88

89

90

91 1834

92

93

94

gloves of white buckskin, the cuffs stiffened and reaching half way to the elbow, a prominent part of the equipment that made up the exact uniformity and military beauty of the whole array.

" We were soon set down and entered the great hall (Buckingham Palace). We were not out of time for by appointment our carriage reached the palace with Lord Castlereagh's ; but whilst hundreds were still arriving hundreds were endeavouring to come away. The staircase branched off at the first landing into two arms and was wide enough to admit a partition which had been let in. The company ascending took one channel those descending the other and both channels were full. The openings through the old carved balusters brought all under view at once.

" The hoop dresses of the ladies, their plumes, their tippets, the fanciful attitudes which the hoops occasioned ; the various costumes of the gentlemen, as they stood pinioning their elbows, and holding in their swords ; the common hilarity created by the common dilemma ; the bland recognitions passing between those above and those below, made up altogether an exhibition so picturesque, that a painter might give it as illustrative of the English Court of that era.

" The party to which I was attached reached the summit of the staircase in about three-quarters of an hour. Four rooms were allotted to the ceremony. In the second was the Queen. She sat on a velvet chair and cushion a little raised up. Near her were the Princesses and Ladies-in-waiting. The doors of the rooms were all open. You saw in them a thousand ladies richly dressed. All the colours of nature were heightening their rays under the fairy designs of art.

" It was the first occasion of laying by mourning for the Princess Charlotte and it was like the bursting out of spring.

No lady was without her plume. The room was a waving field of feathers. Some were blue like the sky, some tinged with red, here you saw violet and yellow, there shades of green, but the most were of pure white like a tuft of snow. The diamonds encircling them caught the sun through the windows, and threw dazzling beams around. Then, the hoops! these I cannot describe, they should be seen. To see one is nothing, but to see a thousand, and a thousand wearers, on such a day! Each lady seemed to rise out of a gilded little barricade or one of silvery texture. This topped by the plume, and the 'face divine' interposing, gave to the whole an effect so unique, so fraught with feminine grace and grandeur, that it seemed as if a curtain had risen to show a pageant in another sphere. It was brilliant and gorgeous. The ceremonies of the day being ended as far as myself and suite were concerned, we sought the corridor to come away. Will it be believed that the channels were as full as ever of hoops and plumes. Positively, it came over the eyes like beautiful architecture, the hoops the base, the plume the pinnacle. The parts of this dress may have been incongruous, but the whole was harmony."

This extraordinary fashion of wearing enormous hoops with Court dresses is illustrated in all the fashion books from 1800 to 1820 and, in spite of the eloquent eulogy pronounced by Mr. Rush, strikes us as both hideous and grotesque, but as a matter of history it is not without interest. A specimen of a Court hoop for 1818 is given in Figure 78.

The advance of manufactures in England called forth the eloquence of a contemporary periodical: " Fashion, that motley divinity, now again is seen welcoming the approach of spring, and from the looms of the British manufacturers are dispersed at her command, silks, ribbands, and gauzes, all of so rich, so exquisite a texture and of such various and tasteful patterns, that we may now dispute the palm of excellence and novelty with every other polished nation on this habitable globe."

With both head-dresses and turbans false curls were worn. We read in a letter of 1818, from Washington : " After breakfast I went forth on a shopping expedition and procured most of the winter clothing for the family, self included. One thing I could not get—Curls, French curls, parted on the forehead, you know how. You must get them for me either in New York or Philadelphia. Now remember *Curls !* " *

" La Belle Assemblée " says : " Amongst the novelties in head-dresses are the Caroline, or Como turban, of pale blue crape, ornamented with white beads ; and the turban *à l'antique*, more costly than becoming, of very fine white net, superbly ornamented with gold, with a gold tassel. Flowers in half dress are but little worn, and gold and silver ornaments are more popular at present in full dress than plumes of feathers, which are better suited to the hussar cap. In jewellery, pearls, rubies, and coloured gems, the initials of which form devices or sentimental words, are now in high favour ; and curiously wrought gold ornaments are very much in demand by the British fashionables. The favourite colours are peach-down, emerald-green, Palmetto green, pale tea-leaf, Spanish brown, scarlet and celestial blue."

Many specimens of the acrostic or anagram jewelry have been preserved, coming into fashion, as we learn, from the authority given above in 1817 ; they were worn in a variety of devices until 1830. An interesting " Regard Ring " worn in Baltimore in the twenties, consists of a small hoop of gold into which is set a ruby, an emerald, a garnet, an amethyst, a ruby and a diamond. This ring was owned by Miss Amanda Nace, afterwards Mrs. Forney.

* First Forty Years of Washington Society.

In a popular magazine of 1819 we read: " The acrostic rage prevails in jewellery. A ring is given with the following expression, *j'aime* (I love). It is accordingly formed of a jacinth, an amethyst, a ruby, and an emerald. Such gems form all the rings of the present day." Also, " A curious romantic fashion is adopted by some young ladies in the ornamenting of their hats; it is aiming at the sentimental, but I call it acrostical. Suppose, for instance, the lady wearing the hat is named MARIA; she accordingly sports a marshmallows blossom, an anemone, a rose, an iris and an asphodel, or evening lily : this forms a mixture of colours, and even of flowers not always in season together."

A Paris gossip describes the short sleeves in vogue with all costumes: (1819) " Let Paris be full or empty, scorching under summer's sun, or freezing under winter's snows, the changes among the hats still continue to undergo their usual motley round. I cannot say the same of our other outdoor covering; high dresses, with only a *sautoir*, or half handkerchief are still the prevailing mode, and these are of Cachemire silk, black lace, or embroidered muslin ; this fashion seems likely to continue till the shivering fair one shall be obliged to resort to the more appropriate spencer and comfortable pelisse. It is true that pelerines buttoned before and trimmed round with muslin or ribbons in cockleshells, are worn by many ladies; the pelerines are made of muslin richly embroidered, and whether the gown is plain, striped, or spotted, the sleeves are worked in a pattern to correspond with that of the pelerine ; but why are these pelerines adopted ? Because a lady cannot have a dress made high that has short sleeves and never were short sleeves so much in favour. Nothing is to be seen but naked arms and as the gowns fall off the shoulders, the bust would be entirely exposed if ladies walked out without a pelerine : let me, however, tell you, as a warning to your fair countrywomen, that never before in Paris were pulmonary and nervous complaints so frequent. This fashion originated in the reign of Louis XIV as may be seen by the portraits of Ninon de l'Enclos, the Duchesse de Fontanges, and that of Madame de Sevigné ; whose cousin, Bussy Rabutin, used to say it was only on account of her arm being beautiful that she displayed it. I sincerely hope, however, that next winter will bring along with its rigour, that modesty which can alone render a female desirable ; and that as soon as ices and melons cease to be eaten, short sleeves will cease to be worn."

This fashion introduced many dainty styles of pelerines or shoulder capes. The most popular were made of muslin richly embroidered by hand, others were trimmed with rows of lace insertion and edged with lace.

Long sashes tied in the back were all the rage in Paris in 1819. According to a local authority : " At the Tuilleries we see nothing but sashes, and they are generally of Scotch plaid ; young, old, handsome, ugly, straight, crooked, hump-backed, tall, short, squint-eyed, one-eyed, black-eyed, grey-eyed, flaxen-headed, every one had a sash tied in a bow behind, with long ends hanging to her heels, or streaming on the wind. These ribbons are like the *aiguillettes* of the *gens d'armes*, permanent signals for the fate of captives. Your countrywomen have introduced the opera cloaks of grey coating, lined with coloured sarsnet ; and every French lady has followed this useful fashion, and folds herself in one while she waits in the vestibule of the theatre for her carriage. We give credit to Mistress Bell for the invention of a silk mantilla of this kind with its *chapeau bras* hood ; it is truly elegant, as well as *très commode* (we have really no word to express what you call comfortable) and has been worn by a lady of high distinction, here."

Bonnets had for many years been worn by young and old, but the plates of 1819 show a revival in favour of hats, and we read: " Hats have a decided preference over bonnets; and one of the former of Carmelite-coloured cloth lined with jonquil coloured sarsnet, has been much admired ; this is of the equestrian shape: London smoke is also a favourite colour for this kind of hat. Black beaver hats are sported by many ladies of fashion ; and a purple bonnet trimmed with gauze spotted with velvet of the same colour as the bonnet, is much in requisition. The beaver hats I mentioned above, are ornamented with a broad band, with a metal buckle on one side. Some have three narrower bands, placed at equal distances, with small buckles. Coloured velvet hats have generally a band of very broad ribbon, made in the form of cockleshells."

From a popular English periodical we glean the following, under the date of December, 1819 : " Grey hats too, lined with rose-colour, and ornamented with a plume of six or eight feathers, half of them grey and the other three or four rose-colour, is another favourite head-dress for the carriage.

" The waists of gowns still continue long, and are made low in the back ; the skirts are plaited very full behind, but without any plaits at the hips. Merino dresses are made with a pelerine of the same ; but instead of flounces they are bordered with velvet, of a colour to suit the dress. Worsted fringe trimming for dresses has in it a mixture of silk, and is headed with plaited satin, forming a rich rouleau ; sometimes three or four rouleaux surmount the fringe ; this trimming is very beautiful."

We read of a new and beautiful manufacture of brocaded gauze fashionable for evening dresses for young people, and are glad to be able to give a picture of a dress of this pretty fabric, that was worn by Miss Elizabeth Smith, in Philadelphia, in 1819 (Figure 61).

About this time the fashionable dance in Europe and America was the Waltz, first introduced in Germany. It attracted almost immediately the popularity which it has enjoyed ever since. It was not, however, as interesting to watch as the old time Minuet with its stately bows and courtesies, nor the Quadrille of the beginning of the nineteenth century, with its intricate figures. An onlooker expressed his feelings on the subject in the following verses which were printed in a Philadelphia magazine of 1819:

" THE WALTZ

" In patent Kaleidoscopes all may discern
A novel attraction at every turn ;
And every movement presents to the sight
A figure more perfect, a colour more bright ;
But waltzing, though charming to those who can do it,
Is rather fatiguing to people who view it :
For though *turns* are incessant, no *changes* you meet,
But giddiness, bustle, embracing and heat.

" At first they move slowly, with caution and grace,
Like horses when just setting out for a race ;
For dancers at balls, just like horses at races,
Must amble a little to show off their paces.
The music plays faster, their raptures begin,
Like lambkins they skip, like tetotums they spin :
Now draperies whirl, and now petticoats fly,
And ankles at least are exposed to the eye.

" O'er the chalk-cover'd ballroom in circles they swim ;
He smiles upon her, and she smiles upon him,
Her arm on his shoulder is tenderly placed,
His hand quite as tenderly circles her waist ;
They still bear in mind, as they're turning each other,
The proverb—' one good turn's deserving another' ;
And these *bodily turns* often end, it is said,
In turning the lady's or gentleman's *head.*"

— *Q. in a Corner.*

FIGURE 95.—1813—A gentleman in a fashionable walking costume of plum-coloured cloth, drab trousers and white waistcoat. From a contemporary print.

FIGURE 96.—1814—Back view of an outdoor costume. The wadded pelisse of golden brown satin with a high rolling collar is copied from an original garment worn in Philadelphia. The hat is from a contemporary print.

FIGURE 97.—1815—White satin afternoon dress with high waist and long sleeves falling over the hands. From an original garment worn in Philadelphia about 1815. The Vandyke ruff and embroidered muslin collarette are copied from plates of that date. Head from a contemporary miniature.

FIGURE 98.—1814—Front view of the pelisse in Figure 96. It is fastened with small gilt catches with snap springs, such as are used for necklaces, showing the collar turned down. Ruff and English walking-hat of brown velvet are taken from a plate of 1814.

FIGURE 99.—1816—Evening dress of a gentleman of this date, taken from a contemporary print. Dark blue coat and white kerseymere trousers and waistcoat. White silk stockings and black slippers.

FIGURE 100.—1828—Dress of very rich corded silk with brocaded flowers arranged in stripes, made with a full skirt and plaited bodice, with a broad belt of the silk. Copied from an original gown worn by Miss Mary Brinton in Philadelphia about 1828.

FIGURE 101.—1820—A walking suit. Long-tailed coat of green broadcloth with silver buttons and black velvet collar. Long pantaloons of white kerseymere. Stock of white satin and hat of rough beaver. From a contemporary print.

FIGURE 102.—1823—Brown cloth pelisse trimmed with bias folds of cloth. Velvet bonnet to match with bows of taffeta and a group of brown feathers on the crown. Brim faced with pink taffeta. A double ruffle of white lawn is worn around the throat and an enormous muff of bearskin completes the costume, which is taken from a plate of this year.

FIGURE 103.—1824—White satin wedding gown made with a deep trimming of white gauze held in place by bows of gauze bound with white satin. Three rouleaux of white satin edge the bottom of the skirt and the low-cut neck of the bodice. The sleeves are made of a full puff of the gauze caught down with satin pipings finished with a tassel of sewing silk. This charming costume was worn by a Virginia bride, Miss Colquhoun of Petersburg, in 1824. The head is copied from a portrait and the veil from a plate of that year.

FIGURE 104.—1820—Full dress of an English gentleman in this year. Blue broadcloth coat edged with white satin and adorned with silver buttons. Knee-breeches of brown satin and stockings of white silk. This figure is copied from a plate in the "La Belle Assemblée."

Women's Dress

1820–1830

" Fashions change with every changing season
Regardless quite of money, rhyme or reason."

ITH the year 1820 we reach the third decade of the nineteenth century, and note a few striking changes in fashion. The first variation to be commented upon is that black dresses came into favour, and two new materials, plume velvet and levantine satin, were used for evening dresses. The former, plume velvet, was distinguished by narrow satin stripes, and the latter, levantine satin, was very soft and rich. Highland tartans had been worn for the last five years off and on but became a pronounced fashion in 1820, even for evening dresses. We read of Caledonian caps of white satin, and of Ivanhoe caps of black tulle and geranium satin, both of these head-dresses being designed for evening wear, and the latter of course named in honour of Scott's delightful romance just published in Edinburgh.

Two new ball dresses for young ladies are described by Mrs. Bell. "One is of figured satin, a new manufacture, with the figures woven into the satin in such a manner that they are transparent; round the border is a beautiful festoon of artificial

141

roses and their foliage in rich clusters ; they are smaller than nature, but faithfully coloured from it. The other ball dress is almost equally attractive on account of its chaste simplicity : it is of fine white net over white satin, and is finished by two flounces of net, richly embossed with fancy flowers and foliage in white satin."

In the letters of the Hon. Stratford Canning, English Minister to the United States in 1820, we find mention of a " revolution in court dress " which was being accomplished at that time. He attended a Drawing-room in London just before he started for America, and remarked, " The great event which at present occupies the public mind is the abolition of hoops, announced in Tuesday's ' Gazette ' preparatory to the Drawing-room fixed for the fifteenth of next month at Buckingham House. I fear we shall regret them in spite of their unbecoming appearance. They have the effect of leaving a little room in the Drawing-room crowds so as to prevent your being squeezed to death." According to Mrs. Bell's magazine, a new style of hoops was introduced for court dress in England in 1817. In Figure 78 we give the sketch of one designed for the Drawing-room of that year, which is undoubtedly an improvement on court hoops shown in the earlier numbers of " La Belle Assemblée." Hoops are not mentioned in the descriptions of ball dresses of that time. They were evidently a court fashion, which lasted until 1820, according to the letter quoted above.

We read of a pelisse of garter blue embroidered in the same colour and lined with white sarsnet, also of black velvet pelisses worn with bonnets of black satin, and as we see by the following extract from " La Belle Assemblée," bonnets were again in the ascendency : " A favourite bonnet for the promenade is of lavender rep silk, with a double quilling of Italian net, edged with narrow satin ribband ; the crown is formed of Italian net and ribbon. On the white lining underneath is a broad layer of pink satin in bias. Another promenade bonnet is of fine black leghorn, trimmed with peach-coloured crape, and crowned with a beautiful bouquet of half-blown roses, lilacs and field flowers ; the trimming at the edge of this bonnet forms a double row of cockle-shells cut in bias. A carriage bonnet of straw gauze is justly admired, the material entirely new ; it is edged with transparent net, embossed with pink ornaments, and is finished with a curtain of blond ; the crown ornamented to correspond with the pattern of the embossed border, and trimmed with a full plume of white uncurled feathers, inter-mixed with three that are pink. Another carriage bonnet is made of fine net, spangled with straw in small figures, and the crown richly trimmed with flowers."

Turbans which had held the popular fancy from the begin-ning of the nineteenth century were still worn in every variety of material, Chinese crape and Peruvian gauze being favour-ites. Many new styles of head-dress had come and gone during the reign of the turban ; among these was the Vevai cap, some-thing like a Tyrolese cap in shape, but less high. It seems to have greatly pleased the fancy of Mrs. Bell, who says of it (1820) : " Nothing can be more chaste or tasteful than this ele-gant little ornament ; its plumage hangs down like the fantastic fretwork formed by frozen snow ; while here and there seem lodged on it a few Christmas berries, either of the red or white berried holly."

We notice at this time frequent mention of flounces as trim-ming for ball dresses, but it soon became fashionable to trim everything with flounces. At first there was but little fullness in them, for skirts were still narrow. In the following description we read of fluted flounces : " Evening dress of black crape, over a black satin slip made with a demi-train, and ornamented round the border with three fluted flounces of crape, each flounce headed by an embroidered band of small jet beads and bugles. Corsage à *Louis Quatorze*, ornamented with jet and bugles to correspond. Tucker of white crape in folds." It was the fashion at that time to trim dancing frocks with artificial flowers, for instance: a ball dress of tulle over white satin was ornamented above the hem with full blown roses. The hair was adorned with silver ears of corn, red roses, and rows of pearl. White satin sandal slippers, white kid gloves, and carved ivory fan were the appropriate accessories.

Spencers were still in favour, the latest being made with a little jacket tail, like that of a riding habit, and a sash the colour of the spencer was worn with it. Long mantles of grey or violet sarsnet were also much worn; they reached as far as the heels, and had hoods drawn with ribbon and stiffened with whalebone, "which latter improvement, to be candid with you," writes our authority, "is, I think, an awkward imitation of Mrs. Bell's *Chapeau Bras.*"

The following chatty letter from Paris is dated September, 1820:

"My last letter contained lamentations on the continued length of our ladies' waists; thanks to all the powers of taste, they begin to shorten, and I hope soon to see them placed on that standard of beauty, without which there can be no claim to the epithet, when divested of all proportion, by being too long or too ridiculously short. A high dress, that marks more justly the contour of a fine shape, is now a favourite outdoor costume; and no other ornament is worn with it, except a cravat-scarf of Scotch plaid gauze, which is gracefully tied on one side. However, when the mornings are chill, a grey sarsnet pelisse, for early walks, is thought very elegant; this silk pelisse has a beautiful falling collar, which takes from it any

winter-like appearance. If a *sautoir*, or half-handkerchief, is
worn with this pelisse it is of rainbow gauze and is tied close
round the throat, like a cravat. These gauze handkerchiefs are
trimmed round with a broad silk fringe. Black lace shawl
handkerchiefs are very prevalent for the public promenade.

" Leghorn hats are very much worn ; they are often ornamented with a bow of ribbon, with long ends (what our grandmothers used to call streamers) on one side. A bouquet of wild
poppies is placed in front, surmounted by a plume of marabout
feathers. The ribbon is either straw colour or striped. Amongst
the newest ribbons is that of Egyptian-sand colour ; the common
sand sold by stationers, to prevent writing from blots, may give
you some idea of this colour. Straw hats are ornamented with
a large cluster of corn poppies, or with ears of corn, mingled
with marabout feathers. The brims of some hats have a quilling of blond, both above and beneath, or a very full *bouilloné*
of gauze : the crown of such hats is simply ornamented with a
bow of ribbon on one side, or a full-blown rose, especially if the
hat is of straw. Lilac linings to hats are popular, but it is not
a becoming colour when placed so near the face unless the complexion is very fair and clear. The flowers are mostly placed in
front of the hat in large bunches, composed generally of wild
poppies and honeysuckles. For the promenade, straw hats are
usually tied under the chin with a plaid ribbon. For the carriage, handkerchiefs of stamped crape are often tastefully disposed on straw hats and bonnets ; the ground of these handkerchiefs is generally white, flowered with lilac. Muslin bonnets
are worn for the *déshabille* morning walk. Rose-coloured hats
are much in favour, with trimmings of the same colour ; lemon-
coloured hats are ornamented with trimmings of lilac, and lilac
hats with lemon-colour. Straw-coloured gauze is much used
in the trimming of straws hats : rainbow gauze is a favourite

trimming for chip hats. Flame-coloured feathers, grouped together so as to resemble flowers, are favourite ornaments on carriage hats; as are all kinds of field flowers, particularly the
woodbine and wild poppy. The brims of some hats are entirely
covered with honeysuckle. Sometimes the hat is trimmed with
either a bouquet of corn poppies or of roses. The semptress
bonnet is again revived for the morning promenade. All bonnets are placed far back, and are generally ornamented at the
edges with tulle quilled in large plaits, with gauze ribbon
bouillonés, coxcombs, or ribbons laid on plain. The bouquets
placed in the front increase in magnitude, and are spread almost over the whole of the brim : tobacco-plant flowers and
others equally spreading are mixed with those most in season.
Scotch caps are not so much in favour as formerly, except those
that have a kind of gauze drapery depending or a quilling of
blond next the face ; and with such appendages they are certainly no longer Scotch caps. Transparent bonnets of rose-
coloured crape are much admired ; they are ornamented round
the crown with a wreath formed of bows of ribbon ; the bonnets are fluted, and they are trimmed at the edge with a double
row of plaited gauze. White gauze hats, chequered with blue,
are generally ornamented with blue larkspur arranged in
parallel lines on one side, while the other remains bare.

"Cambric gowns are often ornamented round the border
with stripes of clear muslin let in full, and as many stripes,
alternately, of hemstitched cambric. The corsage is also formed
of these alternate stripes in bias : when cambric dresses are
flounced, it is always with the same, but the edge of each flounce
is hemstitched and each flounce is headed with a letting in of
muslin, embroidered in openwork. Silk dresses were never in
such favour for evening and half dress as they are now ; they
are ornamented with separate pieces of quilling, like the frill of

a shirt; and these are placed separately, rather in bias, forming
two rows, which have a very elegant and rich effect.   The jockey
at the top of the sleeve, which we formerly called *mancheron*, is
not quite so full as it was; it is very prettily fancied, and so
slashed as to appear a *mélange* of Spanish, French and English;
its latter similitude, perhaps, obtained for it the title of jockey.
The bodies of the silk dresses are all plaited horizontally.
Frocks which button behind are very fashionable.   A favourite
trimming on violet-coloured silk gowns, which are very prevalent, consists of four flounces placed two and two and laid in
flat whole plaits; between the hem of the gown and the edge of
the lower flounce is a space of about two fingers in breadth and
between the first and second row of flounces is a space much
more considerable.   Metallic gauze still continues in fashion for
dress hats and turbans.   Court head-dresses are much lower
than formerly, the hair is divided in front, but is dressed very
full on each side, in regular small curls.   Parasols are lined and
finished with a very broad fringe from which depend balls the
colour of the lining.   The latest ridicules are woven without
seam : they are made in the English fashion, and are drawn up
and ornamented with Scotch plaid ribbon."

A novelty of short duration was in the form of a head-dress
for home costume.   It was a silk handkerchief, called *mouchoirs
aux bêtes*, from the corners being embroidered with different
animals and scenes from the fables of La Fontaine.   These
handkerchiefs were sold at 720 francs the dozen.   A French
wit made a pun on this head-dress, calling the handkerchiefs
" *mouchoirs affables.*"

A great variety of fancy gauzes came into fashion in 1821.
Each variation had a name.   There was the marbled gauze, the
marabout gauze, the deluge gauze, and the flowered gauze.   The
whys and wherefores of these names it would indeed be difficult

FIGURE 105.—1800—Riding habit of blue cloth, black velvet collar and a double row of gilt buttons called Nelson's balls. Tan gloves and half-boots of black Spanish leather. Round cap of beaver with plume and feathers in front, and band of gold braid around the crown.

FIGURE 106.—1801—Dark blue kerseymere habit with three rows of small blue buttons crossed with blue cord ; collar of blue velvet. White beaver hat with very narrow brim and two short white feathers.

FIGURE 107.—1806—Riding habit of lavender blossom cloth. Hat of amber velvet trimmed with loops of black silk. Ruff of lace and muslin ; tan gloves and tan shoes.

FIGURE 108.—1808—Riding habit of dark green cloth trimmed with black braid and gilt buttons. Cap of the same cloth. Gloves and shoes of lemon-coloured kid.

FIGURE 109.—1810—Habit of Georgian cloth, ornamented with military frogs. Hat of green velvet trimmed with white fur.

FIGURE 110.—1817—Riding dress of light brown trimmed with frogs of dark brown. Dark brown hat with feathers.

FIGURE 111.—1812—Habit of bright green cloth, embroidered down the front and on the cuffs *à la militaire*. Hat of black beaver trimmed with gold cord and tassels and a long ostrich feather. Black shoes and tan gloves.

FIGURE 112.—1815—Riding habit of fine blue cloth, front and cuffs embroidered ; lace ruff. Hat of moss silk trimmed with feathers.

FIGURE 113.—1816—Riding hat of black beaver.

FIGURE 114.—1814—Riding hat of blue brocaded silk. Wetherill collection in Memorial Hall.

FIGURE 115.—1812—Riding costume of Marie Louise blue, trimmed with gimp to match. A small blue cloth hat and feathers of the same colour.

FIGURE 116.—1830—Habit of very dark blue cloth. Top hat of black with a blue veil.

FIGURE 117.—1842—Riding dress of black cloth, top hat of beaver and tan feathers. High black satin stock and bow headed with cambric frill.

105 106 107 108

109 110 111 112

113 114 115 116 117

to define, but the materials were especially designed for bonnets and head-dresses.

White silk parasols with borders of flowers painted round them were among the novelties from Paris in that year, and the newest colours were wall-flower and Apollo's hair; the latter must have been difficult to match, but rose, pistachio-nut colour, ponceau, and roasted coffee, were all popular.

In a letter from Paris (1821) we find this: " Vandyke frills, round the back and shoulders of dress gowns, are now much in vogue. Mary has scarcely an evening dress without them. No ornament gives a more becoming finish to the bust; and while it dresses consistently and elegantly the back and shoulders, it has the effect of lessening the appearance of the waist at the bottom. . . . Caps with long lappets are also much in request; and these lappets confine the cap under the chin; this head-dress, on a pretty woman, gives the countenance a resemblance to the beautiful faces of Isabey's. Turbans richly embroidered, and fastened with gold brooches, are much worn by young married ladies; they are surmounted either by marabouts, esprits, heron's feathers, bird-of-Paradise plumes, or curled ostrich feathers. A long veil is often worn with a turban, the veil floating behind à la Reine. The hair is now divided, in equal bands, on the top of the head. If a lady, however, wishes to appear lovely, she will not follow the disagreeable fashion of showing the skin of the head, which has always an unpleasing appearance.

" Jewelry is made chiefly of polished steel. A brooch of polished steel confines the gown to the bust, and another is placed in the back between the shoulders: these brooches are of immense price and of most beautiful workmanship. A very pretty woman appeared in public last week and all her numerous ornaments were of polished steel: her dress was a marsh-

mallow-blossom colour, which admirably set off the superb
brooches she wore in front of her bust, and at her back.

"The white gloves worn with short sleeves are finished by a
sharp point above the elbow, that comes up to the middle of the
thick part of the arm, which the glove is made exactly to fit:
they are therefore so tight that they never fall down or wrinkle.

"The hair is dressed high, and the temples are adorned with
locks of hair which are lightly frizzed before they are curled.   At
the benefit of Mademoiselle Georges, turbans were very general
particularly the Moabitish turban, fastening under the chin.
Toques of satin with white marabout feathers, mixed with ears
of corn, in gold, are much in favour for *grande costume;* and
cornettes of very sheer muslin with broad long ends, are universal in undress.

"The most elegant parasols are of India muslin, embroidered
with a beautiful border in feather stitch, instead of fringe; the
edge is finished with broad Mechlin lace, about four inches in
breadth; the parasol is lined with azure blue, shot with white;
the stick and handle are of polished steel, the thick part is
beautifully wrought and the handle is formed like the leaf of the
acanthus.

"Bouquets are much worn; they consist of a large bunch of
Parma violets, or a full bouquet of roses, jessamine, and helio-
tropes.   Flowers are always offered as an homage to beauty;
every gallant gentleman presents them to a pretty woman, and
she accepts them as her due.

"Very rich bracelets on the wrists, and rings on every finger,
are indispensable ornaments at evening parties.   The clasps of
belts in gold, representing two hands locked together, are very
fashionable."

Reticules of Morocco leather were considered more fashionable than those of silk or velvet.   We hear, too, of Scotch plaid

fringes as a new trimming for gowns and wraps. Bonnets were still large, but they were somewhat flattened on top as in Figures 118 and 119. The newest were transparent and lined with coloured silk to match the trimming. All that could be said on the subject of the latest fashions in hats, will be found in the following extract from a letter by a Parisian correspondent :

" Many carriage hats are made of striped gauze (Figure 272), or crape, of pale straw-colour, and are trimmed with lilac. The hats are somewhat smaller in the brims, though there are some hats which are bent down in the shape of bonnets (Figure 120) : straw hats, of every shape, are now becoming very general for walking ; Leghorn hats have already made their appearance ; the brims much narrower than formerly ; they are ornamented with a narrow scarf of plaid silk, forming a circular drapery. These hats are placed on one side, and the hair that is exposed is arranged in full curls or ringlets. Some of the new carriage hats are of red currant colour, with the strange association of rose-coloured feathers. The most tasteful bonnet for walking is curled plush silk of a beautiful pink ; and grey hats with flowers of the same colour, made of velvet or chenille, are in very great favour. Dress hats for the theatre, or for evening parties, are often seen ornamented with cock's feathers ; and hats of black velvet are trimmed with white marabouts mixed with gold ears of corn. Wreaths of flowers are the chief head-ornament for young ladies ; the flowers with their foliage are thinly scattered in front but very full on the temples ; geraniums and eglantine, with little spiral white flowers from the cups of which issue little tufts of silk, are used for these wreaths. Bandeaux of pearls are worn in the ballroom, and for evening visits bandeaux of white or rose-coloured satin, wreathed round with summer roses.

" Five separate strips of satin form the chief trimming on

the border of merino dresses. On muslin or cachemire there are the same number of full quilled narrow flounces. The dresses for walking are so long that they nearly touch the ground. Black velvet dresses are much worn at evening parties; they are ornamented with beads, with a girdle of rose-coloured or blue velvet; which girdle is adorned with Brandenburghs made of bugles. White cachemire dresses, trimmed at the border with three bands of satin, are much worn at the Parisian tea-parties; those parties, which I recollect so much astonished you when you first beheld them; not only at the sight of the orange flower water mingled with the tea, but at the enormous bowl of punch which made a part of the repast. *Les Thès* are not much improved; and there are none but the British, and more especially the Irish, that know how to make this refreshment a real banquet."

An extract from another letter on French fashions describes the newest designs in fans:

"Two ladies, eminent for fashion, have lately sported at the theatres a kind of fan made of a bunch of feathers like those fans we see in old English pictures; they collect the air, and it is possible that they may become more general. Fans, however, of the last fashion are of sandalwood, mother-of-pearl, horn in imitation of tortoise shell, or of ivory: they are ornamented with garlands of roses, heart's-ease, lilacs, or the little blue flower, forget-me-not. The wreaths are painted at the top very near to the narrow ribbon that confines the mount-sticks."

Turning over the fashion plates of 1821, we notice that the dresses are worn decidedly shorter again. Fluted and plaited trimmings of the material are used on the sleeves and also around the bottoms of the skirts (Figure 120). What was called a matted silk trimming was also very popular; six rows of it were sometimes used, about one inch apart, a little above the hem. Small caps were very much worn with evening gowns. Pelisses were still in vogue. A very pretty one is given in a French magazine of 1821.

"Grey levantine pelisse trimmed down the front, round the border, and at the *mancherons* with full puffings of the same colour and material. The pelisse left open in front of the bust. Marguerite coloured satin bonnet, edged with short white marabouts; and the bow of satin on the bonnet fastened with two rows of pearls. Plain fichu of fine India muslin worn under the pelisse; slippers of grey kid; a ridicule of small beads beautifully wrought, and lemon-coloured gloves."

We hear of Nile-green as a new colour at this time, and Marguerite pink is repeatedly mentioned. Broad sashes of watered, figured, and striped ribbon were now introduced and became very popular.

From a contemporary letter we take the following: "When the corner of the white handkerchiefs of fine lawn had only a little embroidery, then one of these corners served as a purse to the French ladies; and after tying a knot they fastened their ring of keys to it. Now these handkerchiefs are so beautifully embroidered, that they require more management in the display of them; and those fashionable dames who will not take the trouble of carrying a little basket or a ridicule have a silver purse that they fasten to their belt.

"If the *plumassiers* have feathered their own nests, the flower-makers have also their profits. Young ladies have a bouquet of flowers on one side of the head, while a wreath is entwined among their tresses; and every ladies' hat, bonnet, or cap is almost covered with flowers.

"Expense and luxury of every kind increase; I asked a young lady yesterday, who I know has very little fortune, but

whose connections often oblige her to mix much with the gay
world, which obligation, it must be confessed, she fulfills to
the very letter, how much it cost her for every ball she went to,
without reckoning her frock and slip, or indeed her jewels,
which are most of them presents. She told me that what with
hiring a carriage (for her parents do not keep one), the expense
of the hair-dresser, added to other trifles, such as ornamented
white gloves, white satin shoes, flowers for her hair, ribbons,
some slight alteration in the fashion or the trimming of her robe,
or a new corsage by way of change, it cost her every night she
went to a ball or concert about one hundred and twenty francs."

Café au lait was a new colour in 1822, and the favourite trimming seems to have been wadded *rouleaux* of satin. In Figures
61 and 103, pictures of this trimming are given. It was in
favour for several years and was revived about 1870, as is shown
in Figure 315. Feather trimming was also popular. We read of
" a black dress, trimmed with rows of feathers, much in vogue ;
the last row terminates at the knee, the spaces between the rows
of feathers are not very wide ; the gown is made high, with a
standing up collar, edged with feathers. Merino is much worn
in half dress, with wadded *rouleaux* and braided satin trimmings
between."

A note from Paris in the autumn of 1822 says : " Small
fichus, tied carelessly round the throat, are also much worn at
dress parties ; they are of one colour, and often fastened with
a golden arrow."

An interesting bonnet of 1823 may be seen in the Wetherill
Collection at Memorial Hall, Philadelphia. It is made of pink
silk with alternate watered and figured stripes and trimmed
with bows of pink ribbon with a satin border and evidently had
flowers arranged in the bows at the left side. A sketch of it is
given in Figure 272.

Three elaborate bonnets are described in a London magazine of the same date : " Carriage bonnet of pink crape ornamented with *rouleaux* of pink satin, relieved by brocaded crape of the same colour edged with blond lace ; lappets of brocaded crape edged with lace take the place of strings, the back of the bonnet is very richly ornamented with pink satin, and the crown is in the toque form.

" A walking bonnet of white sarsnet, with raised spots, bound and trimmed with Danish blue satin, three bouffont flutings of which material ornament the left side, representing tulip leaves on the edge of the brim ; the other side ornamented with full puffings edged with narrow straw plaiting.

" Park carriage bonnet of white crape over white satin, lined with a fluting of broad blond ; the crown finished by a light gauze puffing, with a leaf end richly trimmed with blond. On the left side a full bunch of Provence roses, surmounted by a marabout plume of feathers."

We read that " a new kind of hat has lately been invented, platted like straw ; but its fabrication is of silk. These were first invented to send out to the United States, where Leghorn hats are prohibited. Leghorn hats, with bands of straw and ripe ears of corn round the crown, are very popular." Why they were not allowed to be imported into America we have not been able to discover.

Chambery gauze, a tough but shimmery material, was popular in 1822, and was much worn also in the seventies. " Broad belts of leather buckled on one side " were preferred by many to the long sashes of ribbon.

The bodices of the gowns were cut square behind and before, and they had a double tucker, one falling, and the other standing up. A great deal of trouble was apparently taken to produce new effects in the trimming of white dresses. Sometimes

1820–1840

118

120

122

119

121

123

the " trimming represented branches of the acacia, the leaves formed by puffs or folds of muslin, the stalks embroidered in cotton, and the branches separated by openwork; the embroidery at the bottom of the skirt reached up to the knee; the branches of acacia were made to twine round the sleeves, and a falling collar was worn edged with this design."

Other cambric dresses were finished at the bottom by two rows of "letting-in lace." Between these rows was an embroidery on the cambric of muslin leaves, the letting-in lace being six inches wide. An apron of cambric, it seems, was often worn with white dresses, trimmed with two rows of quilled muslin.

Some ladies wore a dozen flounces on their dresses, about three fingers in depth, and scalloped at the edges. On sarsnet dresses narrow flounces caught up in scallops were a favourite ornament; six of these flounces might be used, placed at "about a finger's length distance" from one another.

Corsages of silk or satin ball dresses were covered with tulle and a tucker of plaited net drapery was fastened with a brooch as a modest covering for the bust. Barege silk dresses were made with long sleeves of embroidered muslin; when the sleeves were short they were very full.

A Paris correspondent recounts a very extravagant costume and other fashions for 1822: " A wedding dress has lately been made for a very charming young lady of large fortune. It is of tulle embroidered in embossed daisies, which are all of seed pearls. A diadem for her hair is formed of five daisies in pearls; this diadem is valued at thirty thousand francs. At the last evening's musical performance of M. Massimimo, I remarked a white hat of straw, the brim of which was embroidered in white silk flat embroidery. A very full and high plume of marabout feathers was placed on one side.

" Turbans are of two colours, for example : celestial blue and white; cherry colour and white; or pink and straw colour. Small Leghorn hats, à l'Arcadie, are now much worn at balls ; the strings hang down as low as the sash.

" The favourite shoes are black satin, with or without sandal ties, according to the taste of the wearer. Lilac kid shoes are also very fashionable. When gaiters and English half shoes are worn for walking the petticoats are always very short.

" The gloves worn with short sleeves do not come up to the elbow : they are very tight, but are so much rusked that they are only two fingers' breadth higher than the bracelet.

" A cross with a little watch in the centre is the newest ornament in the jewelry line. Some other crosses, with a floweret between each branch, conceal a spying-glass. A new kind of seal, called cachet à la roue, has lately been invented ; it is fixed to a wheel suspended from the watch-chain, and on different kinds of gems are engraved letters, so combined that the initials of these gems form a device. The newest bracelets are of red morocco fastened with a buckle."

The principal change in the fashions for the winter season of 1823 was that bonnets were made of more substantial materials, such as velvet or beaver, the latter being very much in favour. They were lined with coloured satin and trimmed with long feathers hanging down over the shoulder. The latest hats were of black velvet, but there was no marked change in the shapes, except that the brims spread out more like a fan. Hats were faced with a sort of silk plush and the trimming consisted of rosettes, half satin, half plush.

Black velvet dresses were exceedingly fashionable for the winter of 1823, made very short and trimmed with flounces of black lace. A novel combination is described in a French magazine: " The dresses most in favour are of black velvet,

made very short, and flounced with black lace; one of these
flounces is set on at the edge of the hem, and is of a very rich
pattern, which is admirably displayed over a white satin dress
worn under the velvet one, and made as much longer than the
upper garment, as the lace is broad."

"The materials for turbans this autumn (1823) are of the
most effective kind, and well adapted for evening wear. Some
are of white gossamer gauze with green and gold stripes, with
the white spaces between slightly clouded with gold; others are
of a rainbow striped gauze, on a green ground powdered with
gold; the stripes are crimson, royal blue, green and yellow; but
the most superb material for the full dress turban is pactolus,
or golden sand gauze. It combines both lightness and richness,
and makes up beautifully; but much care is required in not
making it appear heavy, and none but a skillful *Marchande de
Modes* can possibly pin up a turban of this material so as to give
it a proper effect. It is peculiarly becoming to ladies with dark
hair and eyes."

According to all the authorities, pelisse dresses were the
favourites for house wear. Made to clear the instep, and opening over a false petticoat trimmed to match the gown, they
were both graceful and dignified. In Figure 62 a charming
morning frock of this style is shown, made of fine cambric,
beautifully embroidered by hand. The hat in the sketch is
taken from a contemporary plate. It was worn by a Virginia
bride, Miss Colquhoun, of Petersburg, the morning after her
wedding in 1823. Evening dresses were made of gauze and
trimmed with puffings of satin or net, and caught down with
rosettes or knots of the gauze. The wedding dress of Miss
Colquhoun, given in Figure 103, was made in this way.

A Paris letter informs us that "at public spectacles and especially at concerts, caps are universally worn; these head-

dresses have, however, undergone a change ; they are no longer of the Mary Stuart shape with the point on the forehead. The fashionable cap now is called the Clotilda cap; it is almost a complete garland of musk roses, white thorn, small daisies and clematis, under a trimming of blond, and this full wreath lies between the blond and the hair and terminates at the ears. Dress hats are made of spotted velvet and are ornamented with three or five plumes, laid round the brim of the hat."

The same correspondent continues : " A dress scarf occasionally thrown over an evening robe is much in favour ; it is of flame-coloured barege silk, each end ornamented with three black stripes and a black fringe ; some of these scarfs have the stripes entwined with rings of gold.

" The fashionable furs are the fox, the white wolf of Siberia, and the chinchilla : the fur tippets have very long ends. The fur trimmed shoes are of violet or dark blue velvet ; they tie up the front and are finished with three large rosettes of satin ribbon, with short ends. . . .

" Half-boots are again very popular for walking ; they are of dark blue, dark green, jean colour, or black ; and made of a new kind of fine morocco leather called Turkish satin.

" A lady has lately arrived here from Louisiana, and has presented some of her friends with very pretty fans, made of feathers, which fans were fabricated in that part of America. They are composed of twenty-five different feathers, each seven inches long, ranged in a half circle, twelve belonging to the left wing, and twelve to the right : these feathers all turn inward ; and it is observed that in fixing one to the other the barbs of the second feather half cover those of the first, and so on to the twelfth. The middle feather inclines neither to one side nor the other, but its barbs half cover the two feathers on each side of it. The stalks of the feathers are all stripped to a certain height; and it is these which form the sticks of the fan; above and beneath each stick is a narrow ribbon the two ends of which, before the rosette at the extremity is formed, leave a loop, whereby to hang the fan on the arm, when not in use. The natural colour of the feathers of the different birds from whence they are taken, gives to the fan the appearance of a shell: the bowed-out part of the mount is painted with flowers or devices and the hollow part is held next the face."

A gown of white cashmere embroidered in jonquil-coloured silk with shoes to match, is a costume described in a contemporary letter that sounds very attractive. Sleeves both short and long were made very full.

The chief novelty of the year (1823) were the plaited blouses. In " La Belle Assemblée " is the first mention of the familiar garment, we have found, and we pinch ourselves to see if we can be awake when we read : " The new blouses are many of them made of clear muslin." " Nothing is thought rare that is not new and follow'd, yet we know that what was worn some twenty years ago comes into grace again." * Several times twenty years brought the " too prevailing " blouses into grace again. Parti-coloured feathers were " all the rage " in the last half of this year; four plumes each of a different colour were often worn on one hat or bonnet.

Although lace has never been manufactured at its best in this country, it is interesting to know that in 1823 a successful effort was made in Massachusetts.

" Medway Lace.—We examined yesterday (says the ' New York Statesman ') at John Nesmith & Co.'s store, Fly-market, two boxes of lace, manufactured at Medway, Mass., by Dean Walker & Co., in a singularly constructed loom, made in this country, from the recollection of a similar machine examined

* Beaumont and Fletcher.

by one of our artists in England, and who, by his genius and memory has thus obtained what he wished, without violating the law of England against the exportation of machinery. . . . The lace is pronounced by good judges to be of a superior quality, and that it will not suffer in comparison with the imported, made from the same material, while the price is stated to be much lower. The widest is very beautiful, and richly and tastefully wrought. We may add that it is destined to become very fashionable as we learn that the proprietor, on a late visit to Washington, was very much gratified to find a liberal purchaser in the lady of one of the honourable members of the cabinet." *

The chief social excitement of this year in the United States was the visit of La Fayette, who came as the guest of the nation invited by President Monroe by order of Congress. The coming of the great Frenchman revived the feeling of gratitude and friendship for France. Our people throughout the country exerted themselves in every way to show their appreciation of the aid of the French troops at Yorktown. Balls, fêtes, dinners, parades, etc., were given in every city. In Philadelphia the celebration lasted for several days. A local newspaper gives the following account:

"THE NATION'S GUEST

" On Monday morning, the 4th inst., about three hundred children of both sexes, from the different schools in Philadelphia, were arranged in the State House yard to receive General La Fayette: the spectacle was most beautiful and highly interesting.

" In the evening he attended a grand ball at the theatre: the lobby of which was converted into a magnificent saloon,

* Niles' Weekly Register (1823-1824).

adorned with beautiful rose, orange and lemon trees, in full bearing, and a profusion of shrubbery, pictures, busts, banners with classical inscriptions, etc., all illuminated with a multitude of lamps. For the dancers there were two compartments, the house and the stage; the upper part of the former was hung with scarlet drapery, studded with golden stars, while the great chandelier, with two additional ones, and a row of wax tapers, arranged over the canopy, shed down a blaze of light. The first and second tiers of boxes were crowded with ladies in the richest apparel, as spectators of the dazzling array. Beyond the proscenium the stage division wore the appearance of an Eastern pavillion in a garden, terminating with a view of an extended sea and landscape, irradiated by the setting sun, and meant to typify the Western world. The company began to assemble soon after seven o'clock, and consisted of two thousand or more persons, of whom 600 or 700 were invited strangers. Twenty-two hundred tickets had been issued. No disorder occurred in the streets, with the arrival and departure of the carriages, which formed a line along the adjoining squares.

"General La Fayette appeared at nine o'clock and was received at the door by the managers of the ball. He was conducted the whole length of the apartments through an avenue formed by the ladies to the bottom of the stage, where Mrs. Morris, Governor Shulze, and the Mayor waited to greet him in form: the full band playing an appropriate air during his progress. As soon as he was seated, the dancers were called, and at least four hundred were immediately on the floor. The dancing did not cease until near five o'clock, though the company began to retire about three. At twelve, one of the managers, from an upper box, proclaimed a toast 'to the nation's guest,' which was hailed with enthusiasm and accompanied by the descent

1840–1848

FIGURE 124.—1847—Bonnet of shirred white satin with *panache* of ostrich tips. From the collection of Miss Dutihl, in Memorial Hall, Philadelphia.

FIGURE 125.—1840—Plain straw bonnet trimmed with brown ribbon. From a plate.

FIGURE 126.—1848—Bonnet of dove-coloured satin with pale pink and green-figured ribbon. From Miss Dutihl's collection, in Memorial Hall, Philadelphia.

FIGURE 127.—1845—House dress of *mousseline de laine*. Hair in Polish braids. From a Daguerreotype.

FIGURE 128.—1840—Walking costume showing lingerie bodice and silk scarf with Roman stripes. From a plate.

FIGURE 129.—1843—Dress of grey satin with black lace scarf. Worn in Boston.

FIGURE 130.—1848—Bonnet of pink uncut velvet trimmed with silk fringe and a band of braided velvet of the same colour. Miss Dutihl's collection, in Memorial Hall, Philadelphia.

FIGURE 131.—1840—Bonnet of white ribbed silk. Blond veil with pink ribbons. Small pink flowers inside the brim. Miss Dutihl's collection, Memorial Hall, Philadelphia.

FIGURE 132.—1845—Quilted hood of ruby silk. Memorial Hall, Philadelphia.

124

125
C.W.T.
After Print

126
S.B.S.

127

128

129

130
S.B.S.

131

132

of a banner from the ceiling. Behind this was suddenly displayed a portrait of the general, with allegorical figures." *

We are told that as each guest was presented to the Marquis de La Fayette, he bowed with much grace of manner and said in very careful English : " How do you do ? "

Speaking of the ball given to General La Fayette in Baltimore a few nights afterwards, the same paper says : "It was the grandest entertainment of the kind ever witnessed in this city, both as regards the style and taste of the decorations and the brilliant and elegant appearance of the company, which was far more numerous than usually assembled here on such occasions. When the music for the dancing ceased, the military band of the first rifle regiment played the most pleasing and fashionable airs. . . . Just before the ladies of the first tables retired, General La Fayette requested permission to give the following toast, which was received in a manner that reflected credit on the fair objects of it : ' The Baltimore ladies—the old gratitude of a young soldier mingles with the respectful sense of new obligation conferred on a veteran.' The ladies rose and saluted the general, and the sensation and effect is not to be described ; when he sat down there was a burst of applause from all the gentlemen present."

> " See the proud eagle now with folded plume
> The form and temper of the dove assume :
> Now free to soar through his own native skies,
> Nor vengeful beak, nor toiling wing he plies,
> But all his struggles o'er, his wrongs redress'd,
> He bends to greet a friend, his country's guest." †

We are so fortunate as to be able to give a picture in Figure 142 of a ball dress actually worn at this important function by Miss Amanda Nace. A badge, with the head of the dis-

* Niles' Weekly Register (1824–1825).   † *Ibid.*

tinguished guest on a white silk ribbon edged with gold fringe, will be seen on the breast. The dress itself is of white chambery gauze and the trimming a deep pink gauze piped with white satin. The costume is complete all but the gloves, about which an interesting anecdote has been related to me by Miss Bittinger, a granddaughter of the owner of the gown, to whom I am also indebted for the picture. The head of La Fayette was stamped on the back of each glove, and as the old courtier bent over the hand of the wearer to imprint thereon a kiss in the old style, he recognized his own likeness, and with a few graceful words to the effect that he did not care to kiss himself, he made a very low bow, and the lady passed on.

As La Fayette went through the streets of Washington on the day of his arrival, a woman dressed to represent Fame recited the following lines:

" Take this wreath, the badge of glory,
    Which thou hast so nobly won,
La Fayette shall live in story,
    With the name of WASHINGTON.

" Warriors known by devastation,
    Who have filled the world with fears,
Never gained my approbation,
    When their wreaths were stained with tears.

" But thou, a suitor, far more true,
    Has courted me with winning wiles,
As thy desert, I give to you
    The crown of laurel, deck'd with smiles."

Less bombastic, but certainly more touching, was the presentation of a ring containing Washington's hair which was made at Mount Vernon with this address: "The ring has ever been an emblem of the union of hearts, from the earliest ages of the world, and this will unite the affections of all the Americans to the person and posterity of La Fayette now and hereafter; and when your descendants of a distant day shall behold this valued relic, it will remind them of the heroic virtues of their illustrious sire, who received it, not in the palaces of princes, or amid the pomp and vanities of life, but at the laurelled grave of Washington."

From 1825 to 1835, the leg-of-mutton sleeves were undoubtedly the most striking article of woman's dress. It is not known who invented these sleeves or gave them the name which so well describes their shape, but like most popular fashions they increased in size until they became absolutely grotesque. Almost as much material was required to make a pair of fashionable sleeves as for the skirt of the gown, although the latter was more voluminous than it had been for many years. Like the hooped skirts and panniers of George IV's time, the sleeves took up so much room that it was necessary for the wearer to go through an ordinary door sideways. A contemporary says of this fashion that walking behind a pair of these sleeves one could always hear a curious creaking sound made as they rubbed together at the back.

The picture of a large Leghorn hat of this period is given in Figure 273. The brim is cut at the back and caught up with a large bow of white ribbon. A rosette is placed over the right ear, and the strings tie under the chin. This style of hat was fashionable from 1825 to 1830. Our illustration is copied from an original hat in the Wetherill Collection at Memorial Hall, Philadelphia.

Bonnets and hats were very much alike and stood up around the face. Fur boas and lace scarfs were in great favour, and the hair was arranged in curls on the temples.

"Fair tresses man's imperial race ensnare."

In a letter of invitation (1827) from Mrs. Mason of Washington to Miss Chew of Philadelphia, which we are courteously permitted to quote, is the following advice about the dresses she should bring with her for the visit :

" Let your dress for the wedding be as simple as you please. The same dress you wore to E. Tucker's wedding will be much handsomer than any you will find here. Virginia will wear a white crape trimmed with large white satin *rouleaux* over white satin, the same dress that she has worn at all the parties she has attended this winter, and T—— will wear a plain bobinet trimmed with a lace flounce she has worked for herself. I shall wear my white satin which is still decent. Nobody here will make dress a matter of moment, and your wardrobe will pass unnoticed and unobserved unless you bring anything very extravagant. The prettiest dress you can wear at the grand occasion will be a white book-muslin trimmed with a wreath of white flowers, or with three rows of plain bobinet quilled double through the middle."

In Figure 63 and in the initial on page 141 pictures of two costumes worn by Miss Chew are given, but the date is earlier than this visit to Washington. One is a short dancing frock of white crape over a slip of white satin, trimmed with white roses with tinsel leaves. The other is a beautifully embroidered India muslin made with a high bodice, long sleeves which fall over the hand, and a very long train.

It is interesting to know that Miss Chew made the journey in her father's coach, travelling from the historic house of Chief Justice Chew, Cliveden, near Philadelphia, to Washington in three days.

A charming little gown of pale blue gauze trimmed with satin of the same shade is given in Figure 64. It is taken from a print of 1828.

Figure 61 shows an opera costume, cloak of silk and hat of

black velvet trimmed with white ostrich plumes. The dress is copied from one of white satin brocade which was worn in Philadelphia in 1829.

Another dress of this period is pictured in Figure 73. It is of a rich yellow brocade and was worn in Philadelphia by Miss Mary Brinton about 1829. The trimming is all made of the material of the gown. The head in the sketch is copied from a contemporary portrait.

Dress does not seem to have been made a matter of moment in the histrionic thought of that time, for we read that Fanny Kemble, the idol of the English stage, on which she made her début in 1829, represented Juliet in a fashionable ball dress of white satin with a long train, short sleeves and low bodice, a girdle of paste brilliants being the only theatrical property of the costume.

At the time of Jackson's election (1829), party spirit ran high in American politics. His lady partisans were to be distinguished by dresses and aprons of calico imprinted in great medallions with the very unhandsome head of their hero. Specimens of the Jackson calico may be seen in the Historical Society at Newport, Rhode Island. This whim of fashion recalls to mind the eighteen tucks in the white dresses of Louis XVIII's adherents in 1815, and the bunches of violets worn by the admirers of Napoleon at the same time.

On the occasion of Jackson's inauguration, we read of a gorgeous costume of scarlet velvet, richly trimmed with gold embroidery, worn by Mrs. Bomford; a "large ruby, for which Colonel Bomford had refused five thousand dollars," in her turban.

It was at this period that Miss Harriet Martineau made her celebrated visit to the United States and was fêted and entertained a great deal in Washington. Having been invited to spend a " sociable day " with a lady who probably thought that form of hospitality would be more enjoyable than a dinner party to the distinguished visitor on account of her deafness, Miss Martineau and her companion, Miss Jeffrey, arrived quite early and were shown to a bedroom to take off their " bonnets and long capes."

" You see," remarked Miss Martineau to her hostess, " we have complied with your request and come sociably to spend the day.   We have been walking all the morning and our lodgings are too distant to return there, so we have done as those who have no carriages do in England when they go out to spend the day."

" I offered her," observed her hostess, " combs and brushes, but having one enormous pocket in her French dress, she assured me that they were provided with all that was necessary and pulled out nice little silk shoes, silk stockings, scarf for her neck, lace mits, a gold chain and some other jewelry, and soon without changing her dress was prettily equipped for dinner or evening company." *

This is the first record we find of a pocket in a gown, but we hope it was not without precedent in America.

The hats were almost as remarkable as the sleeves as will be seen in the illustrations of this period.   Figure 274 shows a very quaint specimen in the Wetherill collection.   It is made of sage green taffeta with a cross-bar of salmon pink, and is corded and bound with pink satin ribbon.   The date given is 1829.

The Cabriolet bonnets shown in Figures 240, 241 and 244 were named for the fashionable carriage of the day.   Both of these novelties were adopted by the eccentric Lady Morgan in 1829.   In a recent memoir we read :

* First Forty Years of Washington Society, by Mrs. Samuel Harrison Smith.

" It was never known where this vehicle was bought, except that Lady Morgan declared it came from the first carriage-builder in London. In shape it was like a grasshopper, as well as in colour. Very high and very springy, with enormous wheels, it was difficult to get into, and dangerous to get out of. Sir Charles, who never in his life before had mounted a coach-box, was persuaded by his wife to drive his own carriage. He was extremely short-sighted, and wore large green spectacles out-of-doors. His costume was a coat much trimmed with fur, and heavily braided. James Grant, the tall Irish footman, in the brightest of red plush, sat beside him, his office being to jump down whenever anybody was knocked down, or run over, for Sir Charles drove as it pleased God. The horse was mercifully a very quiet animal, and much too small for the carriage, or the mischief would have been worse. Lady Morgan, in the large bonnet of the period, and a cloak lined with fur hanging over the back of the carriage, gave, as she conceived, the crowning grace to a neat and elegant turn-out." *

A contributor to the " National Recorder " in 1829 paid a graceful tribute to women, saying :

" The history of woman is the history of the improvements in the world. Some twenty or thirty years ago, when manual labour performed all the drudgery, some five, six or seven yards of silk or muslin or gingham would suffice for the flitting and flirting of the most gay and volatile of the sex. But as soon as the powers of steam are applied, and labour is changed from physical to intellectual, the ladies, in their charitable regard for the operative class of the community, begin to devise means for their continued employment, and as the material is produced with half the labour, the equilibrium must be sustained by consuming a double quantity."

* Little Memoirs of the Nineteenth Century.

137

139

133

138

140

136

134

135

This is certainly a charitable view to take of the new fashion of very full skirts and leg-of-mutton sleeves. An elaborate style of hair-dressing came in at that time, which met with approval on the same grounds.

"I knew of one lady who, for the same reason, sported a large head of puffs and curls, to prove that she not only encouraged but engaged in the support of domestic productions. It does seem peculiarly hard that, while the ladies are thus carrying their principles into practice, even at the expense of their loveliness, they should have to encounter the sarcasm and the ridicule of the other sex. Let us hope that they will not be discouraged in their endeavours by such mean and inconsiderate abuse. They may be assured that there are those who duly estimate their motives and principles and who respect them accordingly."

We do not notice any marked change in riding habits in the twenties, but riding was still the fashionable exercise and we read that Fanny Kemble in 1829 wore a suit of brown cloth with a red waistcoat.

Women's Dress

1830–1840

"Every generation laughs at the old fashion
But follows religiously the new."
—THOREAU.

HERE were not any very marked changes in 1830 in the style and cut of gowns. Although the skirts were somewhat fuller than they had been, they were still worn short, and elaborately trimmed, and were gathered at the waist into a band, which was hidden under a belt made broader than in the previous year and fastened with a buckle in front (Figure 93).

For house wear the shoulders were usually uncovered, the bodices being finished with a tucker or frill of lace. Out-of-doors little capes or pelerines, either matching the dress or of a contrasting colour, were worn (Figures 90 and 94).

Cushions, which were fastened in the tops of sleeves to produce the desired effect, were made larger and larger. The sketch of a pair of these sleeve-extenders, made of brown cambric and filled with down, is given in Figure 82. They belong to the Museum of the School of Industrial Art in Philadelphia. With this order of dress waists looked proportionately slender. Deep collars, sometimes of plain linen but generally

182

of lace or needlework embroidery turned down round the neck, contributed to the broad effect. Scarfs of cachemire, silk or lace were worn universally.

Hats or bonnets still were of the Cabriolet shape, faced with a contrasting silk, and trimmed with large ribbon bows, and wide strings tying under the chin (Figures 87 and 123). The crowns were high and sloped upwards when on the head. In Memorial Hall, Philadelphia, may be seen a bonnet of 1830 made of white silk gauze straw, trimmed with white gauze ribbon with pale yellow and green figures. A sketch of this bonnet is given in Figure 276 and in Figure 293 a picture of a Quaker bonnet of white silk of about the same date, shows a modest adaptation of the fashion from 1830–1840. This bonnet is also in the valuable collection at Memorial Hall. Feathers were still worn, many bonnets being almost overladen with plumes. A wit of the day said of Lady Cork, then over eighty years old, that she resembled " a shuttlecock, for she was all cork and feathers."

In 1830 fashion dictated that the hair should be worn high, and very high it continued throughout that period. This was undoubtedly the ugliest style of hair-dressing ever introduced and could hardly have been becoming to any one, but the coquettish bow-knots and rosettes all made of hair would have been particularly inappropriate in grey, and the use of hair dye became very popular (Figures 73, 83, 121 and 133). Fur boas were in vogue at this time and low thin slippers still prevailed for all occasions.

A letter written about this time points a moral on the subject of dyeing the hair.

" A young lady, a friend of mine residing in the same house, found, to her utter dismay, that her hair was becoming grizzled. It was a terrible misfortune, as she had really a fine head of hair, and false curls were not, at that time, much worn ; so she had no need or excuse for substituting other hair for her own, except that ugly one, growing grey. . . . She purchased, at a very high price, a bottle of 'Imperial Hair Restorer'—I think it was called, or some such sounding name—'warranted to give the hair a beautiful glossy appearance, and restore it to its pristine colour without failure or danger.' The restorative was plentifully applied and in two days' time the curls of the young lady, where the grey hairs had chiefly obtruded, were changed to an equivocal hue, bearing a near resemblance to the dark changeable green of the peacock's feathers. The only truth of the restorative was its glossy qualities. The hair of the unfortunate young lady was glossy enough, and stiff as bristles. I cannot even now, though several years have passed, think of the ludicrous appearance of that patent coloured hair, and the mirth it created in our little coterie, without laughing heartily."

From the "Lady's Magazine," we give an elaborate full dress : " The skirt is of blond gauze. The sleeves and flounce are richly figured with a pattern in white ; but the bouquets embroidered above the deep flounce are in the most delicate shades of French blond. The corsage is of white satin, made plain and tight to the shape both in the back and front. The short *beret* sleeves, beneath those of white gauze, are of white satin, and exceedingly full. The long sleeves narrow a little towards the wrist, but were never made fuller at the top. The belt is of plain satin, corded at the edges. The hem of the white satin dress appears below the flounce ; it is very much puffed, so as to give a great richness to the finish of the costume. The arrangement of the hair is new and beautiful, braids are wound over one high bow, with two folds. A delicate silver sprig is the sole ornament of the head, excepting a long silk scarf, which is gathered slightly on the top of the bows of the hair and falls on each side nearly as low as the knees. The head-dress is called *en barbe.* Necklace, earrings and bracelets of wrought silver and gold. Bouquet of spring flowers."

This odd arrangement of bow-knots and puffs of hair, which we notice in many of the contemporary portraits, was obviously very difficult to adjust without artificial aid. In Figure 83 we give the picture of a cluster of curls of false hair fastened to a comb, showing an easy way of surmounting the difficulty. It is copied from the original article in the School of Industrial Art, in Philadelphia.

Another fashionable coiffure is given in the following description of a ball dress : " Hair braided with gold beads, in Grecian bands, and a low coronet and large knot, ornamented with plumes or silver barley, *à la* Ceres. Dress of white gauze lisse, gathered in front of the corsage with full loose folds. Underdress of deep rose-coloured satin *à la* Reine. The epaulettes and the bottom of the lisse robe are cut into square dents. The upper dress is looped up on the left side to the knees, *à la* Taglioni, with bouquets of gold barley. The rose-coloured satin skirt is finished with a border of full puffs at the feet. Long white kid gloves, fan embossed with gold ; necklace of gold medallions."

And here is another description of hair arrangement for evening dress : " The hair is banded *à la Greque,* small knot on the crown, from which depend a number of ringlets *à la* Sevigné, and is ornamented with a small crown of field flowers. Dress of crape over a slip of satin *à la* Reine ; corsage *à la* Roxalane, over which fall very pretty reveres and epaulettes of satin. The skirt is ornamented with a wreath of cut ribbands *à la* Taglioni, fastened on the right with a few large satin leaves and ends and a bunch of minute field flowers."

We read of many new materials and colours. A pelisse is described of *gros de Tours* in *bleu de Berry*, embroidered down the front, which opened part way showing the underdress. It was close-fitting and finished with a double pelerine embroidered to match the fronts. The sleeves were finished with a plain tight cuff also embroidered. With this was worn a *gros de Naples* bonnet, the colour "a new shade of *vapeur*," trimmed with knots and bows of pink gauze ribbon. These materials and colours are probably known to-day by different and less fanciful names.

The following dress, which sounds unusually pretty, is described in a contemporary magazine :

"Evening Dress.—A straw-coloured crape dress over a *gros de Naples* slip to match. Corsage cut low and square, and trimmed with a falling tucker of *blonde de Cambray*. *Beret* sleeve, finished *en manchette*, with the same sort of lace ; a *noeud* of gauze ribband, to correspond in colour, is placed in front of the arm. The skirt is trimmed with a flounce of *blonde de Cambray*, headed by a cluster of narrow *rouleaux* of satin to match the dress. The trimming is raised a little on the left side, and finished with a single flower with buds and foliage. With this is worn a crape hat of a darker shade than the dress. The brim faced with gauze ribband. The crown trimmed with white feathers placed in different directions ; some are passed through openings made in the brim, and partially shade it. The jewelry worn with this dress should be a mixture of gold and pearls."

Here is another Evening Dress.—"A changeable *gros de Naples ;* the colours blue shot with white. The corsage is cut very low, fits close to the shape, and is ornamented in front of the bust in the fan style with satin *rouleaux* to correspond with the dress. A trimming of rich fringe, the head of which is composed of beads and the remaining part of chenille, goes round the bust. The *ceinture* fastens behind in a rosette with a richly-wrought gold clasp in the centre. *Beret* sleeves, the shortest we have seen."

Two pretty dresses are described by a contemporary London correspondent in 1830 :

" Ball Dress.—White blond gauze over a pale pink satin slip ; from a blush rose on each shoulder a pink ribbon is draped and caught under another blush rose above the centre of a pink satin belt. The skirt is trimmed with blush roses, joined by a loop of pink satin above the hem. The hair is arranged in large Madonna curls, which are somewhat drawn up and heightened by a wreath of blush roses with leaves.

" Dinner and Carriage Dress.—Hat of rice straw, trimmed with bunches of pink azalea. Ribbons of light green, shaded *à milles rayes*, the stripes very minute, and shot with white. The dress is of soft *gros de Naples* of prismatic rose colour, the lights of which are bright lilac. Many other varieties of colour in shot silk are used, but this is a favourite. The corsage is made with large horizontal plaits, confined up the front with a band. The shoulders are trimmed with three falls of silk, the edges worked in loose floss silk into small points ; these falls are seen one below the other, and narrow until they meet in front under the belt, which is broad and made of the same material as the dress. The sleeves are full at top, and are plaited under a band at the elbow and to correspond at the wrist."

An issue of the "Lady's Book" (1830) announced the following :

" Fashions for October.—A frock of changeable *gros de zane*, the body plain behind and full in front, worn occasionally with a pelerine of the same ; the frill of which is very deep and full

1824 - 181   1805 - 152   1820 - 177   1825 - 143

1830 - 144   1830 - 140   1835 - 142   1835 - 145   Carl de Zand, 1847

at the shoulders, becoming gradually narrower and plainer as it descends to the belt. The skirt of this dress is made extremely wide, and is set on the body with five plaits only, one in front, one on each side, and two behind : these plaits are of course very large. The bottom of the skirt is finished with a thick cord sewed into the hem. The sleeves are very wide, till they reach the elbow, and fit tightly to the lower part of the arm. The ruffle round the neck and hands is of plain bobinet quilling. Bonnet of Dunstable straw trimmed with a band, and strings of broad pink satin ribbon. Large scarlet shawl of embroidered Canton crape."

Mrs. Hale, in the "Lady's Magazine," gives advice on the subject of corsets :

"Corsets should be made of smooth soft elastic materials.

"They should be accurately fitted and modified to suit the peculiarities of figure of each wearer.

"No other stiffening should be used but that of quilting, or padding; the bones, steel, etc., should be left to the deformed and the diseased for whom they were originally intended.

"Corsets should never be drawn so tight as to impede regular natural breathing, as, under all circumstances, the improvement of figure is insufficient to compensate for the air of awkward restraint caused by such lacing.

"They should never be worn, either loose or tight, during the hours appropriate to sleep, as by impeding respiration and accumulating the heat of the system improperly, they invariably injure.

"The corset for young persons should be of the most simple character, and worn in the lightest and easiest manner, allowing their lungs full play, and giving the form its fullest opportunity for expansion."

The extreme of fashion was not always adopted in America.

In Figure 86 we give a sketch of a simple costume of brown
taffeta with leg-of-mutton sleeves of modern dimensions which
was worn in Philadelphia in 1830. The hair is arranged in a
simple but dignified coil of braids copied from a contemporary
portrait. An illustration of a bonnet of this period (1830) of
moderate size is given in Figure 275. It is made of fancy
Tuscan straw and trimmed with white ribbon, and belongs to
the Wetherill collection at Memorial Hall, Philadelphia.

Riding has always been a favourite form of exercise in England and considered an essential part of a young lady's educa-
tion. Undoubtedly it was an Englishman who penned the following tribute:

> "How melts my beating heart as I behold
> Each lovely nymph, our island's boast and pride,
> Push on the generous steed that sweeps along
> O'er rough, o'er smooth, nor heeds the steepy hill,
> Nor falters in the extended vale below."

But it was by no means a lost art on this side of the Atlantic
and was probably only less in vogue in the large cities. At this
period of the thirties, habits as well as hats were more severe in
outline, and rather conspicuous for the absence of trimmings.
Not only were they more suitable for their purpose than the
equestrian fashions of the early part of the century, but infi-
nitely more becoming with their short jackets outlining the
waist. Figure 116 represents a habit from a plate of 1830, in
which the effect of the mannish hat is softened by a flowing
veil. Perhaps it was the change of fashion which inspired the
following lines:

> "Her dress, her shape, her matchless grace
> Were all observed, as well as heavenly face."

In the reign of William IV we read of the Marchioness of
Salisbury, a prominent personage of the time, that she was a

fearless horsewoman, and hunted with the Hatfield hounds in
1831, riding hard and clearing fences as ardently as any sports-
man in the field, clad in "a habit of light blue cloth with a
black velvet collar and a jockey cap;" and that when she was
an old lady of eighty years and very feeble, she had herself
strapped into her saddle, and ambled up and down Hyde Park
in the midst of the moving throng.   Locker, in his verses on
"Rotten Row," laments:

> "But where is now the courtly troop
> That once rode laughing by?
> I miss the curls of Cantilupe
> The smile of Lady Di."

Specimens of the very large bonnets worn in 1830–40 are
given in Figures 87, 123, and 276; also in the initial on page 182.

Shawls were so much worn at that time, both genuine India
cachemire and imitations thereof made in France, that it may
be of interest to readers to know something of their manufacture and the origin of the strange names of the different varieties, for like the oriental rugs each design had a symbolic
meaning.

> "Not a vanity is given in vain."

According to an article on the manufacture of cachemire
shawls, nearly "5,000 people were employed in making them
in 1831.   About three weavers were kept at work in each shop,
and when the pattern was especially fine they could not make
more than a quarter of an inch a day, so that the most elaborate shawls were made in pieces.   The weaver was seated on a
bench and a child placed a little below him with its eyes fixed
on the pattern, who every time the frame was turned told the
weaver the colours wanted.   The wages of first-rate workmen
were from four to five pence, and the child labour it is to be

feared counted for nothing. The pattern familiar to us as the palm-leaf is not a palm of the desert, but the cypress, the lover's tree among the orientals, which is sculptured on the ruins of the palace of Persepolis exactly as it is figured on the shawl borders. The cypress adorns the border of a shawl, even as the tree itself overshadows the bank of a stream; and is considered by the Easterns as the image of religion and moral freedom, as Saadi has expressed in verse:

> " 'Be thou fruitful as the palm, or be
> At least as the dark cypress, high and free,'

because its branches never incline to the earth, but all shoot upward towards heaven.

"The original meaning of the wreaths and bunches of flowers woven in the middle of the square shawl pieces, and which so greatly enhance their value, is full of significance. The Turkish and Persian name of these shawls is Boghdscha; the origin of the word is, however, neither Turkish nor Persian, but Indian, from Pudscha, which means a flower offering. When the season of the year will not afford the flowers which the Hindoos offer to their gods, the women spread out shawls, in the middle of which the embroidered basket of flowers supplies the place of fresh blossoms; on this they kneel, as do the Moslems on the little carpets which exhibit a representation of the altar in the holy temple of Mecca, towards which they turn when they pray. The Boghdscha, or square shawl, with the flower-basket in the centre, may here take precedence of the other kinds, from the superiority of its original destination, rather than from its commercial value; for, in this respect, it is usually surpassed by the long scarf shawls, which are commonly denominated Risajii. A third class of shawls are woven without flowers or borders and are generally made into dresses by the

women ; these are called Toulik.   In the shops and warehouses
where the shawls are first sold, they are called Kaschmiri or
Lahori, according as they are the produce of Kaschmire or
Lahor.   The imitations of them, whether they come from Bag-
dad, Paris, or London, are all called Taklid, *i. e.*, imitations.
The workshops of Kaschmire have very lately produced some
splendid shawls, which are always marked with the word new-
tash, signifying new-fashioned.   The patterns of these represent
banners, pinnacles, chains, peacock's feathers, etc. ; they are denominated in Persian, Alemdar (containing banners) ; Kun-
keredar (containing pinnacles) ; Koeschedar (having corners if
the corners are ornamented) ; Lilsiledar (containing chains) ;
Peri-taus (peacock-winged) ; etc.   These denominations are frequently worked on the shawls with coloured silk ; the name of
the manufacturer is also generally inscribed on them, and very
often the epithets of God ; as, O preserver !   O protector ! be a
blessing granted to us ! and single letters, which form the word
Ahmed, or Mohammed, or some talismanic word with the addition of Allah, Allah, ' the highest, the highest ' (of the best
quality)."

> " I long not for rich silks or satins,
> My mind is contented with the schal and woollen stuff,'

is the illustration given in the Persian Dictionary for the word
shawl.

A decided change in the style of dressing the hair is
noticed in 1832.   " The low Grecian arrangement in the severe
classic taste of the antique, is universally adopted by ladies
whose profile will admit of this often most becoming style.
Coronets of pearls, cameos, or flowers are worn very low on the
brow.   Gold beads or pearls are woven with the braided hair.
The high gallery shell combs are now considered vulgar.   In

place of carved shell combs, gold combs, on which four or
five classic cameos are arranged *en couronne*, are worn in full
dress."

An English contemporary authority says : " The last week
has produced a novelty in evening dress, the adoption of
natural flowers for the hair. Wires are made to support them
invisibly. The flowers, which are not wreathed in the hair till
the moment of departure for the ball or *soirée*, are found to
retain their freshness during several hours. This fashion has
been revived from the last century, when little vases were made
on purpose to contain a few drops of water, and were hid
among the hair, with the stalks of the flowers inserted in
them." *

Another style of hair-dressing which was probably more
generally becoming, as it remained in fashion much longer,
was a Grecian knot worn high in the back, the front hair
parted and arranged in soft curls on the temples. (See Figures
72 and 230.)

Black velvet came into fashion for trimmings, for belts, and
for wristlets, in 1832, and has been more or less in favour ever
since. We read, too, of sleeves made plain to the elbow and
very full above.

It was in 1832 that Mrs. Trollope visited the United States
and on her return to England published an ill-natured book
entitled " Domestic Manners of the Americans." She dwells
at length on the unhappy partiality for false hair, forgetting
that the fashion prescribed in Paris was exceedingly popular
in London. Her remarks are shrewd, however, and sometimes
amusing, for instance : " Though the expense of the lady's dress
greatly exceeds, in proportion to their general style of living,
that of the ladies of Europe, it is very far (excepting in Phila-

* Royal Lady's Magazine.

delphia) from being in good taste. They do not consult the seasons in the colours or in the style of their costume ; I have often shivered at seeing a young beauty picking her way through the snow with a pale rose-coloured bonnet, set on the very top of her head. I knew one young lady whose pretty little ear was actually frost-bitten from being thus exposed. They never wear muffs or boots, and appear extremely shocked at the sight of comfortable walking shoes and cotton stockings, even when they have to step to their sleighs over ice and snow. They walk in the middle of winter with their poor little toes pinched into a miniature slipper, incapable of excluding as much moisture as might bedew a primrose. I must say in their excuse, however, that they have, almost universally, extremely pretty feet. They do not walk well, nor, in fact, do they ever appear to advantage when in movement. I know not why this should be, for they have abundance of French dancing-masters among them, but somehow or other it is the fact."

In Figure 75 is a specimen of fashion in America in 1832. The original dress from which the sketch was made is a beautiful shade of blue-green taffeta trimmed with folds of itself. The cape and long undersleeves could be taken off indoors, but were always worn in the street. It belonged to a belle of the thirties, noted for her graceful carriage. The bonnet, copied from a print of 1833, is of white chip trimmed with white satin and pale pink daisies. The dress apron in Figure 89 belonged to the same lady and was worn in 1833. It is made of old gold satin, embroidered in flowers of all colours ; roses of pink chiffon, pansies of arasene (or chenille), small roses of chiffon, forget-me-nots (pink and blue) and jonquils of chiffon, green stems and leaves of arasene, and other small flowers of chiffon.

149

150

152

153
C.W.T.
After Print

154
C.W.Trout
1907.

155
C.W.Trout 1907

156
Cecil W. Trout
1907

A charming old bonnet of 1833 is preserved in the Dutihl collection at Memorial Hall, made of white *point d'esprit* over white silk, with trimmings of white ribbon with a satin spot and a loop edge. The crown is stiff and the brim is formed of slender wires and lined with sarsnet. A picture of this bonnet is given in Figure 278.

White satin was still a favourite material for evening dresses in 1834. A lady writes from Washington: "I was gratified by Julia's good looks. She was dressed in plain white satin, and pink and white flowers on her head. Her hair was arranged by a hair-dresser."

Bodices for evening wear were made close fitting to the figure, and generally were trimmed with a bertha of lace or gauze. The sleeves were short and puffed, and gloves were worn reaching to the elbow. As for the hair-dressers' work, specimens of the prevailing styles are given in Figures 72, 73, 86 and 230.

A beautiful wedding dress, worn by a Quaker bride in Philadelphia in 1834, is sketched in Figure 72. It is of white satin with short puffed (melon) sleeves, over which are full long sleeves of white silk gauze, fastening at the wrist.

Pelisses of velvet and satin, closed down the front, and made with double pelerines, completely disguising the figure, were in great favour in the autumn of 1834. Bonnets were even larger and more flaring than before. Some of the latest were made of velvet and trimmed with a single large rosette of ribbon to match. Morning dresses were made of cashmere, and chintz robes printed in colour were popular. They were made with plain high bodices and fastened up the back. Shoulder capes were much worn with low or square cut bodices in the mornings. Large bonnets were a distinctive feature of costume in the thirties; the flaring brim lined with a becoming tint was surely an appropriate frame for a young face, and attractive indeed must have been Miss Wilkins' * heroine in

"HER BONNET

" When meeting bells began to toll
And pious folk began to pass,
She deftly tied her bonnet on,
The little sober meeting lass,
All in her neat white curtained room before her
      tiny looking glass.

" So nicely round her lady-cheeks
She smoothed her bands of glossy hair,
And innocently wondered if
Her bonnet did not make her fair ;
Then sternly chid her foolish heart for harbouring such fancies there.

·" So square she tied the satin strings,
And set the bows beneath her chin ;
Then smiled to see how sweet she looked,
Then thought her vanity a sin,
And she must put such thoughts away before
      the sermon should begin.

" But sitting 'neath the preacher's word,
Demurely in her father's pew,
She thought about her bonnet still,
Yes, all the parson's sermon through,
About the pretty bows and buds which better
      than the text she knew.

" Yet sitting there with peaceful face,
The reflex of her simple soul,
She looked to be a very saint
And maybe was one on the whole,
Only that her pretty bonnet kept away the aureole."

The bonnet referred to in the following verse must have been especially attractive :

* Mrs. Mary Wilkins Freeman.

" The Love Knot

" Tying her bonnet under her chin,
    She tied her raven ringlets in ;
    But not alone in its silken snare
    Did she catch her lovely floating hair,
    For tying her bonnet under her chin,
    She tied a young man's heart within."

Mantles trimmed and lined with fur were very fashionable. Sable, Isabella bear and a delicate fur called Kolinski were all used. A silk cord fastened the mantle at the waist and hung down low in front, finished with a handsome tassel. Olives and Brandenburgs were used as fastenings on velvet pelisses. Sleeves were very wide from the shoulder to the wrist and there finished with a deep cuff. Satin bonnets were trimmed with satin ribbon to match and bordered by curtain veils of rich black lace. The curtains at the back were very shallow and moderately full.

Among the new materials of the year were Persian taffeta with milk white or cream white ground, covered with small bouquets of roses and satin *moyenage* with a dark blue ground and an arabesque pattern in gold, or black with red figures. A new design for bodices was cut high at the throat, the front laid in plaits from the shoulder to the waist, like a fan. Long full sleeves caught in with two bands giving the effect of three puffs. The short puffed sleeves of 1835 were called melon sleeves ; over them long sleeves of blond lace were sometimes worn. In a fashion column of the " Court Magazine " for July, 1835, we read : " Lightness and simplicity are this month's characteristics, but it is a simplicity as expensive as it is tasteful ; the rich satins, velvets and furs of winter costumes were not in reality more costly than the comparatively plain attire of the present month."

Very dainty but costly must have been the *peignoir* described for that month, made of French cambric trimmed down the front with a deep ruffle of Valenciennes lace caught together at intervals by knots of the cambric edged with lace. The pelerine or shoulder cape was also trimmed with Valenciennes. We read about this time of a new Swiss muslin, with rich foulard patterns stamped on it. The bonnets and hats were enormously big in 1835. The brims were wider, the crowns were higher, and the curtains of bonnets were deeper. Veils of blond, illusion, or *dentelle de soie* were fastened to the brims of some of the newest bonnets.

We hear at this time of a new ribbon. It was of six different colours very tastefully mingled, in patterns of a rather bizarre effect, and was called Chinese ribbon. Flowers of all kinds, as well as feathers, were worn in hats. Printed cambrics, figured organdies, *mousseline de laine* and delicate lingerie continued in favour, and fichus of mull and lace were still very popular. One striking novelty is recorded for this year (1835) : gloves of rose-colour and of flesh-colour were preferred to white.

Turbans, although not as generally popular as they had been, were still worn. A new style was called the turban *à la juive*. It was made of white satin covered with tulle and ornamented with bandalettes *à l'antique*, embroidered with gold, and hanging down in the back almost to the neck. Another turban worn in that same year is described as " of the Turkish form " and as made of white net and maize coloured velvet, ornamented with two aigrettes held in place by a gold ornament set with brilliants.

A popular American periodical which first appeared in 1830, and had a wide circulation, was the " Lady's Book," published by Louis Godey in Philadelphia. It was founded on somewhat the same basis as the " Court Magazine " in London, containing serial stories and verses by recognized authors of the day, as well as fashion plates in colour. Two evening costumes for 1835 are described in the September number :

" A printed satin robe, white ground with a pattern in vivid colours of small sprigs in winding columns. The corsage is cut very low and square at the back and front of the bust, but rather higher on the shoulder than they are generally made, and pointed at the waist. It is trimmed round the top with a single row of narrow blond lace laid on flat. Blond lace long sleeves of the usual size at the top, and moderately full from the elbow to the wrist ; they are made open from the bend of the arm, but are caught together in three places by gold filagree buttons, and surmounted by *mancherons* of broad blond lace. The hair, parted on the forehead, is arranged on each side in a plaited band, which is doubled and hangs low. The back hair, also arranged in a braid, is twisted round the top of the head. Gold earrings, necklace and bracelets. White kid gloves ; white satin slippers.

" A robe of pale rose-coloured *mousseline de soie* over *gros de Naples* to correspond. A low corsage fitting close but with a little fullness at the bottom of the waist ; trimmed round the neck with a blond lace ruche. Short undersleeves of white *gros de Naples*, with an oversleeve of blond lace of the Marino Faliero shape confined by a gold agraffe on the shoulder. Armlets and *ceinture* of gold net, with gold clasps. The hair is parted on the forehead and turned up behind ; the ends form a cluster of curls. A band of fancy jewelry and bunches of gold wheat complete the coiffure. White silk net gloves. White *gros de Naples* slippers of the sandal form."

An attractive costume, which was worn in Pennsylvania, is given in Figure 87. The gown is of soft sage satin with brocaded flowers of the same colour made with bias folds of the satin, broad at the shoulder and tapering in at the waist ; the folds are finished with a shell trimming of the satin, the same trimming being used on the caps of the sleeves and on the cuffs. This unusually pretty dress was worn by Miss Halde-man. The style was fashionable in 1838 and the bonnet is copied from a plate of the same date.

Fashion was by no means an unimportant factor in the social life of rural neighbourhoods throughout the United States. Mrs. Gaskell's tea-party at Cranford might easily have taken place in a small community in Virginia or in New England, for instance. We remember the invitation was discussed and then accepted because " Miss Pole possessed a very smart cap which she was anxious to show to an admiring world." The expenditure in dress in Cranford was principally in the article referred to. If the heads were buried in smart caps, the ladies were like ostriches, and cared not what became of their bodies With old gowns, yellow and venerable collars, any number of brooches (some with dog's eyes painted on them, some that were like small picture-frames with mausoleums and weeping-willows neatly executed in hair inside ; some again with minia-tures of ladies and gentlemen sweetly smiling out of a nest of stiff muslin) and new caps to suit the fashion of the day, " the ladies of Cranford always dressed with chaste elegance and pro-priety," as Miss Barber once fittingly expressed it. " And with these new caps, and a greater array of brooches than had ever been seen together at one time since Cranford was a town, did Miss Forrester, and Miss Matty, and Miss Pole appear on that memorable Tuesday evening. I counted seven brooches myself on Miss Pole's dress. Two were fixed negligently in her cap (one was a butterfly of Scotch pebbles which a vivid imagina-tion might believe to be a real insect) ; one fastened her net neckerchief; one her collar; one ornamented the front of her gown between throat and waist ; another adorned the front of her stomacher. Where the seventh was I have forgotten, but it was somewhere about her, I am sure."

Needlework was still in vogue and was commended in the following verses by a contemporary poet :

'THE NEEDLE

" The gay belles of fashion may boast of excelling
  In waltz or cotillion, at whist or quadrille ;
And seek admiration by vauntingly telling
  Of drawing and painting and musical skill ;
But give me the fair one in country or city
  Whose home and its duties are dear to her heart,
Who cheerfully warbles some rustical ditty,
  While plying the needle with exquisite art.
The bright little needle, the swift flying needle,
  The needle directed by beauty and art.

" If love have a potent, a magical token,
  A talisman ever resistless and true,
A charm that is never evaded or broken,
  A witchery certain the heart to subdue—
'Tis this, and his armoury never has furnished
  So keen and unerring or polished a dart
Let beauty direct it, so pointed and burnished,
  And oh, it is certain of touching the heart.

" Be wise then, ye maidens, nor seek admiration
  By dressing for conquest and flirting with all ;
You never, whate'er be your fortune or station,
  Appear half so lovely at rout or at ball
As gaily convened at a work-covered table,
  Each cheerfully active and playing her part,
Beguiling the task with a song or a fable,
  And plying the needle with exquisite art."

A photograph of the wedding outfit worn by Miss Sarah Hayes who, in 1836, married Major Mordecai, a distinguished officer of the United States Army, in the Synagogue in Philadelphia, is given in Figure 170. The gown is of the sheerest, filmiest India muslin we have seen, and was imported for the

157

158

159

160

161

162

occasion by the bride's father, one of the leading merchants of
the day. The slippers have square toes, the new fashion for
1836, and the short gloves are embroidered and originally were
trimmed with blond lace to match the veil. The handkerchief case was the work of the bridesmaids and also the beautifully embroidered handkerchief with "Sarah" in flowered
letters in one corner. The fan is an exquisite specimen of
carved ivory made in India, with the monogram of the bride in
the centre. The marriage certificate is in Hebrew characters,
which unfortunately do not show in the photograph. We
notice that the sleeves were originally puffed, a very fashionable style in 1836.

About this date the extravagantly large sleeves went out
of fashion, and were followed by a more graceful style, fitting
close to the arm on top and full at the elbows.

In Figure 230 is shown a gown of cream white figured silk
worn in 1837 by a Quaker maiden at a wedding in a Philadelphia Meeting. The sleeves are in the new fashion, which
succeeded the leg-of-mutton in popularity. The hair is copied
from a contemporary portrait.

Some of the costumes worn by Queen Victoria, her coronation
robes as well as some every-day dresses, are exhibited in her
rooms at Kensington Palace, and it is surprising to see what
a little woman the great queen was. One gown of black
poplin, worn on some occasion of court mourning, has very
small sleeves, finished with exquisitely neat little cuffs of embroidered muslin.

In 1837, when President Van Buren took up his abode at
the White House, Mr. Andrew Stevenson was sent as Minister
to Great Britain from the United States, and was of course
present at the coronation of Queen Victoria with Mrs. Stevenson, whose portrait was afterwards painted by Healey in the

costume she wore when she was presented at the Queen's Drawing-room. This picture is well known and we regret space will not permit us to give a copy of it here.

A Philadelphia bride of 1838 wore the attractive gown shown in Figure 228. It is made of white satin and the trimmings are of blond lace. With this costume short gloves with embroidered tops were worn fastening over the band of the long lace sleeves as shown in the illustration. The veil and arrangement of hair are copied from a portrait of the same year. The dress in Figure 74 belonged to the same bride. The colour is a delicate pink and the sash of soft figured satin ribbon to match ; the lace at the neck and on the sleeves is of white blond which was the favourite of fashion at the time. The hair is copied from an English portrait.

Women's Dress
1840-1850

"Change of Fashion is the tax which industry imposes on the vanity of the rich."

WITH the new year, 1840, we notice a decided change in bonnets. The immense flaring brims which had been worn for the last ten years were replaced by a new shape somewhat resembling the capotes of the early years of the nineteenth century. The long veils of brocaded gauze so fashionable in the thirties were also superseded by shorter veils of net or lace, with small figures or with plain centres of lace with figured borders (Figures 128 and 131).

In a letter from the Paris correspondent to the "Court Magazine" for July, 1840, we find the following description of the new bonnets: "They are worn rather close to the face and made of *Paille de riz*, Crêpe lisse, Leghorn and fine straws. The crowns sit back quite flat and the fronts are rather less open but very long at the ears." (See Figures 128, 129 and 131.)

"The most elegant bonnets are covered with what we call a *voilette* of lace or tulle illusion; this little veil does not fall over the face, but merely covers the bonnet, being frequently brought from underneath the front; a long lappet falls as low as the waist from each side of the front."

213

A bonnet worn in Philadelphia in 1840, of white ribbed silk, trimmed with white satin ribbon and a *voilette* of blond lace hanging in long lappets on each side, and with pale pink flowers inside the brim, belongs to Miss Dutihl's Collection at Memorial Hall. A picture of it is given in Figure 131.

"On coloured silk bonnets these *voilettes* are made of the same shade as the silk. Drawn *capotes* are also *de mode;* some have *voilettes* and others a narrow ruche of white tulle round the edge of the front. Straws and Leghorns are trimmed with velvet, violet or dark green being the favourite colours for this purpose; a *torsade* intermingled with straw goes round the crown, and the brim is edged inside and out with a band of velvet more than an inch in depth. A flat ostrich feather is placed at one side and lies perfectly flat across the bonnet, drooping to the opposite side; this feather may be white or the colour of the velvet, or any colour that contrasts well with the trimming. The younger ladies who do not wear feathers prefer a half wreath of field flowers."

The same correspondent announced that long cachemire shawls were coming in and would take the place of square shawls. They were to be worn as scarfs. "White, black and blue grounds with patterns of palms or rosettes joined with light running patterns," were the most desirable combinations. "Black shawls trimmed with lace or fringe, and black silk scarfs trimmed all round with lace, or only with silk fringe at the ends, are universally worn. Coloured silk scarfs are also in fashion," and it was considered *très distingué*, we learn, to have your scarf and your dress of the same colour, and with a white dress a scarf of the colour of the bonnet.

Lace was worn extensively in the forties. Brussels and Honiton lace were perhaps the most fashionable. Queen Victoria's wedding dress (February 10, 1840) was of this beautiful fabric made at the picturesque village in Devon from which the lace gets its name.

The first note on crinoline, so soon to be an indispensable adjunct to the fashionable toilet, is given in the same letter from Paris: "Of course you have heard of the *Jupons de Crinoline;* they are very light and cool, and make the dress sit beautifully, and one perfection in them is that they never crease or get out of form."

Sleeveless jackets, called *Canegous*, came into fashion in 1840. They were open in front, but finished at the neck with small collars, and were either richly embroidered or trimmed with lace. In 1840 we read of white spencers, to be worn like our modern blouses with coloured skirts. Another familiar fashion of to-day seems to be a revival of 1840; cuffs and collars on the sleeves and neck are spoken of by a contemporary author as "indispensable." Spencers of black or coloured velvet were a very becoming fashion.

Close-fitting dresses, called Redingotes, were very popular at this time. We read of one in a London magazine, made of white India muslin lined with pale blue silk and trimmed with lace, and another lined with pink and trimmed with hand embroidery. Sleeves were either tight or full according to the fancy of the wearer; specimens are given in Figures 128 and 136. Bodices were made with a sharp point at the waist in front and round in the back, and were usually open at the throat, and either worn over a chemisette or finished with a ruching of lace for morning or street wear. Evening gowns were cut low and finished with a bertha of lace, or silk to match the dress (Figures 134 and 135).

Very elaborate head-dresses were worn at this date, made of India muslin or organdie, trimmed with lace. Appliqué and English point lace were used instead of the blond lace which had been so fashionable in the thirties. (See Figures 134, 139 and 233.) The front hair was worn either in broad braids, smooth bands, or in long ringlets, while the back hair was braided or coiled very low on the neck. Short gloves were still in fashion and trimmed with lace, swansdown, ribbon, etc. They were either fastened with buttons (two or four) or laced up with a silk cord.

At this period, slender waists being very much admired, the bodices were gradually made with deeper points and worn without belts, and the gathers of the full skirts were distributed at the sides and back to produce that effect. An authority of this time says: " I agree with the doctors in setting my face against tight lacing, the most dangerous practice a lady can persevere in; so have your dress made with a long waist; have your petticoat gathered into a very broad band cut on the cross way, and with a point in front, so as not to have gathers under the point of your dress; let the petticoat be made of crinoline, or of a very thick cotton material with a sort of honeycomb pattern all over; this will make your dress appear sufficiently full and form a proper contrast to the waist, thereby sparing you the necessity and agony as well as injury, of tight lacing."

Wadded cachemire shawls were in vogue, but the newest wrap was a small wadded cape with a pointed hood. We read, too, of the Palatine, a cloak of much the same style made of black satin wadded and lined with blue, rose-colour, or apricot satin trimmed all round with black lace, and reaching to the knees in front, the hood made to be drawn over at pleasure; especially adaptable for an evening wrap.

A walking dress for the winter of 1840 is described in the " Court Magazine ": " Made of satin lined and wadded throughout; the corsage close fitting, and with tight sleeves with two seams. Upon the front of the waist is a trimming consisting of

four rows of black lace set on in regular fluted plaits, extending from the shoulder to the waist in the form of a V, and is
likewise carried across the back in the style of a pelerine; besides
this the trimming is carried down each side of the front breadth
of the skirt *en tablier*, becoming wider as it goes down and also
increasing in distance."

In 1841, we notice that sleeves were worn long and close-fitting for house and street wear, sometimes finished with an
epaulet cap called a jockey (Figure 136).   Evening dresses were
made with voluminous skirts trimmed with flounces; bodices
fitted close to the figure and were stiffly boned and finished
with a point coming a little below the waist line in front.
Berthas of lace or of the same material as the dress were not
only in the height of fashion during the forties, but have been
a favourite style of trimming ever since.

The numerous Daguerreotypes of that period furnish us
with many accurate details of dress.   From these we learn that
it was still the fashion to wear the hair parted in the middle,
and although curls which had been the favourite style for so
many years were still worn, the most fashionable arrangement
was to draw the front hair down in smooth bands concealing
the ears and fasten the ends with the coil at the back.   Often
the front hair was braided in many strands.   The so-called
" Polish braid " was in nine strands and was most becoming to
a delicate face.   When the hair was very long, the braids were
often carried across the head, making a sort of coronet.   (See
Figure 136.)   In many of the portraits of Queen Victoria we
notice this effect, but it was a favourite style in America too;
at that period almost every lady had an abundance of natural
hair, and very little false hair was worn.

In 1841 Mrs. Julia Ward Howe made a visit to England and
records in her " Reminiscences " some of the costumes worn by

1860–1870

163 C.W.T. After Print.

164 C.W.TROUT.

165 C.W.TROUT. after Print.

166 C.W.TROUT

167 C.W.T After Print

168 C.W.T.

169 C.W.T.

English ladies of note in the early days of Queen Victoria's reign. She met the beautiful Mrs. Norton at a dinner, and says : " Her hair, which was decidedly black, was arranged in flat bandeaux according to the fashion of the time. A diamond chain formed of large links encircled her fine head. Her eyes were dark and full of expression. Her dress was unusually *décolleteé,* but most of the ladies present would in America have been considered extreme in that respect." *

On another occasion Mrs. Howe met the Duchess of Sutherland, and describes her costume as follows :

"She wore a brown gauze or barege over light blue satin with a wreath of brown velvet leaves and blue forget-me-nots in her hair, and on her arm, among other beautiful jewels, a miniature of the Queen set in diamonds." A dress of pink moiré worn by the same lady, with a wreath of velvet leaves interspersed with diamonds, is also mentioned. Wreaths of artificial flowers combined with ribbons or jewels were fashionable from 1840 to 1850. (See Figure 139.)

A letter from Paris, written in 1841, describes an evening costume of pale blue satin trimmed with sable round the bottom of the skirt and up the front *en tablier,* the short plain sleeves also trimmed with the fur. The bodice was made with a deep point. A toque of blue velvet was worn with this dress ornamented with a Henri IV plume fastened with a diamond aigrette. The graceful Pompadour sleeves, with ruffles of lace falling very low at the back of the arm, were revived in 1841, and for evening dress the points of bodices were very deep. But tight sleeves were worn for dinner and house gowns. Much fur was used in trimming. Muffs of moderate size (Figure 137) and round pelerines or capes were made generally of ermine, sable, marten and swansdown. Passementerie, Bran-

* Reminiscences 1819-1899. By Mrs. Julia Ward Howe.

denburghs and bias folds were universally used, but ruffles and flounces were temporarily out of favour. Bonnets were made very long at the sides projecting below the chin in a very unbecoming style which did not long remain in fashion (Figure 137). Three new caps are mentioned : *La Coquette*, a half cap with a deep fancy border trimmed with marabout tips ; *La Religieuse*, a nun's cap made of fine materials ; Marie Stuart cap, with point in front, made of lace for morning wear and of velvet for evening dress.

Arrows with diamond heads were worn in the hair and large high backed combs again made their appearance, some plain and others again ornamented with gold and inlaid with precious stones. Coral ornaments were very much worn. A single gold bracelet on the right arm above the glove was very fashionable, and a serpent with ruby eyes was said to be " the most splendid thing of that description ever seen." Several novelties in feathers are also mentioned. " There are willow feathers, *panachées*, the ends tipped in shaded colours running one into another, as green into lilac, thence into orange, and ending in shades of blue. We have also marabouts, *sablés d'or* or *d'argent* having the appearance of gold or silver-dust shaken upon them. For dress turbans they are truly splendid." A certain delicate shade of purple called *pensée* was also new in the winter of 1841–1842, and pearl-grey and watered blue were very popular for street wear.

Many costumes were made *en redingote* buttoned all the way down the front with small buttons. Tight plain sleeves were the best suited for this style of dress, although full sleeves were worn finished with plain cuffs. Gold or silver cord and tassels were twisted in and out among the braids of the back hair, and both tassels brought behind the right ear, and allowed to hang loosely. With this coiffure long English curls were usually arranged on each side of the face, but the front hair was very generally worn in smooth bands throughout the forties, as we notice in many portraits of the day, and turbans of every variety were still in vogue. Bows without ends were used extensively in trimmings for turbans and bonnets. Quillings of tulle were worn inside bonnet brims or, instead of the ruche, plaitings of silk or tulle were sometimes placed on the edge of the brim and flowers worn inside.

Morning dresses of wadded cashmere or merino with loose sleeves showing undersleeves of cambric are noticed in the plates of 1842, and were worn for many years (see Figure 156), sometimes with little caps of India muslin trimmed with lace and ribbon.

Revers worn very low on the shoulders were a noticeable feature of walking dresses in 1842, but many costumes were made without any trimming on the corsage. A new fashion was an arrangement of horizontal puffings of the material of the dress across the front of the bodice; this was called *en coulisses.*

Separate bodices of lingerie were also fashionable at that time made of alternate puffings of thin muslin and embroidery. A picture of one is given in Figure 128, which also shows a scarf of Roman striped silk worn in Philadelphia and a bonnet from a plate of 1842.

During this year skirts were still worn very full over petticoats of crinoline. Sometimes they were made perfectly plain without trimmings, but generally bias folds of the material were put on *en tablier* or in groups above the hem. Bodices were made with rounded points at the waist and laced up the back, and they were usually half or three-quarters high. Sleeves were worn in a great variety of shapes. Long and tight, short and close-fitting, puffed to the wrist with fanciful caps at the top, and even bell sleeves with undersleeves of thin white muslin are seen in the fashion plates of this time. The shoulders are very long and sloping. Black varnished leather shoes were a new fashion. Very fanciful caps were worn. Mits and even gloves of lace were very much in vogue. Bonnets still projected over the face and ears, and were trimmed with feathers, ribbon and flowers. Parasols were very small and muffs moderately large.

In 1842, a French periodical, "Le Follet," was combined with the "Court Magazine" and the descriptions of the new fashions were written in French.

For the spring of this year we are told that soutache braid and passementerie were lavishly used in trimming and that the most fashionable materials were batiste, *mousselline de laine*, and *tissue bayadère*. The crape hats of Mr. Leclerc appear to have been "the rage" in Paris at that time. We read that nothing could be "more delicious" than his hats in rose-coloured crape ornamented with a bunch of moss roses at one side; nothing more dainty than his *capotes* of white crape and Valenciennes insertion trimmed with bias folds of *gros de Naples* in rose-colour. Some of these hats are trimmed with shaded ribbons and marabout feathers shaded to match, producing a very unique effect. Mits of velvet were a Paris novelty described in 1842. They were especially intended to wear with short sleeves and were trimmed with lace and embroidery.

A mourning dress is described in a magazine of 1842: "Dress of black barege made with a deep hem at the bottom of the skirt, and a fold of the same depth above. Bodice cut three-quarters high and laced up the back. A ruche of the material finishes the neck of the corsage, and the edge of the long tight sleeves. A pelerine of black lace cut low in the neck is worn round the shoulders and fastened with a black ribbon bow. An under-dress which shows through the barege is of grey *gros de Naples*. A drawn bonnet also of grey *gros de Naples*, trimmed round the face with a ruche of black tulle, and small black flowers and a long grey feather surrounds the crown and hangs down on the left side. Gloves of black lace, and slippers of black *panet de soie* completed this costume."

A graceful walking dress is described as follows: " Redingote of Pekin stripe, blue and brown. The corsage is tight and almost high in the neck, tight sleeves trimmed with two bias folds of the silk at the top. The skirt is very full, and trimmed with two bias folds (*en tablier*) down each side of the front. Apricot-coloured gloves and parasol. Black shoes and gaiters. Bonnet of rice straw trimmed with pink ribbon ; a large veil of white gauze, drawn into fullness by a ribbon in a hem, is fastened round the crown, and thrown back over the shoulders. Hair is in full ringlets at the sides."

The following extract is from a letter dated Paris, June 25, 1842 : " Bareges, tarlatans and such light textures are the only things that we can wear here just now, but after all can anything be prettier ? The dresses are still very long and the skirts ample though one of our *couturières* has tried to bring in the fashion of not having any fullness in front. Comment! I think I hear you exclaim, ' Can this really be ? ' *Oui, ma chère*, but never mind ; it is an innovation that will not take, so we need give ourselves no trouble about it. In light materials the corsages are invariably made *en coulisses*. They are very becoming to the figure and suitable for muslins and bareges but in anything of a more substantial texture, they do not look well. Corsages with *ceintures* (Figure 127) are a good deal worn in morning negligee ; after all there is something very pretty in seeing the waist neatly supported (the French *soutenue* would suit me better) by a pretty belt and buckle ; it is therefore a fashion not likely to remain long in disuse. We have decidedly triumphed over our antipathy to short sleeves and we wear them at all times now."

From Paris comes the following amusing bit of advice : " I must let you into a little secret about the manner of getting up your fine things which will render them more becoming. It is to put an imperceptible tinge of pink into the rinsing water instead of blue, which our grandmothers for a hundred generations past have been content to use. But now that the other has been discovered, we wonder how we could have put up with such an unbecoming thing as what is called ' snow-white linen.' But recollect your collars must not be pink ; the tinge must be felt, not seen, if I may so express myself."

In the chronicles of 1843, we notice that in spite of the inconvenience of the fashion, street dresses were still worn extremely long especially in the back. They were a little shorter in the front. Corsages were all made tight fitting. Belts and buckles gained in popularity especially for morning wear. In the spring of this year (1843) we read of a new wrap, a Paletot, generally of silk trimmed with black lace, or with a quilling of ribbon, caught in about the waist with a broad ribbon. Mantillas were in the height of fashion at that time and were trimmed with frills and quillings innumerable. A slight change in bonnets is mentioned. The brims did not project quite so much over the face, and the crowns were less deep also. In Figure 126 is given the picture of a bonnet in Miss Dutihl's collection, which shows the change in shape. It is made of dove-coloured satin trimmed with pink and green figured ribbon.

Another bonnet of this year (1843) is given in Figure 129, worn with a dress of grey-green satin and a black lace shawl.

The fashion plates of this decade are very attractive. A certain harmony of colour and feminine grace pervades them. But the bonnets must have been most uncomfortable, projecting beyond the face. It must have been a constant temptation to push the brims back to get a good look at something, and they were worn by young girls, in fact by little children as the pictures show. The newest materials were changeable coloured silks, shot silks and Pekin stripes. House gowns of cashmere and *mousseline de laine* were very popular in winter, and of cambric and printed muslin for summer.

We read in an American publication of a new head-dress for 1844. " A most irresistible coiffure is a wreath of periwinkles with pendant sprigs of the flowers mingled with the curls at each side of the face, or if the hair is worn in bands, the wreath may be most becoming, arranged around the head with small bunches of the flowers and leaves hanging from the coil at the back."

The only change in the form of caps was that they were a little smaller, and often made of plain muslin without any ribbon. The crown was very small, and they had broad lappets of muslin falling on each side behind the ears. But another and decidedly more becoming style, was of plain India muslin, trimmed with two rows of Valenciennes, and ornamented with a broad blue ribbon in the front, and shaded with a second row of lace, falling over the ribbon. A rosette of blue silk with long ends, placed on the left side, was also a tasteful trimming. Another pattern had a very small head piece, with lappets of Mechlin lace reaching only to the edge of the ears on both sides, and ornamented with green satin ribbons. Another is trimmed with two rows of embroidered muslin, slightly fulled, and decorated with two small *coques* of plaited white and blue silk ribbon, a twist or roll of the same encircling the crown. The cap in Figure 233 is on this order without lappets and trimmed with *choux* of pink satin.

170

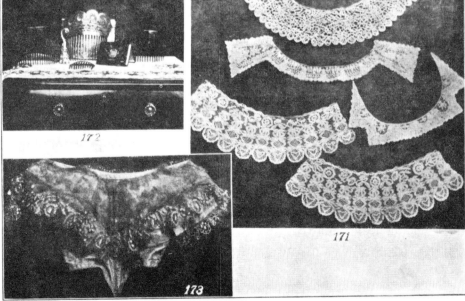

172

171

173

A dainty gown of white cashmere is taken from the same authority : "The front of the skirt is trimmed with a facing of pink ; tight and high corsage, finished with a square collar, full hanging sleeves, bordered and faced to match the skirt. Under-dress of muslin, trimmed round the bottom with two rows of embroidery. Cap of light spotted lace, decorated with roses ; this cap is considered the neatest of the season and is universally admired."

Under the heading "Bonnets, etc., in New York," a corre-spondent of the "Boston Transcript" thus describes the fash-ions there : "Within the past week an invoice of bonnets has arrived from Paris and on Sunday the congregations of the fashionable churches looked like beds of lilies and roses. The latest style is really very beautiful, or as the ladies say 'sweet.' The one I have been most pleased with is a perfect flower. The material is white figured muslin, delicately trimmed with rib-bons and roses, and in form like the cup of a morning glory. If the humming birds and honey-bees don't light upon it on Broadway, I shall think they show a great want of taste. For dresses, chameleon silks are much worn, three distinct colours, by some magic of art, being thrown on a plain ground, looking as if 'Iris dipt the wool.' A new style of evening dress ap-peared at the last 'Hop' at the 'Astor House,' which attracted the attention of connoisseurs as something quite original and beautiful ; a white muslin with two broad and richly coloured borders, looking like an illuminated title page."

As shown in the initial at the head of this chapter skirts were often trimmed with deep flounces in 1845, and they were worn wider and fuller than ever before in the nineteenth cen-tury. Stiffly starched underskirts were worn to keep out the dresses and they were so full over the hips that the waist ap-peared very small in proportion. The shoulders of bodices

were cut long and sloping, and the sleeves continued to be worn
almost skin-tight. Shoulder capes of embroidered muslin and
lace were very fashionable. (See Figure 233.) Turned-down
collars were most popular, but narrow ruchings were also worn
at the throat and wrists. (See Figure 127.) A material called
delaine, a merino without the twill, with figures or spots
stamped in contrasting colours, was popular for house dresses.
It was like the fashionable challis of to-day, but delaines are
mentioned in old letters and books up to the sixties. In Figure
127, a picture is given of a gown of this material worn in
Boston in 1845. Bonnets were now made to flare a little round
the face and were often of tulle or gauze shirred over silk of the
same colour (Figure 124). A pale pink bonnet of this description worn in Philadelphia in 1846 is preserved at Stenton, Philadelphia.

In 1845 we notice that the berthas on evening gowns were
very deep, reaching about to the waist line. Black moiré was
a new fashion for evening dress, and in an English magazine
of February, 1845, is described a costume of this material which
would have suited Lady Dedlock to perfection. " Skirt long
and ample, close-fitting pointed bodice reaching to the throat,
and tight long sleeves. A passementerie trimming, also black,
is arranged at the foot of the skirt, in *bretelles* on the bodice, and
also trims the sleeves. A small embroidered collar is fastened
with a brooch at the throat, and a dress cap of English Point
lace trimmed with pink flowers and ribbons completes the
costume."

A style of dress which came into vogue at this time and remained long in fashion was the bodice opening over a chemisette of white muslin and finished with revers.

In 1846 bonnets were noticeably smaller and the fronts were
less flaring. This change is shown in Figure 136. Caps and

fanciful head-dresses were still in vogue for evening as well as morning dress. Ball dresses were cut quite high in the neck, a very awkward style. House gowns were worn high at the throat and finished with a small flat collar of lace or embroidery, or cut square or surplice and worn over a chemisette with a flat collar; a pretty fashion which afforded an opportunity for the exercise of individual taste, for endless was the variety of dainty lingerie and lace in use at this time. Tarlatan was the most fashionable material for dancing frocks. Parasols were very small in the forties, and in 1846 a new fashion of folding parasols was introduced.

The morning or "undress" costumes of this time were, as we see by the following contemporary verses,* made high neck and long sleeves, and being very comfortable, were adopted both for summer and for winter, and were a great contrast to the full dress for winter balls :

> "She was in fashion's elegant undress,
>   Muffled from throat to ankle ; and her hair
> Was all 'en papillotes,' each auburn tress
>   Prettily pinned apart. You well might swear
> She was no beauty ; yet, when 'made up' ready
> For visitors, 'twas quite another lady.

> "Since that wise pedant, Johnson, was in fashion,
>   Manners have changed as well as moons ; and he
> Would fret himself once more into a passion,
>   Should he return (which Heaven forbid) and see
> How strangely from his standard dictionary
> The meaning of some words is made to vary.

> "For instance, an undress at present means
>   The wearing a pelisse, a shawl, or so ;
> Or anything you please, in short, that screens
>   The face, and hides the form from top to toe ;
> Of power to brave a quizzin-glass, or storm ;
> 'Tis worn in summer, when the weather's warm.

* Fanny, by F. G. Hallack.

" But a full dress is for a winter's night,
    The most genteel is made of ' woven air' ;
That kind of classic cobweb, soft and light,
    Which Lady Morgan's Ida used to wear.
And ladies, this aerial manner dressed in,
    Look Eve-like, angel-like, and interesting."

In 1848, the date of the second Republic in France, bodices were worn opening in front over white chemisettes, and sleeves were wide at the bottom, showing an undersleeve to match the chemisette. This fashion was very generally adopted in the United States and worn more or less for twenty years. (See Figure 135.) We read of a garment called the Kasaveck imported from Russia at this time. It was a sort of jacket reaching to the waist, close-fitting and with wide braided sleeves, and was usually made of cashmere or satin and wadded. This garment was known under several different names : "*Coin du feu*," "*Casagne*," "*Pardessus*," etc. "Women of fashion," we read, "never wore them out of their own houses in the daytime."

A new wrap called the "Cornelia" was introduced about 1848. "It had no seam on the shoulder, and could be gathered up on the arms like a shawl at the pleasure of the wearer." Mantles of cashmere with double capes edged with braid, and the Josephine mantle with one cape, without shoulder seams, reaching to the waist, were popular favourites. Long chains of beads and cameo brooches without clasps were worn.

When Mr. Bancroft was Minister to England (1844–1848) his wife wrote her impressions of the English people she met to her friends in Boston. From her letters, published a few years ago, we quote the following descriptions :

" And now having given you some idea whom we are seeing here, you will wish to know how I like them and how they differ from our own people. At the smaller dinners and *soirées* at this season I cannot of course receive a full impression of English society, but certainly those persons now in town are charming people. Their manners are perfectly simple and I entirely forget, except their historic names fall upon my ear, that I am with the proud aristocracy of England.

"The forms of society and the standard of dress are very like ours except that a duchess or a countess has more hereditary point lace and diamonds. The general style of dress perhaps is as simply elegant as ours. There is less superiority over us in manners and all social arts than I could have believed possible in a country where a large social class have been set aside for time immemorial to create, as it were, a social standard of high refinement.

"Our simple breakfast dress is unknown in England; you come down in the morning dressed for the day until six or seven in the evening when your dress is low neck and short sleeves for dinner. At this season the morning dress is rich silk or velvet, high body cut close in the throat with handsome collar and cuffs and always a cap. I adhere to a black watered silk with the simple cap I wear at home.

"For the Drawing-room my dress was of black velvet with a very rich bertha. A bouquet in the front of *fleurs-de-lis* like the coiffure, and a cachemire shawl. Head-dress of green leaves and white *fleurs-de-lis* with a white ostrich feather drooping on one side. I wear my hair now plain in front, and the wreath was very flat and classical in its effect. I have had the diamond pin and earrings which your father gave me reset and made into a magnificent brooch and so arranged that I can also wear it as a necklace or bracelet. On this occasion it was a necklace."

Describing a Court dinner at Buckingham Palace, Mrs. Bancroft continues:

" My dress was my currant-coloured or *grossaille* velvet with a wreath of white arum lilies woven into a kind of turban with green leaves, and bouquet to match in the bertha of Brussels lace.

" On the occasion of the Queen's Birthday Drawing-room I went dressed in white mourning. It was a petticoat of white crape flounced to the waist with the edges notched. A train of white glacé trimmed with a ruche of white crape. A wreath and bouquet of white lilacs without any green, as green is not used in mourning.

" My dress for the Queen's Ball was a white crape over white satin with flounces of white satin looped up with pink tuberoses. A wreath of tuberoses and bouquet for the corsage." *

Lady Stuart Wortley made an extensive tour in America and evidently found much to delight and interest her. Arriving in New York in the summer of 1849, she was at once attracted by the fashionable attire of the people and dismayed by the " hot weather."

" We soon saw some evidence of the warmth of a New York summer, in the profusion of light cool bonnets furnished with broad and deeply hanging curtains, shading and covering the throat and part of the shoulders, a very sensible costume for hot weather. The fashion just now seems to be for all the ladies to wear large white shawls. I never beheld such a number of white shawls mustered ; the female part of the population seem all *voueé au blanc*. It is very seldom you see any equestriennes in these Northern cities. Every lady chooses rather to walk or go in a carriage. Crowds of carriages, private and public, are to be seen in Broadway, passing and repassing every

* Letters from England, by Mrs. George Bancroft.

moment, filled with ladies beautifully dressed in the most elaborate Parisian toilets." *

A column in the "Lady's Book" (1849) tells of the winter fashions in Philadelphia :

"We will describe three or four of the prettiest costumes of the season, that our lady readers may gather from them some idea of Chestnut Street, and our fashionable concert-room, the Musical Fund Hall :—

"A walking dress of dark green cashmere, with three bias folds upon the skirt, graduating in depth, and edged with a narrow bias velvet binding of the same shade. Corsage and sleeves plain and tight, a velvet fold upon the short cap of the sleeve, and a corresponding trimming also about the throat. White cashmere long shawl folded carelessly. Bonnet of deep green velvet. Marie Stuart brim, edged with blond, and small plume of the same shade as the bonnet.

"A walking dress of rich brocade silk, blue figures upon a fawn-coloured ground. Sacque of fawn-coloured silk, richly embroidered in blue. Bonnet of blue uncut velvet, with folds and bands of the same, mixed with blond.

"Dinner dress of chameleon silk, blue and silver. A small Marie Stuart cap of blond with rosettes of pale blue satin ribbon."

A summer walking costume of 1849 is shown in the initial of this chapter. This dress is of foulard silk trimmed with rows of velvet ribbon at the edge of the flounces. The mantilla is of black lace and the bonnet of white crape trimmed with pink flowers and white satin ribbon.

"Evening Dress.—Crape robe of pale rose-colour, embroidered up the front of the skirt. Girdle of broad brocaded ribbon the same shade, with flowing ends. Hair arranged in

* Travels in the United States, by Lady Stuart Wortley.

FIGURE 174.—1804—Boy in suit of striped calico and ruffled shirt.

FIGURE 175.—1812—Little girl in a scarlet cloth pelisse and bonnet to match. Worn by Mary Brinton, of Philadelphia.

FIGURE 176.—1822—Girl in a buff cashmere gown with long white sleeves. A large hat with brown ribbon. From a contemporary print.

FIGURE 177.—1800—Small child in white muslin gown. From a plate.

FIGURE 178.—1818—Boy in striped duck pantaloons, dark blue jacket and waistcoat. Dark cloth cap with visor. From a contemporary plate.

FIGURE 179.—1826—Little boy in white dress embroidered in blue, over trousers of same material. From a contemporary portrait.

FIGURE 180.—1828—Little girl in pink gauze dress. Worn by Miss Elizabeth S. Smith, of Philadelphia.

FIGURE 181.—1831—Girl in green and white silk gown. Green silk apron. Large white bonnet of *Gros de Naples* with white ribbon. Hair in Kenwig plaits. From a plate.

FIGURE 182.—1832—Boy in high hat, brown kerseymere tunic, and white pantaloons. From a portrait.

FIGURE 183.—1834—Girl in figured lawn dress. Hair in plaits twisted and tied with lilac ribbon.

FIGURE 184.—1837—Little girl of eight in brown and white corded muslin. Bonnet from contemporary plate.

FIGURE 185.—1838—Boy of fourteen. High hat of grey, coat of bottle green, grey trousers.

FIGURE 186.—1848—Little boy of five. The waist is of turquoise blue merino, scalloped with yellow silk and buttoned down the back with gilt buttons. The trousers are of white jean, striped with black.

FIGURE 187.—1848—Little girl from fashion plate of this date. The dress is of pink cashmere trimmed with narrow pink velvet ribbon. Hat of Leghorn trimmed with pink roses and pink ribbon. Pale blue kid shoes.

FIGURE 189.—1856—Boy of three in costume taken from an Ambrotype. The jacket is of black velvet trimmed with black braid and the skirt of plaid poplin ornamented by strips of black velvet ribbon.

FIGURE 190.—1857—Girl of twelve taken from a fashion magazine. Cloak of blue grey cloth trimmed with black velvet. Hat of grey trimmed with blue ribbon and blue feathers. Skirt of old rose. Shoes brown.

FIGURE 191.—1853—Little boy from a Daguerreotype. Suit of brown merino ornamented with gold braid and gilt buttons.

FIGURE 192.—1861—Small child in blue cashmere dress with white apron tied with blue ribbon at the shoulders. From a photograph.

FIGURE 193.—1865—Boy in black velvet suit trimmed with black silk braid. From a photograph.

plain bands with a wreath of mingled sweetbrier and lily of the valley. The contrast of the two flowers is very delicate and beautiful. Robe imported by Levy, wreath by Madam Patot.

"The prettiest style of morning dresses are of cashmere."

The following note on caps and capes is taken from an American authority :

"No unmarried lady should wear a morning cap; it is the mark, the badge, if we may so call it, of the young matron. And if the wife cares as much for her husband's admiration after marriage as before it, she will never dispense with this tasteful, coquettish appendage to a morning toilette.

"There has been an attempt this season to make up delicate India muslin with triple embroidered frills of the same. These are quite simple and require only a bow and strings of some bright coloured ribbon to finish them. A pretty cap is composed of Guipure lace (or what is called Guipure), with a bow and band of ribbon and *noeuds* of the same each side of the face. These are all intended for plain house-costumes and may be worn with propriety by older ladies.

"Capes are rarely worn in the morning, and are more particularly suited to dinner or small evening companies. They are worn of all sizes and patterns, as may be seen from Figures 134, 139 and 233. A favourite style is of lace; Brussels or a fine imitation is allowable. The ribbon knot should correspond or contrast in colour with the dress over which the cape is worn."

Leghorn hats and bonnets were very fashionable in 1849. The "Lady's Book" for the summer of that date says :

"In trimming a Leghorn bonnet, the richest ribbon is required and it should be of some pale shade. Dark blue, green, or brown have a bad effect. White is the most suitable, and straw colour looks well. With white ribbon, small ostrich plumes tipped with marabout are often seen. Chip bonnets are next in cost, and perhaps first in beauty. Their purity allows them to be trimmed with almost anything the wearer's complexion will allow. Bouquets of French flowers fastened with knots of ribbon are graceful. Embroidered crape bonnets are the newest. They are both simple and elegant, and were introduced by Miss Wilson, one of the most fashionable Chestnut Street (Philadelphia) milliners, direct from Paris. The material is *crêpe lisse* of some delicate hue, with silk floss embroidery about the front and on the crown piece. The cape embroidered to correspond. Trimming very simple. The prettiest one we have seen was a pale green bonnet, with a bouquet of purple lilies on each side, the ribbon just crossing over the top of the bonnet; there was not a single bow in the whole arrangement. A tulle quilling and a single lily inside the brim. Mourning bonnets are of drawn crape, trimmed with crape ribbon which is a new material."

The following note on new fashions is also from the same authority :

"Slippers, as we have before said, threaten to supersede gaiters for the street. The toes are rounded, and the instep ornamented with a small bow, quite as our grandmothers recollect them.

"The hair is dressed considerably higher than formerly, and puffed, as in old pictures, over a cushion at the back. Combs are principally of shell with round tops, that curve close to the head at the side. They are valued according to the newness of the pattern, those which sold for fourteen dollars in the spring being only eight dollars now.

"A new style of dress is made with a double skirt lined with paper muslin, which has a facing of the silk eight inches in depth. Just over this comes the real skirt, the edge of which is scolloped, and bound ; it does not meet at the waist, but opens over a plain breadth faced up the lining. This has exactly the effect of a tunic. Plain waists are still the rage, there being two seams each side the centre. Sleeves are mostly plain, or slightly full, with a band at the wrist. Belts are universally worn ; some have them set into the dress."

Looking over the pages of the " Quarterly Review " we came across the following appreciation of the dress of the forties :

" The present dress has some features worth dwelling on more minutely. The gown is a good thing, both in its morning and evening form, and contains all necessary elements for showing off a fine figure and a graceful movement. There is something especially beautiful, too, in the expanse of chest and shoulder, as seen in a tight plain-coloured high dress, merino or silk, like a fair sloping sunny bank, with the long taper arms and the slender waist so tempting and convenient between them, that it is a wonder they are not perpetually embracing it themselves. And then the long full folds of the skirt which lie all close together above, like the flutings of an Ionic column, as if loth to quit that sweet waist, but expand gradually below as if fearing to fetter those fairy feet. And the gentle swinging of the robe from side to side, like a vessel in calmest motion, and the silver whisper of trailing silk. Flounces are a nice question. We like them when they wave and flow as in a very light material, muslin or gauze or barege, when a lady looks like a receding angel, or a dissolving view ; but we do not like them in a rich material where they flop, or in a stiff one, where they bristle ; and where they break the lines of the petticoat, and throw light and shade where you don't expect them. In short we like the gown that can do without flounces, as Josephine liked a face that could do without whiskers ; but in either case it must be a good one. The plain black scarf is come of

too graceful a parentage—namely, from the Spanish and Flemish
mantilla—not to constitute one of the best features of the present
costume.   It serves to join the two parts of the figure together,
enclosing the back and shoulders in a firm defined outline of
their own, and flowing down gracefully in front, or on each side,
to mix with that of the skirt.   That man must be a monster
who would be impertinent to a woman, but especially to a
woman in a black scarf.   It carries an air of self-respect with it
which is in itself a protection.   A woman thus attired glides on
her way like a small close-reefed vessel, tight and trim, seeking
no encounter but prepared for one.   Much, however, depends
on the wearer ; indeed no article of dress is such a revealer of
the wearer's character.   Some women will drag it tight up their
shoulders, and stick out their elbows (which ought not to be
known to exist) in defiance at you, beneath.   Others let it hang
loose and listless like an idle sail, losing all the beauty of the
outline, both moral and physical.   Such ladies have usually no
opinions at all, but none the less a very obstinate will of their
own.   Some few of what are nowadays called mantillas, which
are the Cardinals and Capuchins of a century ago, are pleasing
and blameless.   A black velvet one turned up with a broad
dull black lace, the bright metal chased with dead, is very good.
But whatever piece of dress conceals a woman's figure is bound
in justice to do so in a picturesque way.   That a shawl can never
do with its stiff uniformity of pattern, each shoulder alike, and
its stiff three-cornered shape behind with a scroll pattern standing straight up the centre of the back.   If a lady sports a shawl
at all, and only very falling shoulders should venture, we
should recommend it to be always either falling off or putting
on, which produces pretty action, or she should wear it up one
shoulder and down the other, or in some way drawn irregularly,
so as to break the uniformity."

Women's Dress
1850–1860

" Fashions that are now called new
  Have been worn by more than you ;
  Elder times had worn the same
  Though the new ones get the name."
                          —MIDDLETON.

NOTICEABLE feature of the dress of 1850 was the basque, a bodice with short skirt or tails below the waist line. According to the fashion plates of that period an attempt had been made to introduce this style of dress late in the forties, but it did not become a popular fashion until early in the fifties.

Basques made of velvet of some dark colour were worn with silk skirts of contrasting design. A black velvet basque which could be worn with any skirt was in almost every woman's wardrobe. Even riding habits were made in this popular style, as will be seen in the pages of " Punch " for 1850.

At that time Prince Albert had proposed to have the Industrial Palace built in Hyde Park, which would have spoiled the famous resort of English horsewomen, Rotten Row. The suggestion caused a flutter of indignation which found expression in the following verses :

245

" Then take our lives and spare our ride the only place we know,
Where ladies pent in London for exercise can go.
'Tis not with us as with our lords for they, the park beside,
Have got the House of Commons where their hobbies they can ride.
The Prince looked grim, it was his whim, humbugged he would not be,
When lo ! a stately lady is kneeling at his feet
I too would ride, she sweetly said, so Albert if you please
Don't there's a darling, for my sake please don't cut down the trees."

India muslins, embroidered in colours, were popular at this period. In Figure 266 is given a picture of a dainty gown of this material which was worn in Philadelphia about 1853.

Chemisettes and undersleeves were still worn and were more or less elaborate for different occasions. Flounces were extremely popular ; as many as five were worn at a time, the upper flounce being gathered in with the skirt at the waist.

Early in this decade a novel and very hideous costume was devised by Mrs. Bloomer, editor of a temperance journal in the United States, who went about the country giving lectures in 1851–1852, on Woman's Suffrage, and advertised the new dress henceforth known as the " Bloomer costume." By way of manifesting the independence of her sex she advised the women to adopt a part at least of the customary costume of the men. This was her idea of a reform in woman's dress :

" A skirt reaching to about half-way between the knees and the ankles and not very full. Underneath the skirt trousers moderately full, and in fair weather coming down to the ankle and there gathered in with an elastic band. The shoes or slippers to suit the occasion. For winter or wet weather the trousers should be fastened under the top of a boot reaching three or four inches above the ankle. This boot might be sloped gracefully at the upper edge and trimmed with fur or embroidery according to the taste of the wearer, the material might be cloth or morocco, and waterproof if desired."

The upper part of this costume was left to be determined by the individual fancy of the wearer. Mrs. Bloomer had a picture taken exemplifying her favourite dress, a copy of which is given in Figure 152. "The fashion," we read, "did not fail to make itself apparent in various parts of the United States." The "Washington Telegraph," the "Hartford Times," the "Syracuse Journal" and many other leading papers "noticed the adoption of the costume and generally with commendation." In the autumn of 1851 an American woman dressed in a black satin suit of jacket, skirt and trousers gave lectures in London urging the adoption of the reform dress, but succeeded only in raising a storm of merriment on the subject. Even in America the Bloomer costume soon became a thing of the past. In Figure 211 we give a photograph of a doll dressed in this eccentric fashion, which was the cherished plaything of a little Quaker girl in Pennsylvania.

The invention of Mrs. Bloomer was soon cast into oblivion by the marvellous creations of the beautiful Empress Eugénie, whose dresses became the envied models of the world of fashion in 1853. We read that "a glimpse of the Empress in the drive through the Bois de Boulogne sufficed to set the fair observers to work upon a faithful reproduction of her costume, and her toilette on the occasion of a ball at the Tuileries afforded food for thought during many days to those who had been present." At the civil marriage on the evening of January 29, 1853, which took place in comparative privacy, Eugénie wore a white satin gown trimmed with lace, with two rows of magnificent pearls around her neck, and flowers in her hair, and at the religious ceremony on the following morning, in Notre Dame, she wore a gown of white velvet with a long train covered with lace in a design of violets which is said to have been worth at least 30,000 francs. Around her waist was a belt of diamonds and

1806–1870

FIGURE 194.—1806—Boy in brown suit of kerseymere; collar and ankle ruffles of white cambric. Cap with full soft crown and visor. From a print.

FIGURE 195.—1807—Boy in short sleeved tunic of blue cloth over white full trousers. Black slippers and straw hat. Mother in short dress of jaconet muslin, black silk mantle trimmed with lace. Shirred muslin bonnet. Pagoda parasol. From a print.

FIGURE 196.—1822—Girl in dress of apricot gauze, worn in Philadelphia.

FIGURE 197.—1833—Boy in suit of brown kerseymere, white waistcoat and black tie. From a portrait.

FIGURE 198.—1833—Boy in leg-of-mutton trousers of green kerseymere. From a print.

FIGURE 200.—1860—Child's turban hat and feather. From a photograph.

FIGURE 201.—1862—Girl in a checked silk over a white guimpe. Braids tied at the back with a ribbon and ends. Gaiter boots. From a photograph.

FIGURE 202.—1862—Boy in a grey tweed suit and striped stockings. From a photograph.

FIGURE 203.—1806—Child's hat with straw buttons and strings of white ribbon. School of Industrial Art, Philadelphia.

FIGURE 204.—1864—Boy in a brown suit braided in black. Little girl in pale blue cashmere trimmed with quilled ribbon to match and worn over a white guimpe. From a plate.

FIGURE 205.—1861—Girl in a Zouave jacket and skirt. Hair in a net of chenille. From a photograph.

FIGURE 206.—1865—Boy of sixteen in a short round coat and long trousers. From a photograph.

FIGURE 207.—1870—Little girl of this date. From a fashion plate.

C.W.T.
After Tin.
194

195   S.B. STEEL. &
          after a print

196   C.W. Trout
          1907.

197   C.W. Trout
          1907.

198   C.W. Trout

200   C.W. Trout
          From Photograph.

203

201   C.W.Trout
          After
          Photograph

202   C.W.T.
          After Photograph

204   C.W. Trout
          After Photograph

205   C.W. Trout.
          After Photograph.

206   C.W.T.
          After
          Photograph

207   C.W.T.
          1907.

she had the same coronet of brilliants which Marie Louise had worn on her wedding day, to which was fastened a long lace veil and a wreath of orange blossoms.

The description of the famous dressing-room of the Empress Eugénie at the Tuileries, with its revolving mirrors, etc., has often been recounted. On the upper floor over this dressing-room, and connected with it by a lift and a speaking tube, were the rooms set apart for her personal attendants and her wardrobe. "Separate rooms," we are told, "were devoted to hats and bonnets, boots and shoes, sunshades, dust cloaks. Each morning a life-sized doll made to resemble the figure of the Empress was carefully dressed in every particular and sent down by the lift and exhibited before her. In spite of the pains taken by the dressmakers and tailors to please her it was a rare occurrence for a gown to satisfy her entirely; she criticized, altered and rejected incessantly until she succeeded in recomposing the costumes to her satisfaction." The second empire of the hoop-skirt was inaugurated in 1854, and in spite of jeers, jibes and caricatures held its sway over feminine taste to the exclusion of beauty and convenience. We read that "the first form of this invention was a whalebone skirt not unlike a beehive; the largest circumference was around the hips whence the rest of the dress fell in perpendicular lines; others preferred hoops arranged like those on a barrel." But the most popular form of hoop-skirt was made of graduated steel wires covered with a woven cotton netting held together by perpendicular straps of broad tape. A picture of a genuine skirt of this description is given in Figure 154. It was worn in Pennsylvania about 1856. More unassuming followers of fashion lined the edges of their gowns with horsehair and their flounces with stiff muslin. Petticoats were also made with casings around them at intervals, into which canes were run.

Numerous are the tales of accidents which happened to the wearers of the fashionable hoops. A very thrilling escape is recounted by Lady Neville in her recently published diary. She speaks of the offending garment as " that monstrosity the crinoline, which once came near costing me my life ; in fact I only escaped a terrible fate through mercifully retaining my presence of mind. It was in the drawing-room one evening after dinner, before the gentlemen had joined us there, that my dress caught fire. I was showing a lady an engraving of Mr. Cobden which he had just given me and which hung over the fireplace. Somehow or other my voluminous skirt caught fire and in an instant I was in a blaze, but I kept my presence of mind, and rolling myself in the hearth rug by some means or other eventually put out the flames. None of the ladies present could of course come to assist me for their enormous crinolines rendered them almost completely impotent to deal with fire." *

In Watson's " Annals " (1856) a caustic arraignment of this fashion appeared under the heading " Hoops Again " :

" We had hoped that our ladies would never again be brought to use such ill-looking, useless and deforming appendages to their dresses. They are, too, so annoying and engrossing of place and room in omnibuses, rail cars, and in church pews and aisles, and why all this ; but as spellbound subservients to some foreign spell ; one feels scandalized for ' the Land of the Free ! ' Nor is this all. Ladies who profess to be Christians and communicants too, pledged ' to renounce the vain pomp and vanities of the world, and not to be led thereby,' go up to the sacramental altar, showing before the eyes of all beholders an unseemly vanity ! "

The prices current in Philadelphia in 1856 provoked the aged annalist to an outburst of righteous indignation :

* Reminiscences of Lady Dorothy Neville.

"EXTRAVAGANCE IN DRESS

"At this time a fashionable dry goods store advertises a lace scarf for 1,500 dollars! Another has a bridal dress for 1,200 dollars. Bonnets at 200 dollars are also sold. Cashmeres from 300 dollars and upwards are seen by dozens along Broadway. And 100 dollars is quite a common price for a silk gown. Think of such a scale of prices for 'un-ideaed' American women! Can the pampering of such vanities elevate the character of our women?"

"The Rise and Fall of Crinoline" is delightfully set forth in "Punch." Figure 153 is copied from a cartoon of 1857, and shows, besides the crinoline, the fashionable wrap and bonnet. A glimpse of a head-dress of bows of ribbons, which was also characteristic of the period, is shown on the left side of the picture.

The dress shown in Figures 255 and 268 is made of a rich lustrous silk which stands out by itself, although it was evidently assisted by crinoline in the days of its youth. The prevailing colour is brown, the alternate stripes being a cross-bar pattern of two shades of brown, and a pattern of variegated roses *en chiné*. The trimmings are, according to the fashion of the fifties, made to match the dress, the colours brown and pink being woven into the fringe and the guimpe heading. The lace collar and the brooch are also copied from originals and were worn in Philadelphia in 1855. The hair is taken from a contemporary portrait.

Deep collars were worn at this time (see Figure 255) and bonnets were shallower in the crown and worn back from the face as in Figures 149, 268 and 269.

Cashmere shawls and inexpensive imitations of them were worn very generally throughout the fifties. A very beautiful specimen of the former is shown in the initial to this chapter.

It was worn in Philadelphia by Mrs. Emlen Cresson. Tunisian shawls, manufactured from silk refuse and usually woven in stripes of two colours, were worn in summer, and a very graceful wrap, the Algerian *burnous*, was introduced at this time, and became a favourite garment for theatre wear. The material was a mixture of silk and goat's hair, and the full flowing lines of this Arab mantle with a sort of hood finished with a tassel, were not ungraceful even over the fashionable hooped skirt. Beaver hats with long ostrich feathers were worn by young ladies in 1859. At least one American girl bears witness to this fashion :

"I wonder if my descendants, should they ever read these memoirs, will be shocked at the levity of an ancestress who frankly acknowledges that the most vivid recollection left in her mind is a grey merino pelisse and black beaver hat and plumes, with which her small person was decked during the winter of 1859." *

The fashionable shape for several years was a shallow crown and soft, wide drooping brim like the picture of a fine straw hat trimmed with ribbon copied from a fashion plate of 1857 given in Figure 253 and the soft felt hat in Figure 258.

Mrs. Clay, the wife of the Senator from Alabama, spent many years in Washington at that prosperous and pleasant period of American history, "before the war." In her most entertaining Diary she gives very valuable notes on the fashions of the fifties, although we may not agree with her in pronouncing them "graceful and picturesque."

"In 1858–59 the hair was arranged on the top of the head in heavy braids, wound like a coronet, over the head (Figure 255), and the coiffure was varied now and then with a tiara of velvet and pearls, or jet, or coral. Ruffled dresses gave place to panelled skirts in which two materials, a plain and embossed or

* A Southern Girl in 1861.

brocaded fabric, were combined, and basques with postillion backs became the order of the day.   The low-coiled hair, with brow free from frizzes and bangs, was the style adopted by such prominent beauties as Mrs. Pugh and Mrs. Pendleton, who in Lord Napier's opinion had the most classic head he had seen in America.   Low necks and lace berthas, made fashionable because of their adoption by Miss Lane,* were worn almost universally, either with open sleeves revealing inner ones of filling lace, or sleeves of the shortest possible form allowing the rounded length of a pretty arm to be seen in all its perfection. Evening gloves were of half length only, or as often reaching half way to the elbow.   They were of kid or silk with backs embroidered in delicate silks with now and then a jewel sparkling among the colours.   Our gloves and our fans and handkerchiefs and bonnets and the larger part of our dress accessories, as well as such beautiful gown patterns as were purchased ready to be made up by a New York or Washington dressmaker, were all imported directly from foreign houses and the services of our travelling and consular friends were in constant requisition for the selection of fine lace shawls, flounces, undersleeves and other fashionable garnitures.   Scarcely a steamer but brought to the Capital dainty boxes of Parisian flowers, bonnets and other foreign novelties despatched by such interested deputies."†

Speaking of shopping in Washington, another gifted woman of the South has recorded her own experiences in a book which we venture to say will always hold a high place among contemporary histories of that unhappy period of our national life. ‡

" . . . There were few shops.   But such shops !   There was Galt's, where the silver, gems and marbles were less attract-

* Niece of President Buchanan.
† A Belle of the Fifties : Memoirs of Mrs. Clay, 1855–56.
‡ Reminiscences of Peace and War, by Mrs. Roger A. Pryor.

ive than the cultivated gentlemen who sold them; Gautier's, the palace of sweets, with Mrs. Gautier in an armchair before her counter to tell you the precise social status of every one of her customers and, what is more, to put you in your own; Harper's, where the dainty, leisurely salesman treated his laces with respect, drawing up his cuffs lest they touch the ethereal beauties; and the little corner shop of stern Madame Delarue, who imported as many (and no more) hats and gloves as she was willing to sell as a favour to the ladies of the diplomatic and official circles, and whose dark-eyed daughter, Léonide (named for her godmother, a Greek lady of rank), was susceptible of unreasoning friendships and could be coaxed to preserve certain treasures for humbler folk.

"Léonide once awoke me in the middle of the night with a note bidding me 'come *toute de suite*,' for '*Maman*' was asleep; the boxes had arrived and she and I could peep at the bonnets and choose the best one for myself. Thus it was that I once bore away a 'divine creation' of point lace, crape and shaded asters before Madame had seen it. Otherwise it would have been reserved for Miss Harriet Lane or Mrs. Douglas. Madame had to know later; and Léonide was not much in evidence the rest of that season. At Madame Delarue's, if one was very *gentil*, very *convenable*, one might have the services of François, the one and only hair-dresser of note, who had adjusted coronets on noble heads, and who could (if so minded) talk of them agreeably in Parisian French."

" Le Follet " was the great Parisian authority whose dictates were published every month not only in England but also in the United States. At the close of this decade, a tendency to exaggeration in the prevailing fashions may be noticed which called forth the following satire from Mr. Punch: *

* Punch, 1859.

"From 'Le Follet' of this month, we have the pleasure of learning that 'the robes are generally made with five or seven flounces, the top one not reaching higher than the knee.' This is extremely moderate, and husbands, with incomes under £300 a year, will be delighted to learn that the number is so limited. For ourselves, we think 'seven flounces' positively absurd, and you might as well have none at all, if they are not to go any higher than the knee. We had hoped to see a lady who was all flounces—a regular muslin *La Scala*, tier upon tier of flounces rising right up to the proscenium. The time was when you could not distinguish the dress from the profusion of the trimmings. If they keep falling off in this way, we shall soon be able to see what the pattern of a lady's dress is like.

"Further on 'Le Follet' tells us confidentially that it 'prefers a skirt completely *bouillonneé*, notwithstanding the inconvenience of its holding the dust.' We do not know what *bouillonnée* exactly means. We are perfectly aware that *bouillon* means broth, but still it is a mystery to us how any one can prefer a skirt that is *bouillonéed* all over, for we have noticed ladies, who at dinner have had a little soup spilt over their dress, look as though they did not altogether like it; nor can we see how 'broth' and 'dust' would go very well together. Supposing they do, the recommendation of this new fashion seems to be that it enables every lady to be her own Dust Carrier. The scavengers ought to be very much obliged to them.

"With regard to bonnets we are informed that 'thin bonnets are usually made with double curtains.' Why not have your bonnet like an old four-post bedstead, with curtains all round it? It would be much cooler, though we have a difficulty in seeing what great use there is in having a bonnet at all, when you have a couple of curtains to hide it! We cannot help star-

1829–1855

208

209

210

211

ing also at the notion of a 'thin bonnet.' The thinness may be in consequence of the weather."

The custom of wearing mourning has always been combated by the masculine mind. Trollope's veiled satire on the conventional costume of an English widow is a touch of nature that awakens an echo of kinship in men the whole world over. We recall Mrs. Greenow in " Can You Forgive Her ":

" The Widow was almost gorgeous in her weeds. I believe that she had not sinned in her dress against any of those canons which the semi-ecclesiastical authorities on widowhood have laid down for outward garments fitted for gentlemen's relicts. The materials were those which are devoted to the deepest conjugal grief. As regarded every item of the written law her *suttee* worship was carried out to the letter. There was the widow's cap, generally so hideous, so well known to the eyes of all men, so odious to womanhood. Let us hope that such head-gear may have some assuaging effect on the departed spirits of husbands. There was the dress of deep, clinging, melancholy crape, of crape which becomes so brown and so rusty, and which makes the six months' widow seem so much more afflicted a creature than she whose husband is just gone, and whose crape is therefore new. There were the trailing weepers, and the widow's kerchief pinned close round her neck, and somewhat tightly over her bosom. But there was that of genius about Mrs. Greenow, that she had turned every seeming disadvantage to some special profit, and had so dressed herself that though she had obeyed the law to the letter, she had thrown the spirit of it to the winds. Her cap sat jauntily on her head, and showed just so much of her rich brown hair as to give her the appearance of youth which she desired. . . . She spent more money, I think, on new crape than she did on her brougham. It never became brown and rusty with her, or formed itself into old lumpy folds, or shaped itself round her like a grave cloth. The written law had not interdicted crinoline, and she loomed as large with weeds, which with her were not sombre, as she would do with her silks when the period of her probation should be over. Her weepers were bright with newness, and she would waft them aside from her shoulder with an air which turned even them into auxiliaries. Her kerchief was fastened close round her neck and close over her bosom; but Jeannette well knew what she was doing as she fastened it, and so did Jeannette's mistress."

In Figure 271, a *peignoir* or house gown of pink cachemire, trimmed with a Persian border, is given. It opens over a white embroidered petticoat. The sleeves are full, showing white undersleeves at the wrist. In Figure 264 a mantilla of black velvet, trimmed with Chantilly lace, pictures a fashionable outdoor garment in the fifties.

Women's Dress
1860-1870

" L'acoutumace nous rend familier
Ce que nous parassait terrible et singulier."

N the year 1860 Fashion had set its seal on the most exaggerated form of the hoop-skirt. We are told that it was not really ungraceful when first introduced by the Empress Eugénie, but there was no grace whatever about the hoop-skirt of the sixties. From our point of view, accustomed to many years of clinging draperies, it seems almost incredible that women of judgment and taste could ever have adopted this monstrosity of Fashion. Nevertheless there are reams of contemporary evidence to prove that it was universally worn and by women of all classes. A popular song runs thus:

" Now crinoline is all the rage with ladies of whatever age,
A petticoat made like a cage—oh, what a ridiculous fashion!
'Tis formed of hoops and bars of steel, or tubes of air which lighter
    feel,
And worn by girls to be genteel, or if they've figures to conceal.
It makes the dresses stretch far out a dozen yards or so about,
And pleases both the thin and stout—oh, what a ridiculous fashion!"

The noted historian, McCarthy, in his " Portraits of the Sixties," although not without prejudice in matters of much

greater importance, bears such witness to the prodigious spread
of the crinoline in circumference and popular esteem as cannot
be denied. We give his animadversion in his own words :

" There is one peculiarity belonging to the early sixties which
I cannot leave out of notice, although assuredly it has little
claim to association with art or science, with literature or
politics. The early sixties saw in this and most other civilized
countries the reign of crinoline. It is well for the early sixties
that they had so many splendid claims to historical recollection, but it may be said of them that if they had bequeathed no
other memory to a curious and contemplative posterity, the
reign of crinoline would still have secured for them an abiding-
place in the records of human eccentricities. I may say, without fear of contradiction, that no one who was not living at the
time can form any adequate idea of the grotesque effect produced on the outer aspects of social life by this article of feminine costume. The younger generation may turn over as much
as it will the pages of ' Punch,' which illustrate the ways and
manners of civilization at that time, but with all the undeniable
cleverness and humour of ' Punch's' best caricatures, the
younger generation can never fully realize what extraordinary
exhibitions their polite ancestresses made of themselves during
that terrible reign of crinoline. . . . The fashion of crinoline defied caricature for the actual reality was more full of unpicturesque and burlesque effects than any satirical pencil could
realize on a flat outspread sheet of paper. The fashion of
crinoline, too, defied all contemporary ridicule. A whole new
school of satirical humour was devoted in vain to the ridicule
of crinoline. The boys in the streets sang comic songs to
make fun of it, but no street bellowings of contempt could
incite the wearers of this most inconvenient and hideous article
of dress to condemn themselves to clinging draperies. Crino-

line, too, created a new sort of calamity all its own. Every day's papers gave us fresh accounts of what were called crinoline accidents, cases, that is to say, in which a woman was severely burned or burned to death because of some flame of fire or candle catching her distended drapery at some unexpected moment. There were sacrifices made to the prevailing fashion which would have done the sufferers immortal honour if they had been made for the sake of bearing some religious or political emblem condemned by ruling and despotic authorities. Its inconvenience was felt by the male population as well as by the ladies who sported the obnoxious construction. A woman getting out of a carriage, an omnibus, or a train, making her way through a crowded room, or entering into the stalls of a theatre, was a positive nuisance to all with whom she had to struggle for her passage. The hoop-petticoats of an earlier generation were moderate in their dimensions and slight in the inconvenience they caused when compared with the rigid and enormous structure in which our ladies endeavoured to conform to the fashion set up by the Empress of the French. I remember well seeing a great tragic queen of opera going through a thrilling part at one of the lyric theatres. Her crinoline was of ultra-expansion, was rigid and unyielding in its structure as the mail corselet of the Maid of Orleans. The skirt of silk or satin spread over it, so symmetrically and so rigidly conformed to the outlines of the crinoline that it seemed as if it were pasted to the vast arrangement beneath. The thrill and tragedy of the part were wholly lost on me. I could only see the unpicturesque absurdity of the exhibition. I could feel no sympathy with the dramatic sufferings of the melodious heroine thus enclosed. Every movement and rush of passion, of prayer, of wild despair, or distracted love was lost on me, for each change of posture only brought into more striking display the fact that I was looking at a slight and graceful woman boxed up in some sort of solid barrel of preposterous size over which her skirt was artificially spread. To this day I can only think of that glorious singer as of a woman for some reason compelled to exhibit herself on the stage with a barrel fastened round her waist. A lyrical heroine jumping in a sack would have been graceful and reasonable by comparison. Do what we will, we who lived in those days cannot dissociate our memories of the crinoline from our memories of the women of the period." *

The obnoxious hoop-skirt was usually made of graduated rows of steel wire with a woven cotton casing, held together by broad strips of tape running lengthwise. It was collapsible and very easily broken, adding another inconvenience to its use. The earlier form of reeds run into casings made in a petticoat of cotton, proved to be too heavy and clumsy, and was almost entirely abandoned in 1860.

Mrs. Pryor narrates an adventure during the Civil War, of which the derided hoop-skirt was the heroine.

" One day I was in an ambulance, driving on one of the interminable lanes of the region, the only incident being the watery crossing over the ' cosin,' as the driver called the swamps that had been ' Poquosin ' in the Indian tongue. Behind me came a jolting two-wheeled cart, drawn by a mule and driven by a small negro boy, who stood in front with a foot planted firmly upon each of the shafts. Within and completely filling the vehicle, which was nothing more than a box on wheels, sat a dignified-looking woman. The dame of the ambulance at once became fascinated by a small basket of sweet potatoes which the dame of the cart carried on her lap.

" With a view to acquiring these treasures, I essayed a tenta-

* Portraits of the Sixties, by Justin McCarthy.

67

tive conversation upon the weather, the prospects of a late spring, and finally the scarcity of provisions and consequent sufferings of the soldiers.

"After a keen glance of scrutiny the market woman exclaimed: 'Well, I am doing all I can for them! I know you won't speak of it. Look here!'

"Lifting the edge of her hooped petticoat, she revealed a roll of army cloth, several pairs of cavalry boots, a roll of crimson flannel, packages of gilt braid and sewing silk, cans of preserved meats, and a bag of coffee! She was on her way to our own camp, right under the General's nose! Of course I should not betray her, I promised. I did more. Before we parted she had drawn forth a little memorandum book and had taken a list of my own necessities. She did not 'run the blockade' herself. She had an agent, 'a dear, good Suffolk man,' who would fill my order on his next trip."

Another hoop-skirt story seems worthy of repetition and offers a practical suggestion to the Women's Society for the Prevention of Cruelty to Animals. A young lady in San Francisco dressed in the height of the fashion of the summer of 1865, which of course included a wide-spreading crinoline, was out walking and had with her a pet spaniel, for whose protection she had neglected to take out a license. Suddenly the dog catchers, with their horrible paraphernalia of nets, etc., and followed as usual by a mob of idle boys and men, came into sight, and in a few minutes the officials of the law confronted the young lady and tried to seize her dog. Tilting her hoop-skirt a little to one side, she called the dog who wisely took refuge under the protecting shelter that offered, and with flaming cheeks, the lady held her ground despite the vituperation of the dog catchers. The crowd cheered her with shouts of "Good for you, Lady," "Don't let them have him, Lady," etc., and

212   C.W.TROUT

213   C.W.TROUT

214   C.W.TROUT.
       1907.

215   C.W.TROUT
       1907

216   J.B.Slid
       after photo

217   C.W.TROUT
       1907

218

219

220   C.W.TROUT
       1907.

finally the enemy retreated and the lady took her dog into her arms and fled homeward.

The reign of the hoop-skirt was beginning to decline in 1865, and the change for the better was joyously recorded by "Punch."

" RHYMES TO DECREASING CRINOLINE

"With exceeding satisfaction
A remarkable contraction
Of thy petticoat our eyes have lately seen ;
The expanse of ladies' dress,
Thank its yielding arbitress,
Growing beautifully less,
Crinoline."

A maker in London offered a prize of a hundred guineas for the best poem on the hoop-skirt by way of advertising the garment, and with the purpose of keeping it in favour. This fashion "finally and reluctantly disappeared" about the time that the rule of the beautiful Empress and the Second Empire of France was drawing to a close.

As we will see by the following story, vouched for by a contemporary, the fame of one crinoline outlived its fragile frame.

"Some time after the close of the Civil War, about 1869–70, a story was published by a Northern writer of a somewhat facetious nature, purporting to explain the failure of the Southern cause. The title as well as can be remembered was 'How the Southern Confederacy Was Lost,' and the story was about as follows: In the South during the war it was very hard for the women, shut off as they were, to keep up with the fashions in dress. From time to time an illustrated paper or magazine would get within the lines, showing what was being worn in the outside world. This was quite provoking as many of the things were not to be had in the Confederacy. Among others, the hoop-skirt of the period, made of steel wire woven into a cotton cover, was much coveted and very hard to get. In a certain part of the South it was the ambition of a young lady to obtain one of these much-wished-for garments, shall we call them? and after much trouble and a large expenditure of paper money, the object was achieved. Here, as they say on the play bills, 'a period' is supposed to have elapsed and the erstwhile stylish and proud fabric of steel and cotton has suffered the inevitable fate, and, although mended and tied up in places, is at last, sad to say, no longer a sustaining force, but rather a depressed object, and from the amount of cotton casing considered more fit for the rag bag than the metal scrap heap. Now it happened that a critical time had come in the history of the South. It was becoming more and more evident that without foreign recognition, the effort to establish a nation would fail. A ray of hope came; it was reported that England would not only recognize them, but would take millions of their bonds, and everything was hurried with the object of getting these bonds out as quickly as possible. In fact, it was declared that they must be ready on a certain day for shipment on an English ship which could not remain beyond a certain date. The paper mills were working night and day making the paper for the bonds, then they were to be printed, signed and shipped, but alas, a catastrophe occurred. Among the rags now being made into paper was what remained of the old hoop-skirt and still sticking to part of the webbing there was a small piece of the steel wire. Need we tell more? This, getting into the machinery, soon ruined it; no more machines could be procured, the works stopped, and before matters could be again arranged, the ship for England had to sail and the hopes of the Confederacy were blasted forever."

This period, known in the history of our country by the ambiguous title of the "Civil War," offers for our observation two sides to the question of dress, as well as of politics. With the latter we need not meddle, but the picture of the restricted social life of the South and the economies in dress practised by the once most fashionable element of our people is very interesting.

While pathetic scenes were being enacted in camp, the ladies of Richmond were entertaining, dressing, and dancing by way of keeping up their courage.

" President and Mrs. Davis gave a large reception last week, and the ladies looked positively gorgeous. Mrs. Davis is in mourning for her father." *

During the progress of the war Mrs. Pryor was reduced to finding some means of feeding her household, and, out of a trunkful of " before the war " finery, which had been long stored away, manufactured articles of lingerie, collars, undersleeves, neckties, etc., which brought good prices in the inflated Confederate currency. In her endeavour to keep in the neighbourhood of General Pryor's brigade, she stopped for a while at Petersburg, and describes the ingenuity of the women there.

Mrs. Pryor also mentions the advanced prices during the war times in the Southern states.

Calico of the commonest kind in those days was sold at twenty-five dollars a yard, " and we women of the Confederacy cultivated such an indifference to Paris fashions as would have astonished our former competitors in the Federal capital."

Invention, that clever daughter of Necessity, devised a costume for a Southern belle (for in peace or in war the women of Dixie were always belles) which made such an impression on an English newspaper correspondent, that he sent a description of it to his London paper. This was a gown of unbleached

* Reminiscences of Peace and War.

muslin (made at Macon, Georgia) and trimmed with gourd seed buttons dyed crimson.

"My Petersburg beauties were all wearing hats of their own manufacture, the favourite style being the Alpine with a pointed crown. For trimming, very soft and lovely flowers were made of feathers, the delicate white feather with a tuft of fleecy marabout at its stem. The marabout tuft should be carefully drawn off, to be made into swansdown trimming. A wire was prepared and covered with green paper for a stem, a little ball of wax fastened at the end, and covered with a tiny tuft of the down for a centre, and around this the feathers were stuck, with incurving petals for apple blossoms, and half open roses, and reversed for camelias. Neatly trimmed and suitably tinted, these flowers were handsome enough for anybody, and were in great demand. Cock's plumes were also used on hats, iridescent, and needing no colouring."

The becoming fashion of wearing black velvet around the throat was revived in 1860, a gold locket or a jewel pendant usually being worn on it in the evening. Gold chains and rows of gold beads were also very popular.

A prevalent style of coiffure during the ten years between 1860–1870 was popularly known as the waterfall. A frame of horsehair was attached to the back of the head by an elastic, and the back hair brushed smoothly over it, the ends caught up underneath. A net was usually worn over this "chignon" to keep the hair in place. Often the whole structure was made of false hair and fastened on with hairpins. Augustus Hare tells a good story about a "waterfall" or "chignon" of this kind. "How well I remember the Aumales riding through the green avenues near Ossington; Mary Boyle was with them. She was a most excellent horsewoman, but a great gust of wind came and the whole edifice of her ' chignon ' was blown off before she could stop it. The little Prince de Condé was very young and he was riding with her. He picked it up and said, 'I will keep it in my pocket and then when we reach Thorsby you can just go quietly away and put it on '—and so she did."

Many illustrations of this arrangement are given in "Punch." In Figure 140 the back hair is done in a "waterfall," and in Figure 168 the hair under the net is arranged over a horsehair rouleau attached to the head by a narrow elastic cord. The latter was generally adopted by schoolgirls, and was very easily adjusted.

"In the arrangement of the hair," says an acknowledged American authority of this period, "regard ought to be paid to the style of the features as well as to the general appearance of the wearer. When the features are large or strongly marked, the hair should be arranged in masses, in large curls or well defined bows, so as to harmonize with the general cast of the countenance. If, on the contrary, the features are small and delicate, the greatest care should be taken not to render too striking the contrast between them and the magnitude of the head-dress. Small and delicately formed curls or ringlets, braids, or light and airy bows are the most pleasing varieties for this style. The features of the greater number of young ladies, however, cannot be classed under either of these extremes. When such is the case, the fancy of the individual is of course allowed greater latitude, but ought to be no less subject to the dictates of taste."

While on the subject of hair, it is interesting to note that "Miss Reed (of Tennessee) was the original girl with a curl in the middle of her forehead," the "coquettish item of coiffure" being speedily imitated by a hundred other girls in Washington.

A new fashion in 1866, introduced by Eugénie, was known as the "Empress peplin." It consisted of a belt with basque tails cut square in front and back and very long at the sides.

A French authority remarked of this innovation : " The peplin marks an epoch in history, and deserves our gratitude, for with it crinoline was decidedly an anomaly and its fall was assured."

Nets for the hair (Figure 168) and the still popular *en tout cas*, between a parasol and an umbrella, were also novelties stamped by the approval of the Empress. Not the least popular of the fashions adopted by this lady was the arrangement of hair which is still known by her name. A photograph is given (Figure 138) showing the curls hanging from the coil at the back, etc. The Empress was a most accomplished equestrienne, and for this exercise preferred an almost masculine costume. The long full skirt was worn over grey cloth trousers and on her feet were patent leather boots with high heels and spurs. The curls were concealed by a trig coil of braids under the long plume of her hat. It was, we are told, her custom to ride astride and she " despised the side saddle ordinarily used by her sex."

A contemporary American authority speaks of " Foulard," a silk first introduced in 1860 which still retains popular favour.

" In the foulards for ordinary wear, pansies, clusters of berries, fruit, as the cherry and plum, are among the newest designs."

Specimens of the fashions in bonnets of this decade are illustrated in Figures 282 and 283 from originals in the interesting collection of Miss Dutihl in Memorial Hall, Philadelphia. One of these bonnets (Figure 282) is made of emerald green velvet with a brim of white bengaline, a full trimming next the face of blond lace, green velvet and white roses, and two sets of strings, one of white ribbon and the other of green velvet. The other (Figure 283) is of brown horsehair braid and brown silk with a quilling of the same. White tulle, black velvet ribbon and red poppies inside the brim.

These bonnets are much flatter on top and more open at the ears than formerly. A variety of fancy braids, and some delicately fine Dunstables and split French straws were popular. We find the following under the heading " Spring Bonnets " :

" A Neapolitan braid, grey and white, trimmed with Solferino and grey ribbon drawn into rosettes on one side, with straw centres, which give them much the appearance of poppies, a long loop of ribbon and two straw tassels complete the trimming of the left side, and on the other side the ribbon is drawn down perfectly plain. The cape and front of the bonnet are finished with a puffing of Solferino crape.

" An English chip bonnet, with pansy-coloured velvet cape. On the right side of the bonnet are two bows of pansy ribbon worked with gold stars, and on the other a large bunch of scarlet flowers.

" Fine split straw with dark crown, trimmed with a sapphire blue ribbon and a white ribbon. On the right side of the bon- net is a large water-lily with buds and leaves. The inside trimming is a roll of sapphire blue velvet, black tabs, and a small lily on one side.

" A Tuscan braid trimmed on one side with white ribbon bound with black velvet, and black lace rosettes with jet centres, and on the left side are handsome jet tassels fastened by medallions of white gimp. The inside trimming is in a puffing of white illusion, and large black rosettes with jet pendants. This is a beautiful style of bonnet for light mourning." *

Hats were very small in the sixties. The mushroom hat of 1907 is a revival of a style introduced in 1862. Another shape much worn at that time had a round crown and small rolling brim, and was usually trimmed with a drooping ostrich feather. Illustrations of both these fashionable hats are given in

* Godey's Lady's Book (1861).

1808–1830

FIGURE 222.—1808—Specimen of hand-painted trimming, a popular fancy-work in the first quarter of the nineteenth century. Chinese shawl of muslin embroidered in a design of pagodas and trees. White mull shawl. White satin slippers. Part of the wedding outfit of Miss Lydia Leaming, worn in Philadelphia.

FIGURE 223.—1808—Wedding veil, fan and reticule. Linen gloves cut out and sewn by hand.

FIGURE 224.—1808—Black lace scarf.

1820—Three-cornered shawl.

FIGURE 225.—1810—Baby dress.

1830—Embroidered pelisse.

222   225

223

Figures 163 and 165 and in Figure 169 will be seen the picture of a walking hat decorated with a feather which came into favour in 1865, and was celebrated in the following verses of a popular song:

"THE JOCKEY HAT AND FEATHER

"As I was walking out, one day,
    Thinking of the weather,
I saw a pair of roguish eyes
    'Neath a hat and feather;
She looked at me, I looked at her,
    It made my heart pit-pat,
Then, turning round, she said to me,
    How do you like my hat?

"CHORUS—Oh! I said; it's gay and pretty too;
        They look well together,
        Those glossy curls and Jockey hat,
        With a rooster feather.

"She wore a handsome broadcloth basque,
    Cut in the latest fashion,
And flounces all around her dress
    Made her look quite dashing;
Her high-heeled boots, as she walk'd on,
    The pavement went pit-pat,
I will ne'er forget the smile I saw,
    Beneath the Jockey hat.

"CHORUS—Oh! I said," etc.

The pork-pie was the name of another style of hat. It was not unlike the turban hat in shape, but there was a little space between the brim and crown. (See Figure 164.)

In the year 1863, the game of croquet was introduced and became very popular on both sides of the ocean. "Punch" has described it in the following verses:

"CROQUET

"Aid me, ye playful nymphs that flit around
The Pegs and Hoops of every Croquet ground !
Ye gentle spirits do not mock, nor blame
My humble efforts to describe the Game.
Eight's the full complement of players : more
Than six is bad, I think ; let two or four
Of equal skill for Croquet's laurels fight,
This the best form of game.   Say, am I right?
Let Messrs. Robinson and Jones choose sides ;
Miss Smith, Miss Brown ; perchance their future **brides,**
Events do happen strange as those we **read,**
And Croquet may to Hymen's Altar lead.
Jones wins the toss, and cunning dog, forthwith,
Takes for his partner blonde Miss Emmy Smith,
While Robinson, who'd just begun to frown,
Looks happy and selects brunette Miss Brown.
On Emmy, Blue her partner's care bestows,
And her with Yellow does Brunette oppose ;
Jones chooses Green ; two laugh : 'he laughs who wins' :
To Robinson the Red : and Red begins."

A croquet costume is shown in Figure 166 from a fashion
book of 1868, in which the dress is made with an apron front
and looped up over a gay coloured under petticoat and the high
walking boots are finished with a silk tassel at the ankle.   A
short sacque or loose jacket is worn with this dress, and a small
hat with a long ostrich feather falling over the hair.

In Figure 246 illustrations of shoes worn during the sixties
are given.   Congress gaiters were made of cloth and, instead of
opening up the front, were finished with a broad piece of elastic
on each side.   They were cut rather low, and were made in different colours and tipped with patent leather.   Balmoral boots,
depicted in Figure 166, were very popular.   They laced up the
front and were considered very stylish, and were effectively worn
in the game of croquet, or with seaside costume.   A sketch by
Leech in "Punch" has the following squib printed underneath it :

"That the mermaids of our beaches do not end in ugly tails,
Nor have homes among the corals, but are shod with neat balmorals,
An arrangement no one quarrels with,
As many might with seals."

A riding habit of 1865 is given in the initial at the beginning of this chapter. It is taken from a contemporary English print. It is similar to the costume worn by Queen Victoria as represented in the equestrian statue at Liverpool. Several attractive riding habits are described in the magazines of the sixties :

A black cloth with a long basque with revers in front, standing white collar with cherry silk necktie. Black felt hat with dark blue grenadine veil.

A blue cloth habit made with a square coat tail in the back, and point in front. Standing linen collar with necktie of white muslin. Black straw hat with blue feathers.

Habit of grey cloth made with a short point back and front. Standing collar and blue silk necktie. Veil of grey tissue.

Among other innovations introduced in this decade was the Garibaldi blouse, which for a while attained great popularity in America as well as in Europe. Two new colours which mark that dramatic period of Garibaldi's career, "Solferino" and "Magenta," were in favour during the sixties. A costume worn by Eugénie, grey woolen skirt looped in festoons over an under-petticoat of Solferino cashmere with a Garibaldi blouse of the same new colour, small hat with feather, may be considered typical of the middle of that decade. (See Figure 165.)

A popular song of that time describes these prevailing fashions.

"RED PETTICOAT
"You may talk about the fashions,
Of bonnets neat and small,
Of crinoline and flounces,
But the stripes exceed them all.

I'm fond of little bonnets,
    Of skirts quite full and wide,
But they want the striped petticoat
    To show them off beside.

" There's a beauty in the gaiter,
    That defies the clumsy foot,
But the tidy little slipper,
    Looks best upon the foot.
And if you wish to show it,
    Or have it well display'd,
Then with the striped petticoat
    Just take a promenade.

" All women take the fashions
    Of Empress and Queen,
Victoria wears the petticoat,
    And crinoline—Eugene ;
Victoria is a model,
    As every woman knows,
And every girl should imitate
    Her virtues, well as clothes."

The Zouave jacket, made either with or without sleeves, rivalled the Garibaldi blouse in popular favour. Like the spencers of an earlier date, these little jackets were made in every colour and combination. Zouave trousers for riding were among the new fashions for women in 1869. A plate of that date, in the collection of the Salmagundi Club of New York, shows a suit of dark green cloth, Zouave jacket and full Turkish trousers fastened at the ankle, and a fez to match with a black tassel hanging over the left side.

Printed calicoes and chintzes were worn by maids, with white aprons and, in many households, white caps with a bow of ribbon, as in Figure 167, which is taken from a contemporary print.

In the winter of 1869–1870 the hoop-skirt, which had been gradually diminishing in circumference since 1865, was superseded by dress improvers or bustles. These articles of attire were made either of horsehair with a series of ruffles across the back, or of cambric with steels run through a casing, their object being to hold the dress skirt out at the back. They were made like a petticoat with a plain breadth in front and the full trimming in the back breadth only, but they gradually grew smaller and smaller.

Overdresses were worn with every costume in 1870, caught up at the sides and decorated with numerous bows or rosettes. Bodices were cut high and sashes to match the dress were very much worn in the street as well as with evening dresses. Very long trains were worn with the latter, but street costumes were made to clear the instep. Bonnets and hats were very small and flat.

At this period (1869–1870) the hair was usually arranged in braids at the back and turned up and pinned close to the head, while the front hair was crimped, parted in the middle and drawn back above the ears, and the ends made into finger-puffs on top of the head. Curls were much worn, sometimes hanging in a soft cluster over the braids, but the favourite style was a long ringlet coming out from the braids at the left side and hanging down over the shoulder. For full dress occasions the coiffure consisted entirely of finger-puffs and small artificial flowers were placed at intervals through them. Bonnets were worn for visiting, etc., by every lady from the age of eighteen upwards.

A *débutante* costume for fashionable street wear in 1870 was usually a dress of black silk trimmed with ruffles of the same, a close-fitting basque coat of black velvet trimmed with fur or with ostrich feather trimming, a bonnet of coloured velvet trimmed with flowers and, instead of strings, a bridle of velvet under the chin. Such a combination would be considered much

1836–1847

FIGURE 227.—1838—A gentleman in full dress. Taken from a plate.

FIGURE 228.—1838—A white satin wedding dress trimmed with blond lace, worn in Philadelphia by Miss Mary Brinton. Head and veil from a contemporary portrait.

FIGURE 229.—1839—Gentleman in morning suit of mixed tweed. From a print of that date.

FIGURE 230.—1836—A soft white figured silk gown worn in Philadelphia. The trimming is of the same material plaited and arranged in a fan-shaped bertha. Head is from a contemporary portrait.

FIGURE 231.—1837—Bottle-green broadcloth coat, white figured silk waistcoat; worn in Philadelphia. Pantaloons, stock, etc., from a print of that date. Head from a portrait.

FIGURE 232.—1847—Blue changeable silk pelisse, wadded and lined with white silk; worn in Boston. Bonnet and gown from a print. Head from a contemporary portrait.

FIGURE 233.—1845—Greenish-gray satin gown, worn in Boston. Embroidered muslin cape from a plate. Head from a portrait of the same date.

FIGURE 234.—1845—Blue coat with gilt buttons and white silk waistcoat; worn in Philadelphia. Stock, hat, etc., from a plate. Head from a contemporary portrait.

1838·227   1838·228   1838·229   1836·230

1837·231   1845·232   1845·233   1845·234

too sedate for a grandmother in the present day. Black silk was also worn for evening dresses with sashes and trimmings of a bright colour or with a flat trimming of jet passementerie.

Possibly the popularity of black may be traced to France, which was in great trouble in 1870. During the disastrous siege of Paris, Challomel tells us, " Fashion veiled her face. The ' Magazine des Modes ' was silent and under the melancholy circumstances black was universally worn, but it was not like ordinary mourning, being richly trimmed."

Gloves with one button had been worn throughout the sixties even with short sleeves, but at the end of that decade a pronounced change was introduced. Picturesque Musquetaire gloves of "Suède," reaching almost to the elbow, at once claimed popular favour for evening dress. For street wear from two to six buttons were in vogue. Soft shades of tan and grey were the fashionable colours. The following verses by Locker gracefully express the sentiment attached to the glove at all periods :

> " Slips of a kid-skin deftly sewn,
> A scent as through her garden blown,
> The tender hue that clothes her dove,
> All these, and this is Gerty's glove.

> " A glove but lately dofft, for look
> It keeps the happy shape it took
> Warm from her touch ! who gave the glow ?
> And where's the mould that shaped it so ?" *

> * London Lyrics.

CHILDREN'S GARMENTS
1800–1870

"NEW DRESSES

"New dresses ? Ay, this is the season
  For ' opening-day ' is close by :
Already I know the ' Spring fashions '—
  Can tell you, I think, if I try.

"Of colours, the first thing to mention,
  There's a great variety seen ;
But that which obtains the most favour
  Is surely a very bright green.

"True, the elderly portion are plainer,
  And choose, both in country and town,
To appear in the shades which are sombre,
  And keep on the garment of brown.

"Miss Snowdrop, the first of the season,
  Comes out in such very good taste—
Pure white, with her pretty green trimmings ;
  How charming she is, and how chaste !

"Miss Crocus, too, shows very early
  Her greetings of love for the sun,
And comes in her white, blue or yellow ;
  All dresses of hers are home-spun.

"And who is this handsome young master,
  A friend to Miss Crocus so true ?
He comes dressed in purple or yellow,
  And sometimes in pink, white and blue.

"In form he is tall and majestic ;
  Ah ! the Spring has just whispered his name :
' Hyacinthus '—the beau of the season !
  And sweet and wide-spread is his fame.

"Madame Tulip, a dashing gay lady,
  Appears in a splendid brocade ;
She courts the bright sunbeams, which give her
  All colours—of every shade.

" She came to us o'er the wide ocean,
    Away from her own native air,
But if she can dress as she chooses
    She can be quite at home anywhere.

" Narcissus, a very vain fellow,
    Has a place in the Spring fashions, too—
Appears in his green, white and yellow,
    In his style, though, there's nothing that's new.

" Miss Daisy wears white, with fine fluting ;
    A sweet little creature is she,
But she loves the broad fields and green meadows,
    And cares not town fashions to see.

" Another style, pretty and tasteful,
    Green, dotted with purple or blue,
Is worn by Miss Myrtle, whose beauty
    In shade and retirement grew.

" I've borrowed these styles from Dame Nature,
    Whose children are always well drest :
In contrast and blending of colours
    She always knows what is the best.

" Already her hand is arranging
    More elaborate trimmings for May ;
In silence, unseen it is working,
    Accomplishing much every day.

" Her 'full dress' and festive occasion
    Will take place quite early in June,
Ushered in by low notes of sweet music,
    Which her song-birds alone can attune."
                                —S. H. BARKER.

Children's Garments
1800–1835

"Oh, what a silken stocking,
And what a satin shoe;
I wish I was a little toe
To live in there, I do."

HE dressing of babies and little girls in the early part of the nineteenth century was very simple and very pretty. The prevailing fashions for women were in fact more suitable for children than for their mothers, and the numerous portraits of that period show infants and children dressed in soft muslin, made with low necks, short sleeves, high waists, and scanty skirts just reaching to the ankles. Slippers or low shoes made of kid or satin were worn at all seasons, and a sash of ribbon and a necklace of coral or of gold beads were the favourite adornments.

The little shoes sketched in Figure 219 belonged to a baby girl in Philadelphia and recall another rhyme of Kate Greenaway's:

"As I stepped out to hear the news,
I met a lass in socks and shoes,
She'd shoes with strings, and a friend had tied them,
She'd a nice little pair of feet inside them!"

The hair was generally cut short, which is not a becoming fashion even to a pretty face. Curls, however, came into vogue

295

1804–1860

FIGURE 235.—1812—Morning cap of embroidered muslin, called "coiffure à l'indisposition." From a plate.

FIGURE 236.—1812—Dinner cap of lace and muslin trimmed with white satin. From a plate of the day.

FIGURE 237.—1812—White "Hyde Park" bonnet. After a print.

FIGURE 238.—1816—Bonnet of white chip trimmed with rouleaux of gauze and bunch of white flowers. From a plate.

FIGURE 239.—1810–13—Hat of Leghorn trimmed with pale blue ribbon and straw rosettes around the crown. Wetherill collection.

FIGURE 240.—1817—Straw bonnet trimmed with green ribbon rosette. From a plate.

FIGURE 241.—1825–29—Leghorn hat with blue satin ribbon in a brocade scroll pattern. Wetherill collection.

FIGURE 242.—1818–19—Hat of white straw with gauze ribbon; white flowers and gauze plaits under the brim. Wetherill collection.

FIGURE 243.—1804—Bonaparte hat of white gauze trimmed with wreath of laurel.

FIGURE 244.—1819—Bonnet of white spotted satin trimmed with white satin ribbon. Wetherill collection.

FIGURE 245.—1816—Muslin morning bonnet. From a plate.

FIGURE 246.—1820–60—Pale blue ribbed silk slippers with satin rosettes. Gaiters of drab cloth laced up the side. Bronze kid slipper with red inlaid rosette. White kid slipper.

235 S.B.S.
after print

236 after print.

237 S.B.S. after print

238 S.B.S. after print.

239 S.B.S.

240 S.B.S. after Print

241 S.B.S.

242 S.B.S.

243 G.W.T. 1907.

244 S.B.S.

245 S.B.S. after print

246 C.W.TROUT 1907

soon after 1800 and were encouraged and cultivated whenever it was possible. In a few years the fashion became so popular that curl papers were the torment of almost every little girl in the nursery. Caps, which as we have seen were ordinarily worn by grown people, were also worn in the house by children from 1800 to 1825, and will be noticed in many of the portraits by Sully, Stuart, and St. Memin. Over the caps, hats of beaver or straw, according to the season, were worn out-of-doors, demurely tied under the chin, for

" Little Fanny wears a hat
Like her ancient Grannie."

Mits of thread and silk, which were fashionable in the latter half of the eighteenth century, were still worn by children from 1800 to 1830.

During the First Empire period the gowns of children were of the plainest. In Figure 77 a picture of the little niece of Napoleon shows a very unpretentious costume of sheer muslin trimmed with Valenciennes lace, which has been selected as a typical specimen of the garb of little girls from 1800 to 1820 in France, England and America. For outdoor wear pelisses or wrapping cloaks, lined or wadded and often trimmed with fur, were fashionable during the first quarter of the century, made as in Figure 175, with a standing collar, high waist and buttoned closely down the front. This particular pelisse is of red cloth and was worn in Philadelphia by little Mary Brinton in 1812. It is not unlike the green pelisses of Kate Greenaway's verses :

" Five little sisters walking in a row,
Now isn't that the best way for little girls to go?
Each had a round hat, each had a muff,
And each had a new pelisse of soft green stuff."

These outdoor garments were often made with capes, as in the following description taken from a fashion book of 1808:

"A frock and short trousers of cambric, with Turkish pomposas [slippers] of jonquille kid. A wrapping coat with deep cape, formed of fine scarlet kerseymere. A beaver hat and feathers of dove colour."

The hats of that period, illustrated in Figures 194, 195 and 203, were quaint enough to find favour with Miss Greenaway when she started the picturesque revolution in the dress of children, which is still known by her name. Bonnets much like their elders were worn by small girls from the age of seven up, and remained in fashion all through the century (Figures 157, 175, 181, 184, 187 and 280.)

" Polly's, Peg's and Poppety's
    Mamma was kind and good,
She gave them each, one happy day,
    A little scarf and hood.

" A bonnet for each girl she bought,
    To shield them from the sun ;
They wore them in the snow and rain,
    And thought it mighty fun."

An infant's dress worn in Boston in 1824 is illustrated in Figure 217. It is very dainty and a beautiful specimen of plain needlework. Another little dress of about the same date (see Figure 218) is trimmed with openwork insertion. A christening frock shown in Figure 215, which is of a much later date, was worn by a Philadelphia baby in 1855.

Long cloaks of merino, wadded and lined with silk and trimmed with embroidery or swansdown fur, were the usual outdoor garments of babies from 1800 to 1870. The picture of one in Figure 220 is taken from a baby cloak of fawn-coloured merino embroidered with silk of the same colour, and lined throughout with silk to match.   It was made in England, and was sent to Philadelphia as a present to a little Quaker baby in 1834.   The bonnet was made to match the cloak and the ribbon trimmings are all of the exact shade of brown.   A coat and bonnet of the same material and colour and made for an elder sister of three years of age are shown in Figure 216.   Both of these costumes are beautifully embroidered and nothing but the colour, which is rather sober for babies, suggests that they were especially designed for the children of Quaker parents. In the early part of the century, however, Quakers were much more rigid in their regulations with regard to dress. In the "Autobiography of Mary Howitt" she describes the austerely plain costumes of a little Quaker girl in 1809 as follows:

"How well I remember the garments that were made for us. Our little brown cloth pelisses, cut plain and straight, without plait or fold in them, hooked and eyed down the front so as to avoid buttons, which were regarded by our parents as trimmings, yet fastened at the waist, with a cord.   Little drab beaver bonnets furnished us by the Friends' hatter of Stafford, James Nixon, who had blocks made purposely for our little ultra-plain bonnets.   They were without a scrap of ribbon or cord, except the strings, which were a necessity, and these were fastened inside.   Our frocks were, as usual, of the plainest and most homely fabric and make."

Nothing could be more sad and doleful than the garb in Figure 288, copied from the woodcut in the book.

The love for pretty things is almost an instinct with young children, and it is not easy to imagine the "Sophia" of Jane Taylor's verses entitled:

" SOPHIA'S FOOL'S CAP

" Sophia was a little child,
    Obliging, good and very mild,
    Yet, lest of dress she should be vain,
    Mamma still dressed her well but plain —
    Her parents, sensible and kind,
    Wished only to adorn her mind ;
    No other dress, when good, had she,
    But useful, neat simplicity.

" Though seldom, yet when she was rude,
    Or even in a naughty mood,
    Her punishment was this disgrace,
    A large fine cap adorned with lace,
    With feathers and with ribbands too ;
    The work was neat, the fashion new,
    Yet, as a fool's cap was its name,
    She dreaded much to wear the same.

" A lady, fashionably gay,
    Did to Mamma a visit pay.
    Sophia stared, then whispering said,
    'Why, dear Mamma, look at her head !
    To be so tall and wicked too,
    The strangest thing I ever knew,
    What naughty tricks, pray, has she done,
    That they have put a fool's cap on ?' "

A story is told of a little Quaker girl whose soul yearned for
bright colours. Having made an engagement to take a country
walk with a boy neighbour, she stole quietly out of the house
and gathered in the orchard some ripe cherries with which she
adorned her plain straw hat and drab ribbons, being very careful to throw away the bright cherries on her way home.

Another story of the days of pantalets is told of a little
Quaker girl and her sister, who laid a deep scheme to procure a
pair of those uncouth garments which, being in the height of
fashion among children of the world, were forbidden to the children of Friends, and consequently much coveted by them. Be-

fore the grown people were stirring, these two children got up and fashioned for themselves two pairs of pantalets out of one of the sheets from their bed. They were busy plying their needles when the door suddenly opened and their mother appeared. Needless to say, an emphatic demonstration of maternal disapproval ensued and the little Quakeresses never finished the pantalets.

In 1815 great changes in fashion for everybody were introduced. The big hats and full skirts were well enough for little girls, but alack! the pantalets reaching to the ankles spoiled everything. These obnoxious articles must have been very troublesome to make and very uncomfortable to wear, but they held their sway from about 1818 to about 1858. There are several specimens to be seen in the collection at Memorial Hall, Philadelphia. It was the custom of thrifty mothers to make the pantalets for school and every-day wear of stout calico or nankin, but for afternoon and dress occasions they were always of white and often elaborately trimmed with lace and embroidery. Occasionally they were trimmed with deep gathered ruffles, and awkward indeed must have been the wearing of these stiff and starched vanities. Pantalets were usually adjustable and made to button on to the edge of the drawers, but occasionally they were made to full into a band and finished with a ruffle at the ankle, as in Figures 157 and 181.

Old fashion books tell us that when children were dressed in mourning, a general custom on the death of a parent in the first half of the nineteenth century, they had pantalets made of crape; could anything be more hideous?

From 1825 to 1835, leg-of-mutton sleeves figured in the children's corner of Fashion's kingdom, as elsewhere. Broad belts or sashes were universally worn too, and everything was made to stand out about the shoulders. Hats were rather aggressively trimmed with projecting bows of ribbon, etc. In Figure 208 will be seen pictures of a paper doll dressed in the very height of the fashion of 1829. It was owned by a little girl in Philadelphia named Elizabeth Randolph. The costumes are all well preserved, as the photograph shows, but the original doll has been lost in the course of time and the modern representation who now displays the wardrobe wears high heels, which no fashionable doll of 1829 would have thought of doing.

Perhaps the original doll is still lamenting her fate in some obscure closet like the heroine of Eugene Field's pathetic verses:

"LAST YEAR'S DOLL

"I'm only a last year's doll!
    I thought I was lovely and fair —
But alas for the cheeks that were rosy,
    Alas for the once flowing hair !
I'm sure that my back is broken,
    For it hurts me when I rise,
Oh, I'd cry for very sorrow,
    But I've lost out both my eyes.

"In comes my pretty mistress,
    With my rival in her arms,
A fine young miss, most surely,
    Arrayed in her borrowed charms !
My dress and my slippers too,
    But sadder, oh, sadder than all,
She's won the dear love I have lost,
    For I'm only a last year's doll.

"Oh, pity me, hearts that are tender,
    I'm lonely and battered and bruised,
I'm tucked out of sight in the closet,
    Forgotten, despised and abused !
I'm only a last year's doll,
    Alone with my troubled heart,
Sweet mistress, still I love thee,
    Inconstant though thou art."

Fancy aprons were fashionable for little girls in the period of the thirties. They were usually made of silk and were considered very stylish when made with bretelles and trimmed with a ruching of the silk as shown in Figure 181. But fine muslin aprons, trimmed with lace or embroidery, were also worn; and printed calico and white cross-barred cambric, trimmed with narrow frills of the same, were used for the aprons of less fashionable children for many years.

The costumes in fashion for little boys from four to ten were not quite as simple as those for girls. Sometimes, it is true, we notice a short-waisted jacket with low neck and sleeves, like a girl's, but the ruffled shirt collars and close-fitting jacket and trousers devised by Marie Antoinette for the unfortunate Dauphin, were very generally worn by boys upward from the age of four years.

The sketch of a small boy from a print of 1808 is given in Figure 194 showing a cloth cap with a full soft crown and a visor worn with a kerseymere suit.

In Figure 195 a boy in a short-sleeved tunic with full trousers reaching to the ankle, copied from a fashion plate of 1810, is given. The straw hat is turned back in front and is not very unlike the hat shown in Figure 203, which is in the interesting collection at the School of Industrial Art, Philadelphia.

In Figure 174 we give a picture of a suit worn by a little American boy, about four years old, in 1804. The material is a striped brown and white calico, and the pantaloons, which fit close to the leg, are fastened with a fly front like a man's. The short waisted jacket has tight long sleeves and revers at the neck in front, allowing the ruffled collar of the linen shirt to show. It is a fascinating costume and we consider ourselves most fortunate in securing a picture of it for this book. It

1840–1851

247

250

248

249

252

251

is much too small for a modern boy of four, however; in fact, it
was a tight fit for the little fellow of two and a half who posed
in it. Evidently this was the style of suit worn by Miss Austen's little nephews in 1801 and mentioned in the following extract from a letter of that date:

"Mary has likewise a message: she will be much obliged
to you if you can bring her the pattern of the jacket and
trousers, or whatever it is that Elizabeth's boys wear when they
are first put into breeches; so if you could bring her an old
suit itself, she would be very glad, but that I suppose is
hardly done."

Some years later, in 1809, Miss Austen writes of getting black
suits for her nephews whose father had just died, establishing
for us the fact that it was customary for little boys, as well as
girls, to wear mourning for their parents.

"Mrs. J. A. had not time to get them more than one suit of
clothes; their others are making here, and though I do not believe Southampton is famous for tailoring, I hope it will prove
itself better than Basingstoke. Edward has an old black coat,
which will save his having a second new one, but I find that
black pantaloons are considered by them as necessary, and of
course one would not have them made uncomfortable by the
want of what is usual on such occasions."

Before promotion to trousers, an event which usually took
place when a boy had reached his fourth year, queer little
tunics of merino opening down the front and reaching below
the knees were worn over white trousers reaching to the ankle
either of material to match or of white linen. (See Figure 179.)

In the thirties exaggerated leg-of-mutton sleeves were worn
even by boys. In Figure 197 a suit of dark green merino is
shown, copied from a portrait of 1833, in which not only the
sleeves are of this shape, but the long pantaloons follow the same

lines, being cut very full from the hip to the knees, and tapering to the ankle. This was worn in England by a boy of
about ten years, while the suit with very pronounced leg-
of-mutton trousers in Figure 198 was worn by a younger brother
of eight.

From 1830 to 1835 the ordinary costume of boys over ten
years of age was a suit of long, rather loose-fitting pantaloons,
a waistcoat cut rather low and showing a white shirt beneath,
and a short jacket reaching to the waist line.

The hats for boys of the early part of the nineteenth century
were extremely ugly. The jockey cap with a round crown and
a visor is seen in many of the prints from 1801 to 1810, a long
tassel hanging down over the left ear being the only decoration.
Then came the stove-pipe hat, made of straw in summer and of
beaver in winter, which was actually worn for several years
even by little boys in frocks. During the Regency period
(1810–1819) caps were worn with crowns of cloth and visors of
enamelled leather as in Figure 178, taken from a drawing of
Boutet de Monvel. From 1820 to 1830 hats worn by small
boys were like that shown in Figure 351, with rather high
crowns and straight brims. In 1830 high hats were worn by
very fashionable boys in trousers (see Figure 182) which looked
like inverted flower pots. Beauty and fitness seem not to have
been considered.

Children's Garments

1835–1870

"Young ladies then wore gowns with sleeves,
  Which would just hold their arms;
  And did not have as many yards
  As acres in their farms."

THE leg-of-mutton sleeves, which in 1835 had indeed reached extravagant proportions, declined in favour for the gowns of little girls towards the end of that year. In 1836 sleeves were made less full and gathered into three puffs from shoulder to wrist, or the fullness was laid in flat plaits at the top of the arm, hung loose about the elbow and was finished with a cuff at the wrist. A little later straight, close-fitting sleeves trimmed with frills and puffings were popular. In 1840 sleeves to the elbow were introduced. This fashion still retains its popularity and is very appropriate as well as becoming. In the forties sleeves for little girls were often made to reach a little below the elbow, showing undersleeves of white muslin. A small plaited frill of the muslin was worn at the throat. For girls of fifteen pelerines were in vogue. They were fastened at the waist, both front and back, and trimmed with frills of lace or muslin. In the fifties big sleeves with muslin undersleeves were worn by girls from twelve years up.

After the decline of the leg-of-mutton sleeves and trousers,

311

boys wore tight sleeves, but the pantaloons, as we notice in many of the portraits between 1835 and 1850, were usually loose at the ankle. The following extract is from an American book, late in the forties:

"Small jacket, open and rounded in front, of dark velvet, cloth, or cashmere, with buttons of the same. Small square linen collar turned over, a ribbon necktie. Loose trousers of blue and white striped linen. Cap of dark cloth."

From 1835 to 1850 we notice in the fashion plates as well as in portraits that most of the skirts were trimmed with flounces, and until 1846 the pantalets covered the tops of the shoes, but at the end of the forties pantalets were worn shorter and gradually disappeared. In fact in the fifties they were visible only on very small children and under very short skirts. Plaids and graduated stripes were very fashionable for both boys and girls throughout that decade.

Before 1835 the hair was usually worn parted in the middle by girls of all ages. Curls were fashionable and by the help of curling tongs were easily acquired by every one. Maggie Tulliver's short mop of hair was a special vexation, we know, to her mother, who always felt a pang of envy at the sight of Lucy's neatly arranged curls. But for a time between 1835 and 1870 a very popular fashion was to plait the hair in two long braids, like the two eldest Kenwigs who, as we recall, "had flaxen hair tied with blue ribbons in luxuriant pigtails down their backs." Some time in the forties it became fashionable to comb the hair back from the forehead without a part, and springs of steel covered with ribbon or velvet were introduced to keep it in place. Back-combs were another novelty introduced for the same purpose. Older girls arranged the back hair in a net of silk or chenille, as in Figure 205, or fastened the "pigtails" in a coil at the back, as in Figure 201.

Boys wore the hair parted very much to one side at that time, and it was not cropped close to the head as is the fashion of to-day. About 1860 the fashion of parting the hair directly in the middle was introduced and followed for some years by big boys as well as men, although this change was considered effeminate at first, and consequently disliked by little boys ambitious for promotion to long pantaloons.

Bonnets and hats were equally fashionable for girls from 1835 to 1860. Illustrations of the prevailing styles of both are given in Figures 181, 184, 187, and 190. In Miss Whitney's " Stories of New England " a great deal is said about the clothes of girls from 1840 to 1850. We learn that when Augusta Hare, who was almost grown up, appeared to the unsophisticated eyes of Anstiss Dolbeare in mourning for her father, wearing "a black merino shawl and long veil that made her face so sweet and fair, these garments were to my childish fancy the very poetry of bereavement, there seemed a grandeur and solemn distinction in having lost a friend. My openworked straw bonnet with blue gauze ribbons seemed so tawdry, so little girlish."

The adventures of this straw bonnet were very interesting. Anstiss, having seen some scarfs of silk with fringed ends, which Augusta Hare had brought, longed to have one too, but knew that " Aunt Ildy " would never listen to such an extravagance.

The next morning, however, Anstiss saw the pretty face of Miss Augusta smiling at her from the doorway. She was dressed on this occasion "in a clear black muslin with the tiniest dash of white, and a knot of black ribbon in her hair. In her hand, streaming down in brilliant contrast over her dress, was a rich broad bonnet scarf of blue with fringed ends." In a short time the despised bonnet was completely transformed and not until this change was accomplished did Anstiss realize how difficult it would be to gain her aunt's approval. Hastily the bonnet was put away on a shelf in the closet and when finally the aunt discovered the change, the little girl was sent to bed under most aggravating circumstances and the old trimming replaced by the angry fingers of Aunt Ildy, whose displeasure was visibly expressed in the hopelessly flattened bows of the old gauze trimming. And yet the fashion which was new in 1840 was by no means elaborate. A scarf " was passed up from under the chin across the bonnet in the depression between the brim and crown and tied at one side with a careless knot, long ends fluttering down upon the shoulder." According to the simple habits of New England village life, a Dunstable straw was worn by girls until Thanksgiving and then replaced by a bonnet of beaver.

Sunbonnets of calico, stiffened with many rows of cording, were much worn in summer time by little country girls. In winter quilted hoods, like the sketch in Figure 132, were substituted. A specimen of a pink sunbonnet of the above description worn by a little girl in Pennsylvania is shown in Figure 132.

A little girl of twelve " was allowed one clean print gown and two aprons each week, a change and one for best, and if she spilled or tore she went to bed." Calicoes that were well covered and would wash, silk that would wear and turn, and above all, things that were " in the house " and could be made over were usually allotted to little girls. They were undeniably calculated to discourage vanity.

Infant caps were small and close-fitting and were trimmed with ruchings of lace and ribbon from 1835 to 1870. A picture of one trimmed in this way is given in Figure 160. A narrow satin ribbon with a loop edge was used for this purpose up to 1870.

The following description of a costume for a little girl four or five years old is quoted from the " Lady's Book " for 1849 :

"Dress of shaded silk (grey and rose-colour). The skirt very full and edged at the bottom by a broad hem, headed by a row of gimp in tints corresponding with the shades of the silk. The corsage is half high, square in front, and plaited in broad folds, which are confined by a band at the top and at the waist. Short sleeves edged by two bias folds of silk headed by gimp. Under the corsage is worn a spencer chemisette of jaconet muslin drawn on the neck in fullness, and set on a band at the throat. The chemisette has long sleeves, slightly full, and drawn on wrist bands. Loose trousers of cambric muslin, edged at the bottom by a bordering of needlework. The hair divided on the forehead and combed straight to the back of the neck, where it hangs down in long plaits. Boots of black glazed leather, with grey cashmere tops."

For an older girl an English magazine gives the following for the same year:

"Coarse straw bonnet lined and trimmed with blue silk. White openworked muslin waist, and a skirt of some light and delicate material. It may either be a glacé silk, as in the plate, or lawn, French cambric, etc. Pantalettes quite plain and finished by a narrow frill."

In the hoop-skirt days (1855–1865) little girls of seven years and over wore those weird inventions too, but the decline of the pantalets was heralded at the same time. White lingerie blouses were worn very much by young girls and Zouave jackets worn with skirts to match or of a contrasting colour were in vogue from 1860. (See Figure 205.) Garibaldi blouses were the next novelty and they won universal favour. Suits consisting of a grey skirt, trimmed with a broad band of plain colour above the hem, and a Garibaldi blouse, of the same colour as the trimming, were "quite the rage" during the struggle for independence in Italy. Solferino and Magenta were the fa-

1850–1860

FIGURE 253.—1857—Straw hat with drooping brim and streamers of ribbon. From a plate.

FIGURE 254.—1856—Bonnet of pale blue uncut velvet and white blond lace. Miss Dutihl's collection in Memorial Hall, Philadelphia.

FIGURE 255.—1855—Dress of silk with alternate stripes of brown and white plaid and coloured flowers. The basque and bell sleeves are trimmed with fringe and gimp heading of pink and brown. The picture is taken from a dress worn in Philadelphia. Head showing a braided coronet of hair. From a contemporary portrait.

FIGURE 256.—1859—Bonnet of black velvet and corded silk. Has had a bunch of currants and a red feather around on the side. Miss Dutihl's collection.

FIGURE 257.—1850–60—Black velvet wrist-band with mosaic clasp.

253

254

255

256

257

vourite shades of red, named of course for the famous battles. Boys wore these blouses too, with long pantaloons. Later a fancy for plaid materials prevailed over the plain colours. (See Figures 183, 189 and 201.)

It was the fashion in 1840 and after, to make dresses for girls with low or half-low bodices, to be worn over guimpes of white muslin (Figure 201). The skirts were made very full and were often lined with crinoline or worn over petticoats of crinoline like their mothers'. Instead of a bodice an arrangement of bretelles was often worn by little girls, as in the initial at the head of this chapter. Shoes made of morocco or leather, with cloth tops, called gaiter boots or gaiters, were much worn from 1835 to 1870 (Figures 181, 183, 184, 186 and 189). Sashes of ribbon tied at the back with long ends reaching to the end of the skirt were in general vogue.

In the sixties velvet ribbon and braid were the favourite trimmings and were used in a great variety of designs.

Bonnets at last went out of fashion in 1860 and even big girls began to wear hats instead. All the shapes worn by grown people were adopted for children at this time. The mushroom, the turban, and the pork-pie were worn very generally by girls of from ten to eighteen. For little girls under ten hats with low crowns and wide flapping brims were fashionable. They were popularly called " flats," and when simply trimmed with a wreath of small flowers or a band and ends of ribbon were exceedingly pretty and becoming.

The little girl of Austin Dobson's verses, " Little Blue-Ribbons," probably wore a hat of this shape :

" 'Little Blue-Ribbons.' We call her that
　　From the ribbons she wears in her favourite hat;
　　For may not a person be only five
　　And yet have the neatest of taste alive ?

As a matter of fact, this one has views
Of the strictest sort as to frocks and shoes ;
And we never object to a sash or bow,
When 'Little Blue-Ribbons' prefers it so."

For dressy occasions in the fifties suits of black velvet or velveteen were worn by little boys under ten and made often with full short trousers to the knee. Queen Victoria adopted the Highland suit of Scotch tartan for the English Princes on a visit to Balmoral in 1854, and the Highland dress, especially the kilts, soon became popular for boys from five to ten all the world over (Figure 162).

"THE COMING MAN

"A pair of very chubby legs
Encased in scarlet hose :
A pair of little stubby boots
With rather doubtful toes ;
A little kilt, a little coat
Cut as a mother can,
And lo ! before us strides in state
The Future's coming man."

Another fashion which at once became popular, and which probably had a similar origin, was the sailor costume, which was worn by boys from about seven to fourteen (Figure 161). Larger boys, of fifteen and upward, at this period wore long pantaloons like their fathers, with round short jackets to match, as in Figure 206. In England the high hat was still the regulation head-gear for little boys and for young men in the winter, but soft felt and straw hats of the sailor type will be seen in most of the contemporary illustrations.

Although dolls of the nineteenth century were not used as fashion models, they were always dressed according to the prevailing styles, and the few of them that have outlived their

generation record the fashions of their time. For instance, the
doll in Figure 211 is dressed in the Bloomer costume, which
was introduced in 1851. Although it is happily quite out of
fashion, this costume has become historic. In Figure 209, a
photograph of an interesting doll of the forties with her front
hair in (painted) braids in the fashion adopted by Queen
Victoria is given. Her wedding gown is of white satin trimmed
with silver and her veil and wreath of white flowers are worn in
the height of the fashion of 1840, the year of the Queen's marriage. This doll also possesses a stylish bonnet of white tulle
and white flowers. Another doll of about 1850 is shown in
Figure 210, wearing the fashionable pantalets and an apron
with bretelles, which were thought almost indispensable for
little girls at that time. The two last mentioned are wooden
dolls " with necks so white, and cheeks so red." They have
probably outlived more than one waxen rival like the wooden
doll of Jane Taylor's verses.

"THE WOODEN DOLL AND THE WAX DOLL

" There were two friends, a charming little pair
  Brunette the brown, and Blanchidine the fair :
  This child to love Brunette did still incline,
  And much Brunette loved sweet Blanchidine.
  Brunette in dress was neat yet wond'rous plain,
  But Blanchidine of finery was vain.

" Now Blanchidine a new acquaintance made,
  A little miss, most splendidly arrayed :
  Feathers and laces most beauteous to behold,
  And India frock, with spots of shining gold.
  Said Blanchidine, a miss so richly dressed,
  Most sure by all deserves to be caressed ;
  To play with me if she will condescend,
  Henceforward she shall be my only friend.
  For this new miss, so dressed and so adorned,
  Her poor Brunette was slighted, left, and scorned.

" Of Blanchidine's vast stock of pretty toys,
A wooden Doll her every thought employs ;
Its neck so white, so smooth, its cheeks so red,
She'd kiss, she'd hug, she'd take it to her bed.

" Mother now brought her home a Doll of wax,
Its hair in ringlets white and soft as flax ;
Its eyes could open, and its eyes could shut,
And on it with much taste its clothes were put,
My dear wax doll, sweet Blanchidine would cry :
Her doll of wood was thrown neglected by.

" One summer's day, 'twas in the month of June,
The sun blazed out in all the heat of noon,
My waxen doll, she cried, my dear, my charm,
You feel quite cold, but you shall soon be warm.
She placed it in the sun—misfortune dire !
The wax ran down as if before the fire !
Each beauteous feature quickly disappeared,
And melting left a blank all soiled and smeared.

" She stared, she screamed with horror and dismay,
You odious fright, she then was heard to say ;
For you my silly heart I have estranged,
From my sweet wooden Doll, that never changed.
Just so may change my new acquaintance fine,
For whom I left Brunette, that friend of mine.
No more by outside show will I be lured,
Of such capricious whims I think I'm cured :
To plain old friends my heart shall still be true,
Nor change for every face because 'tis new.
Her slighted wooden doll resumed its charms,
And wronged Brunette she clasped within her arms."

QUAKER COSTUME

and

Dress of the Shakers

1800–1870

"THE FRIEND

" In patriarchal plainness, lo ! around
  The festive board, a friendly tribe convene ;
  Chaste, simple, neat, and modest in attire,
  And chastely simple in their manners too ;
  To them her gay varieties in vain
  Fashion displays, inconstant as the moon.
  Them to allure, in vain does chymic art
  For human vestments multiply its dyes.
  One mode of dress contents them, and but few
  The colours of their choice—the gaudy shunned
  E'en by the gentle sisterhood. In youth,
  The rose's vivid hue their cheeks alone
  Wear, dimpling ; shaded by a bonnet plain,
  White as the cygnet's bosom ; jetty black
  As raven's wing : or if a tint it bear,
  'Tis what the harmless dove herself assumes.
  The hardier sex, an unloop'd hat, broad brimm'd,
  Shelters from summer's heat and winter's cold ;
  That from its station high ne'er deigns to stoop,
  Obsequious not to custom nor to king ;
  Yet, though precise, and primitive in speech,
  Restrain they not the smile, the seemly jest,
  Nor e'en the cordial laugh, that cynics grave
  Falsely assert ' bespeaks a vacant mind.'
  Serenely gay, with generous ale they fill
  The temp'rate cup : no want of new-coined toast
  To give it zest ; ' Good fellowship and peace'
  Their sentiment, their object, and their theme."
               —From " The Evening Fireside."

Quaker Costume

1800–1870

" While Quaker folks were Quakers still some fifty years ago,
  When coats were drab and gowns were plain and speech was
      staid and slow
  Before Dame Fashion dared suggest a single friz or curl.''

N the first years of the new century a very distinct costume was worn by the Quakers. Not only were all colours but grey and brown and white eschewed by strict members of the sect, but black was considered worldly. Everything they wore was of the best quality, most durably made and most neatly adjusted. Beaver hats with brims especially broad were worn by Quaker men for the greater part of the century. In the words of an English essayist: " A Quaker's hat is a more formidable thing than a Grandee's," and " Broad Brim " is one of the most familiar soubriquets by which members of the Society of Friends are known.

Short clothes were worn by more than usually conservative Quaker gentlemen throughout the thirties. A picture of Gabriel Middleton, said to have been the last man in Philadelphia to wear knee-breeches, is given in Figure 351. It is copied from a daguerreotype taken in 1840, and shows the dress fashionable in the beginning of the century, and " the hat

1838–1866

FIGURE 258.—1852—Outdoor costume; dress of cashmere, cloak of soft English cloth. From a contemporary portrait.

FIGURE 259.—1840—Typical Quaker dress of 1840 and after, with slight variations in the fullness of skirt and sleeves. This costume was worn in Pennsylvania in 1840.

FIGURE 260.—1866—Fashionable indoor gown of black taffeta trimmed with velvet ribbon. From a photograph.

FIGURE 261.—1850—Gown opening over a chemisette of shirred muslin and insertion, with undersleeves to match. From a portrait of the day.

FIGURE 262.—1865—Old lady in Quaker dress. The shawl is of a soft woven fabric called Chenille. The bonnet is a grey silk shirred over small reeds. From a photograph.

FIGURE 263.—1838—Widow's mourning; bombazine dress with trimming of crêpe. Collar and cap trimmed with goffered frills. From a portrait of Queen Adelaide.

258   259   260

261

262   263

which had not yet lost all its original beaver," but was still adhered to by the Friends. The coat is cut high, but is made without a collar and the plain buttoned waistcoat is also high and collarless. In the initial to this chapter the picture of a Quaker gentleman of Philadelphia is given, taken from a pencil sketch made by Dr. Valentine in 1838.

The subject of Quaker costume has been so ably covered by Mrs. Gummere* that it is not necessary to attempt a description in these pages. Only one to the persuasion born could master the subtle differences in the garb of the two factions, the Orthodox and Hicksite Friends. To the worldly eye the most obvious distinction seems to be that the Orthodox Quakers wear unorthodox garments, while the followers of Hicks dress in ordinary apparel. The division of the sect took place in 1827. The Orthodox members were at one time so strict in matters of dress that even buttons were forbidden as unnecessary ornaments. It has been narrated that on one occasion a Friend was publicly rebuked at a Meeting in Philadelphia for a breach of this regulation, whereupon the spirit moved Nicholas Waln, a famous preacher of his day, to remark that "if religion consisted of a button, he did not care a button for religion."

The Friends of the first quarter of the nineteenth century were conservative in customs as well as in costumes. In the diary of William Howitt we read of the observance of mourning in England in the year 1820 :

" A day I have not forgotten was when I was sent on Peter to the Friends' families for some miles round, to invite them to the burial of my paternal grandmother. This was called ' Biddin' to the berrin'.' At all the country funerals then people got their black crape hatband and pair of black gloves, but the Friends not wearing mourning, we gave a pair of drab

* The Quaker, a Study in Costume.

gloves. At the funeral the guests were treated to wine and cake made for the purpose, called ' berrin' cake,' and when the funeral left the house each person received the customary gloves and a square piece of ' berrin' cake ' wrapped in white paper and sealed."

The following extract from a letter of Mary Howitt describes the wedding costume of that most gentle poetess :

" On the 16th of Fourth month, 1821, we were married, I wearing my first silk gown, a very pretty dove-colour, with bonnet of the same material, and a soft white silk shawl. Shawls were greatly in vogue, especially amongst Friends, and my attire was thought very appropriate and becoming. For a wedding-tour my husband took me to every spot of beauty or old tradition in his native country, romantic, picturesque Derbyshire."

A very interesting portrait miniature of Miss Woolston, a Hicksite Friend, is given in Figure 70 ; the hair is arranged in curls and held in place by combs at the side, and a very high comb of the prevailing fashion of 1824 is worn at the back. The very sheer lawn collar is of an unusual design, and the low cut dress is of black which was considered worldly by Ortho- dox Friends. Another costume of interest is shown in Figure 259. The short waist and the scanty skirt, as well as the little cap with the bridle of ruffled lawn under the chin, will be noticed in portraits of the twenties, although this costume was worn by a Quaker in Pennsylvania until 1840.

The bonnets worn by Quaker ladies were decidedly distinct- ive. Pictures of them will be seen in Figures 293 and 286. Figure 286 shows the bonnet worn with the costume in Figure 289, which is also of brown satin.

An ingenious device to protect bonnets from the rain was used by the Friends. It consisted of a carefully fitted cover which could be folded into a small parcel and carried in the reticule until needed. In Figure 291 a picture of one of these rain covers is given, drawn from the original in Memorial Hall, Philadelphia. The shape suggests that it was in use during the forties.

The slight changes in Quaker fashion are exemplified in the interesting costume in Figure 289, which resembles with absolute fidelity the dress of Elizabeth Fry in the portrait by Richmond painted in 1824, although it was worn by Mrs. Johnson of Philadelphia about 1860.

DRESS OF THE SHAKERS

Although the belief and rites of the sect called "Shakers" are very different from the tenets and practice of the Quakers, there is a similarity in dress which it seems appropriate to describe at this point in our history. The most flourishing settlement of their community is at New Lebanon, New York.

As this sect is gradually dying out and their ways and ceremonials will before many years have become obsolete, we will give the following account of a visitor to this Shaker village in 1829, describing the costume which still remains unchanged.

"The Elders wear long plain coats and wide brimmed hats, but the Sunday costume of the ordinary man consists of pantaloons of blue linen with a fine white stripe in it, vest of a much deeper blue linsey-woolsey, stout calfskin shoes and grey stockings. Their shirts are made of cotton, the collars fastened with three buttons and turned over. The women wear, on Sunday, some a pure white dress, and others a white dress with a delicate blue stripe in it. Over their necks and bosoms were pure white kerchiefs, and over the left arm of each was carried a large white pocket handkerchief. Their heads were covered

with lawn caps, the form of all, for both old and young, being
alike. They project so as to fully conceal the cheeks in profile.
Their shoes, sharp-toed and high-heeled, according to the fashion
of the day when the Society was formed [1747], were made of
prunella of a brilliant ultramarine blue. And there were children too, with cheerful faces peering out from their broad hats
and deep bonnets, for they were all dressed like old men and
women. I marvelled at the sight of children in that isolated
world of bachelors and maidens, forgetting that it was a
refuge for orphans who are unsheltered in the stormy world
without."

Perhaps a brief account of Shaker worship by an eye-witness may be of interest to our readers in connection with their
severe costumes.

" As I entered the room, the Shakers were arranging themselves on both sides of it ; the women on the right and the men
on the left. Some of the men had taken off their coats, and
placed them aside. They formed themselves into figures,
leaving an open space in the centre which I afterwards found
was for any one who chose to address the society. They stood
in this position for some time, without a word being spoken by
any one ; and their countenances wore a serenity and fixedness
very unusual among any denomination or class of people. The
hands of all were pressed together ; and the women had handkerchiefs hanging vertically from their arms, clean from the
drawer, and half unfolded. They stood thus nearly ten minutes, with their eyes bent upon the floor, and you might have
heard a pin drop, so very still was every one in the building.
They forcibly reminded me of the sleeping scene in the En-
chanted Castle, if I may not be thought making an ir-
reverent comparison. Presently, a man who seemed the chief
among them, broke the silence, by suddenly commencing a

tune upon a base key, and ascending suddenly to a sharp one. His next hand neighbour joined and the next, and the next, each a little behind the other ; and then by degrees the females, till every voice in the room swelled the fitful chorus ; yet they seemed as incapable of motion as statues ; except their hands, which were gently lifted to keep time to their voices and of which you would know nothing unless your eyes were turned to them. This tune continued about ten minutes ; after which followed a breathing time of several more, during which a death-like silence again prevailed. The man whom I took to be the chief among them, then came forward into the space I have mentioned, and addressed the society, calling the members of it brothers and sisters. His voice was so low that I could only catch a few words ; enough, however, to assure me that his speech was directed alone to the Society, and was not intended for others. The burthen of his remarks was, as well as I could hear, the importance of the Gospel to mankind, and the inducements they had to exertion, under the Christian revelation. Then followed another tune, in which all joined with the same devotion as before, after which another member came forward and spoke substantially to the same effect as the former speaker. He was listened to with attention, and though his language was very simple and often unhappy, yet his words were uttered with that kind of solemnity that never fails to carry conviction to the mind. He had no sooner withdrawn to his place, than another hymn followed ; which to my ear seemed of a piece with the preceding ones. It was loud, faint, quiet and slow by turns, and the change was very sudden, from one pitch to another. As soon as it was concluded they all bowed and separated in such disorder that I thought the exercises over. Not a man went near a woman, though they all seemed separating in confusion and wild disorder. They

1850–1856

FIGURE 264.—1850—Black velvet mantilla trimmed with Maltese lace, worn in Philadelphia. Head from a portrait.

FIGURE 265.—1850—Gentleman in walking dress. From a portrait of that date. Brown cloth coat and pantaloons of brown and white plaid.

FIGURE 266.—1853—A white muslin gown embroidered in colours, worn in Philadelphia. Head from a contemporary portrait.

FIGURE 267.—1855—Gentleman in morning dress; black coat, buff nankin pantaloons and white waistcoat. From a contemporary print.

FIGURE 268.—1855—A gown of brown silk with chiné stripes, made with a basque trimmed with fringe to match. Worn in Philadelphia. Bonnet from a plate of that date. Head from a contemporary portrait.

FIGURE 269.—1856—Blue poplin gown trimmed with black velvet ribbon. Bead bag of crochet work. Worn in Philadelphia. Bonnet and head from a Daguerreotype.

FIGURE 270.—1855—A suit of black broadcloth, waistcoat fastened with oblong mosaic buttons. Worn in Philadelphia. Head from a contemporary portrait.

FIGURE 271.—1856—A peignoir of old-rose cashmere with Persian trimming; worn in Philadelphia. Head from a contemporary portrait.

1850 · 264   1850 · 265   1853 · 266   1855 · 267

1855 · 268   1856 · 269   1857 · 270   1858 · 271

came together by degrees and soon arranged themselves into two solid squares, the women composing one and the men the other. This was done by way of preparing for what they call the labour-dance ; of which I will endeavour to give some idea.

"After arranging themselves into two squares, with their faces towards the singers, who, about ten in number, male and female, stood in one row at the farther part of the building, they commenced a slow dance, keeping time with the singers not with their voices, but their hands, and feet. They danced two steps forward, then turned suddenly, as before ; danced two steps forward again, and so on, till they reached the point from which they started. This they repeated, until the tune ended, which was very long. As soon as it ended, they all bounded and had a short breathing spell, standing in the same spot and attitude they happened to be in when the dance ended ; but yet, though one would have supposed them nearly exhausted when they stopped, judging alone from their loud breathing, the chief speaker called upon them to labour on. 'Let us on, brothers and sisters,' said he, throwing his hands forward, suiting the action to the word, ' let us on, and take the kingdom of heaven by violence ! ' They rested about three minutes after which they commenced the dance again, though with a more lively step, quicker gesticulation, and a brisker voice than before. After this, they scattered in confusion, but came together again in the form of a circle, preparing for what they call the labouring march ; they marched round the room in a circle, the singers being in the centre, pouring forth a high and low keyed hymn, to which the rest kept time, as they went round, with a quick rise and fall of their hands. When this was over, and after a sufficient pause, they began a quicker march, which they went through after the same fashion as the last. After about five minutes of deep silence, one of the

society arose, came forward into the space between the males
and females, and addressed those whom curiosity had brought
there to witness their mode of worship. He spoke with fervour
and animation, and expatiated, with a fluency that would have
shamed many public speakers, upon the happiness attending
their mode of life and worship. They then all arose, and
joined in a hymn much the same as the one which commenced
their exercises. The words of the hymn or psalm accompany-
ing the slow labouring march were these, as well as I could
catch them, now and then :

"So let us live in this world below,
Serving our God where'er we go,
That when we quit this frame of clay,
We may rise to glory's eternal day."

We believe that the Shakers have never had an established
community in England, although Mr. Meredith's weird poem,
"Jump to Glory Jane," is very suggestive of the vigorous mode
of worship we have described above.

"A Revelation came on Jane,
The widow of a labouring swain :
And first her body trembled sharp,
Then all the woman was a harp
With winds along the strings ; she heard
Though there was neither tone nor word.

"For past our hearing was the air,
Beyond our speaking what it bare,
And she within herself had sight
Of heaven at work to cleanse outright,
To make of her a mansion fit
For angel hosts inside to sit.

" They entered, and forthwith entranced
    Her body braced, her members danced ;
    Surprisingly the woman leapt ;
    And countenance composed she kept ;
    As gossip neighbours in the lane
    Declared, who saw and pitied Jane.

" These knew she had been reading books,
    The which was witnessed by her looks
    Of late : she had a mania
    For mad folk in America,
    And said for sure they led the way,
    But meat and beer were meant to stay.

      *   *   *   *   *   *

" It was a scene when man and maid,
    Abandoning all other trade,
    And careless of the call to meals,
    Went jumping at the woman's heels.
    By dozens they were counted soon,
    Without a sound to tell their tune."

MEN'S APPAREL
1800–1870

" May he who writes a skillful tailor seem,
    And like a well made coat his present theme ;
    Tho' close, yet easy, decent but not dull,
    Short but not scanty, without buckram full."
                                —SAMUEL FOOTE.

Men's Apparel
1800–1810

"Be not the first by whom the new is tried
Nor yet the last to lay the old aside."
—POPE.

CCORDING to Mr. Ashton, in his "Dawn of the Nineteenth Century," "there is little to chronicle concerning the dress of the men as the radical changes during the last ten years of the eighteenth century maintained popularity for the first years of the nineteenth." The changes from season to season were trivial, it is true, from 1800 to 1810. A modification of the Jean Debry coat, popular in Paris after the Revolution and of which a copy of Gilray's caricature is given by Ashton, was worn in England and America, the shoulders much padded to give breadth and the coat buttoned at the waist to make the wearer look slender, and cut short enough to show the waistcoat which was usually of a contrasting colour. Sometimes two waistcoats were worn, an undervest of a bright colour showing above and below a drab or brown outer garment. Hessian boots were worn with this style of costume (Figure 345) and a high hat which in the early years of the century was usually very large. (See Figure 361.) Collars were worn extravagantly high, and slippers, according to Mr. Ashton, were preferred by

347

FIGURE 272.—1825—Bonnet of white silk gauze, with crown pattern of white carnations and stripes of yellow straw. Trimmed with white gauze ribbon with pale yellow and green figures. Wetherill collection, Memorial Hall, Philadelphia.

FIGURE 273.—1825-30—Leghorn hat trimmed with white ribbon. Piece of the brim cut away at the back and drawn up to the crown with a large bow. Strings and rosette over right ear. Wetherill collection, Memorial Hall.

FIGURE 274.—1829—Hat of sage green and salmon pink taffeta bound and corded with pink satin ribbon. Wetherill collection, Memorial Hall.

FIGURE 275.—1820—Bonnet of Tuscan straw trimmed with white ribbon. Wetherill collection, Memorial Hall.

FIGURE 276.—1830—Bonnet of white taffeta trimmed with white ribbon with fringed ends. Wetherill collection, Memorial Hall.

FIGURE 277.—1835—Bonnet of chip, brim faced with pale pink silk and trimmed with pink ribbon and white lace. Spray of small white flowers on top. From a plate.

FIGURE 278.—1833—Bonnet of white *point d'esprit* over white silk. Ribbon with satin spots and loop edge. Stiff crown; brim made over slender wire frame and lined with white sarsenet. Miss Dutihl's collection, Memorial Hall, Philadelphia.

FIGURE 279.—1838—Bonnet of fancy straw trimmed with blue ribbon. From a plate.

FIGURE 280.—1840—Quilted silk hood. Wetherill collection, Memorial Hall.

FIGURE 281.—1839—Leghorn bonnet trimmed with plaid ribbon. Wetherill collection, Memorial Hall.

FIGURE 282.—1860—Bonnet of light velvet with white roses and green velvet leaves; frills of blond lace inside the face; two sets of strings—white ribbon and green velvet. Miss Dutihl's collection, Memorial Hall, Philadelphia.

FIGURE 283.—1863—Bonnet of brown horsehair braid; black velvet ribbon, white tulle and red poppies inside the brim. Miss Dutihl's collection, Memorial Hall, Philadelphia.

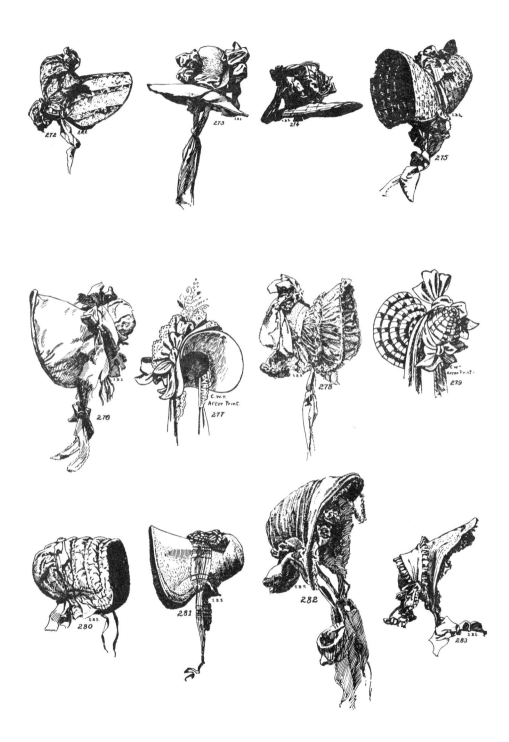

many to boots. Gay gallants still sported short trousers or "shorts," as they were familiarly called, and white waistcoats displaying ruffled shirts and high white stocks. Pantaloons, however, were a new fashion from Paris in 1800, and were chronicled in contemporary English verse:

> "The French we conquered once
> Now give us laws for pantaloons."

Trousers were not worn with evening dress, however, in the first quarter of the century.

The "Port Folio" for 1801 tells us of the fashions in the United States:

"All our young men of fashion wear frocks of dark blue, dark green, or dark brown cloth, with convex metal buttons, round hats with broad brims, short breeches and white stockings, or pantaloons with Hessian boots."

The frock coat of this period is illustrated in Figure 57 which is copied from a portrait by Sully painted in 1807. It was fashionable from 1800 to 1810, as well as the hat and short breeches for dress occasions which are shown in the same figure. The "Port Folio" is also the authority for the following items of fashion in this country:

"Mixed grey, bottle-green, Vandyke brown, and Spanish blue are the prevailing colours for morning coats, which are made in every respect the same as the dress coats, except that they have gilt basket buttons, sleeves with slits and three buttons, and pockets in the plaits of the skirts. Waistcoats are made of striped marseilles, and light-coloured double-milled cassimere pantaloons are worn with half-boots, or nankeen trousers and gaiters. We must not omit noticing in this place an ingenious article just invented, called Key's travelling waistcoat, which by folding answers the purpose of two waistcoats. It may be made either single or double-breasted, and of any material."

President Jefferson began his administration with an effort to set aside conventionality in dress and shocked the Federalist party by a certainly ill-timed exhibition of his democratic ideas. We are told by an eye-witness of his first inauguration, March, 1801, that " he made no preparation for the ceremony as far as his appearance was concerned. His indifference was ostentatious and evidently intended to cause comment. He wore a blue coat, a thick drab-coloured waistcoat with a red under-waistcoat lapped over it, green velveteen breeches with pearl buttons, yarn stockings, and slippers." Another contemporary says Jefferson's democratic simplicity was affected. " It was part of his political policy to dress badly, although he did not adopt it until he was elected President. While Minister to France he lived in great elegance, not only expending his entire salary, but drawing on his private income to maintain an appearance befitting his position. While a member of Congress and Secretary of State in Philadelphia, he occupied a beautiful place near Gray's Ferry outside the city. He was passionately fond of good horses and owned five beautifully matched bays, four to draw the carriage designed by himself, and one for his man, Burwell, who always rode behind. Two servants rode on horseback each guiding a pair, for he never trusted a driver with the lines." Many anecdotes are told of Mr. Jefferson's unceremonious treatment of the ambassadors from foreign countries during his eight years as President of the United States, but there has been much controversy published on the subject and it is difficult to get at the exact truth. The well-known portrait of Mr. Jefferson reproduced in Figure 296 is certainly not lacking in dignity nor propriety of dress.

In an American periodical of 1802 appeared the following paragraph under the heading " Parisian Fashions " :

" The young men still wear their coats very short, excessively *degagé*, and with the lapels buttoned. . . . Each lapel has now seven buttons instead of six. The three cocked hat is strictly and exclusively for full dress. The cockade is subject to almost daily changes in the combination of the three colours. The cravat is no longer so large. A great many wear frills. They wear at the knee-bands very small plain gold buckles, round or square, with rounded corners ; and in their shoes silver buckles of the same shape " (Figure 52).

The " Port Folio " printed this ridiculous satire in 1802 :

" RECIPE TO MAKE A MODERN BEAU

" Take anything . . . put it into a pair of pantaloons, put a binding on the top of the pantaloons (called a vest) and attach to the bosom of the shirt an oval glass case with a wig on it, pare away the skirts of its coat to the width of a hat-band. If the subject is doomed to pass its time in the house, it will require a heavy pair of round toed jack boots, with a tassel before and behind. Lift up by the cape of the coat, pull its hair over its face, lay a hat on its forehead, and spectacles on its nose.

" N. B. Its hands must, on no occasion, be suffered to escape from the pantaloon pockets, nor the spectacles from its nose."

It will be noticed that the fashionable high collars are often spoken of as capes in the printed descriptions of this period.

In another paper we find under " Fashions for September " (1802) :

" The following is now all the rage with the fashionables in London :

"Blue coat made very scant, with pockets in the skirts; blue velvet cape, high up in the neck ; pantaloons of mix'd broadcloth made very loose, with pockets. Suwarrow boots (all the vogue) and black hat with a narrow brim ! "

Of this new fashion in boots, which were made without any apparent seam, we read " the artist who has discovered the mode of kneading the leather so as to make solid boots, without any apparent seam, uses for the purpose a glossy gum, which prevents stains."

Hats were extravagantly large in 1802, and the shafts of " Mr. Oldschool's " ridicule are aimed at them in the following paragraph :

"Our High-street loungers sport a hat of an enormous circumference. A small beau is so overshadowed by one of Tiffin's best, that his dimensions to any thick sight are invisible."

The fashionable coat is the next target for his wit :

" I believe it is remarked in ' A Merry Connoisseur ' that the winter fashions of London reach this country in sufficient season to be in full bloom at midsummer. Our coats, on this side of the Atlantic, are copied from the London model generally after the original has become quite faded at home. If an early autumnal scheme of dress can be of any use now, let the beau of Philadelphia copy the following, taking especial care, however, to avoid the old hat. Gentlemen's coats are very short and loose, the collars are merely turned over ; round, concave middle-sized buttons of yellow metal are put on the facings at each side."

A curious anecdote concerning silk stockings, which were still worn with knee-breeches in Washington, in 1802, is told by Rev. Manasseh Cutler :

" On Thursday evening about ten, Mr. Dayton, going to bed, pulled off a pair of silk stockings, laid his stockings on his slippers at the bedside ; he perceived some sparks as he pulled them off. In the morning both stockings were burnt to a cinder, threads appearing to lie in their position in a coil; slippers burnt to a crisp; carpet burnt through and floor to a coal, so as to cause the resin to run. Many gentlemen noted the sparking of their silk stockings as they went to bed. I wore silk stockings that day, but did not notice sparks."

In 1803 coats were made somewhat broader in the waist, and cut lower in the neck, and the collars were less high. Knee-breeches were still in favour and boots with high tops. High shirt collars were worn with stocks, and beaver hats with rolling brims. Mr. Ashton mentions an advertisement of a London firm in 1803, which offered " to make a gentleman's old hat as good as it was when new; gentlemen who prefer silk hats may have them silked and made water-proof." Late in 1803 long coats not cutaway came into fashion, also pantaloons reaching to the ankle, and in 1804 coats were worn much longer in the waist and slightly cutaway. Ruffled shirt fronts were fashionable and low cut waistcoats. High close-fitting boots were worn over long pantaloons (Figure 360). Hats changed a little in 1804, the brims drooped back and front and were rolled slightly at the sides (Figure 347). It became the fashion in this year to carry very short canes and a satirical couplet in the " Port Folio " for December, 1804. proves that the new fashion was in vogue in America also.

"SHORT CANES

"Two bucks, having lost their bamboos in a fray,
Side by side swagger'd into a toy-shop one day,
Each, by a new purchase his loss to repair—
But, lo ! when for payment our heroes prepare,
All the cash in their pockets, together combin'd,
For the purchase of *one* scarce sufficient they find.
In common they buy it ; and, nice to a hair,
In two they divide it, and each takes his share.

284 *S.B.S.*

287 *S.B.S.*

285
*C.W.Trout.
After Print.*

286
*C.W.TROUT.
1907.*

288

289
Cecil W. Trout.

290
*C.W.Trout
After Print.*

291 *S.B.S.*

292
*C.W.T.
After Print.*

293 *S.B.S.*

Our beaux economic, improving the hint,
The length of their canes have determined to stint :
And when they would buy, a whole company splice
Their pence and their farthings, to make up the price,
Hence, view the smart beau, and you soon ascertain
The depth of his purse, by the length of his cane."

Coats in 1805 were long and not cutaway, with tails full in the back. Waistcoats were cut high and single-breasted, and the long close-fitting trousers were shaped over the instep like gaiters and fastened under the boot with a strap. Long gaiters were also in fashion reaching as high as the knee. The newest hats were very big, having wide brims and high crowns. Top-coats with three capes were very generally worn.

Many varieties of dress must have been observed in Washington in the first decade of the nineteenth century, when the foreign legations displayed so many rich colours and such a wealth of embroidery. A contemporary makes the following mention of a foreign minister at the President's levee in 1805 :

" We went at twelve. The French Minister, General Tau-reau, had been in, and was returning. We met him at the door, covered with lace almost from head to foot, and very much powdered. Walked with his hat off, though it was rather misty ; his Secretary, one Aide, and one other with him. When we went in the number was small, but soon increased, until the Levee room, which is large, was nearly full. A large number of ladies, Heads of Departments, Foreign Ministers and Consuls and the greater part of both Houses of Congress. The British Minister was in a plain dress, but superb carriage."

But even a civilian's dress could be made gay with one of the fanciful waistcoats in vogue. At the Historical Society in Philadelphia is preserved a quilted vest of bright gold-coloured satin which was once worn by Mr. George Logan of Stenton, a Quaker gentleman of some renown. It is wadded slightly and lined with heavy linen probably with a view to warmth, but the edge of the brilliant satin evidently showed above an outer waistcoat of a sombre tint. Waistcoats were apparently the most important article of masculine costume at that time, and it is amusing to read that the great English statesman, Fox, and Lord Carlisle " made a journey from Paris to Lyons for the sole purpose of procuring something new in waistcoats, and talked of nothing else by the way."

In 1806 we read of fashionable full dress coats cutaway and made with small rolling collars and revers, the tails reaching to the knee. With these coats very short waistcoats were worn, and knee-breeches fastened with small buttons on the outside of the leg, black pumps and stockings of white silk, ruffled shirts and fine cambric stocks. A cocked hat or a *chapeau bras* completed this full dress costume, which is illustrated in Figure 57. The *chapeau bras*, which is mentioned in many descriptions of court dress, is shown in Figure 340 from a print of 1807.

A walking suit of that time consisted usually of a blue coat with black buttons, buff breeches buttoned a little below the knee, over which boots with turned-down tops of buff kid were worn. High stock of white linen and high hat of beaver as shown in Figure 361.

From " Follies and Fashions of our Grandfathers " we transcribe the following :

" GENERAL OBSERVATIONS ON GENTLEMEN'S DRESS FOR 1807

" The general mourning ordered on account of the death of the venerable Duke of Brunswick has prevented much alteration in gentlemen's dress ; evening parties in the fashionable world have been a mere assemblage of sables ; and as many gentlemen's wardrobes furnished them with what was deemed sufficient for the purpose, the inventors of fashion found themselves completely cramped and disappointed in the great field of taste." *

The short period of court mourning over, a great variety of costumes were announced as follows :

" Morning coats of dark brown mixtures, or dark green mixtures, made either according to the same style as the evening coats, or single breasted and rather short, are still fashionable. These we observe to have generally a moderate-sized metal plated button ; and though collars of the same cloth are much used, a black velvet collar is considered as carrying a greater degree of style. For morning wear : Drab-coloured cloth coat, single-breasted, with pantaloons to match, which for the sake of avoiding the weight or incumbrance of boots, are made with buttoned gaiters attached ; with the addition of a striped waistcoat. This costume has undoubtedly a very genteel appearance."

" A single-breasted coat of a dark green or green " mixture with a collar of the same cloth, and plated buttons ; light coloured striped waistcoat made single-breasted, and light drab-coloured or leather breeches, with brown top boots " is a costume suggested for riding or walking."

We read now for the first time of the " parsley mixture, which is beginning to usurp popular preference ; coats of this colour are worn single-breasted with collars of the same cloth, and almost universally plated buttons ; they are shorter than the evening coats, made without pocket flaps, and rendered as light as possible." Quilted waistcoats are also mentioned " printed in stripes, single-breasted and without binding." " Light coloured kerseymere pantaloons or breeches and gaiters," and " white or nankin trousers with or without

* Follies and Fashions of Our Grandfathers, by Andrew W. Tuer.

gaiters " are fashionable details announced for 1807, but worn for several years afterwards.

"We have noticed many gentlemen in plain buff kersey-mere waistcoats of a very pale colour, which certainly have a neat appearance; others of a sort of pearl colour, and also some of scarlet kerseymere, which after being rejected for several years seem to be again coming into notice; but as they do not correspond with the coats usually worn, nor afford a pleasant contrast, they are not likely to become by any means general; indeed, blue or dark brown or corbeau colour coats are the only ones that can well be worn with a scarlet waist-coat. Brown top boots seem to be more worn than they have been for some time past, and with kerseymere breeches, in preference to leather. We have also observed that many gentle-men in their morning walks have attempted to introduce a sort of shooting dress, a short coat of any light colour, and with drab colour cloth or kerseymere gaiters to come up to the knees; but, however well such a dress may suit a watering place or a walk over the grounds of an estate, we do not think it adapted to the promenade of Bond Street. There is also a new article in the waistcoat fashion, which is a sort of silky shag well adapted to the season; and has a good appearance in riding dress, but we think does not seem perfectly in char-acter, unless accompanied with brown top boots and a riding whip."

For September, 1807, we read: "Morning coats of various mixtures are worn; the parsley mixture is decidedly the most fashionable, and that made single-breasted, with a collar of the same cloth, large size plated buttons, and without pocket flaps. Striped marseilles waistcoats single-breasted, or plain buff kerseymere waistcoats, of a pale colour, single-breasted, but not bound. Drab colour kerseymere pantaloons with Hessian boots, or India nankin trousers and gaiters. Dark olive cloth mixtures with covered buttons vie with dark forest green in favour, but blue cloth with gilt buttons is likely to retain popularity. White marseilles waistcoats, single-breasted, and light drab cloth or nankin breeches are still considered the most genteel."

Mixed cloths apparently gained in favour, for another morning dress for gentlemen of this material is given : " A coat, single-breasted, cut off in the front, and made of pepper and salt mixture, with covered or plated buttons, and collar of the same cloth ; the skirt rather shorter than the dress coats, and the pockets in the plaits behind. Waistcoats of printed marseilles made single-breasted are most popular and are made without any binding. Light drab kerseymere pantaloons are still worn ; as also drab kerseymere breeches with gilt buttons and brown top boots. Nankin pantaloons and trousers are becoming very prevalent as well as nankin gaiters."

In November of the same year, we are told : " Morning coats are still popular of greenish-olive or mixtures, and are worn both double-breasted and single ; they are seen with plain plated buttons and collars of the same cloth, and made without pocket flaps, the pocket being put in the plaits behind. Striped toilinet waistcoats of clear distinct stripes, bound with silk binding. Drab kerseymere breeches to come down over the knee with gilt buttons, and brown top boots, or pantaloons of the same colour and Hussar boots. The great coats are generally made of olive browns, single-breasted, with collars of the same cloth, and covered buttons ; the skirts lined with silk of the same colour. Many gentlemen who wish to appear in the height of the fashion have the front lined with silk, and if the weather permits the coat to be worn open, this has certainly a very dashing appearance."

1800–1860

FIGURE 294.—1800—Natural hair and high stock. Portrait of Charles Carroll, by St. Memin.

FIGURE 295.—1800—Powdered hair and queue. Portrait of Mr. Brumaud, by St. Memin.

FIGURE 296.—1801—Natural hair and ruffled shirt. Portrait of Thomas Jefferson.

FIGURE 297.—1802—Powdered hair and queue. Portrait of Dr. Rush, by St. Memin.

FIGURE 298.—1802—Powdered hair and queue. Portrait of DuBarry, by St. Memin.

FIGURE 299.—1804—Natural hair and side whiskers. Portrait of Nathaniel Williams, by St. Memin.

FIGURE 300.—1809—Natural hair and clerical stock. Portrait of Rev. Dr. Simons, by St. Memin.

FIGURE 301.—1809—Hair in queue. Portrait of James Madison.

FIGURE 302.—1821—Natural hair parted in the middle. Portrait of James Monroe.

FIGURE 303.—1845—White hair and judge's robe. Portrait of Judge Story.

FIGURE 304.—1840—Black stock and standing collar. Portrait of Franklin Pierce.

FIGURE 305.—1860—Low white stock and high collar. Portrait of James Buchanan.

The colours and combinations for evening dress for gentlemen in 1807 long remained in fashion, as will be seen from the illustrations given for the first half of the century.

" Dark blues with flat gilt buttons, with collars of the same, or of black velvet, according to the fancy of the wearer. The buttons on green coats are guided by fancy. White waistcoats are universal. Breeches are generally of nankin, or light drabs and pearl-coloured kerseymeres."

There were many changes in cut and design from time to time. An evening suit is described in 1809 consisting of a " double breasted dark blue coat with large yellow double gilt buttons; white marseilles waistcoat; light brown kerseymere breeches, with strings to the knees; white silk stockings; shoes with buckles," and at that date we learn "the collar though made to rise well up in the neck, is, however, not so extremely high as it was formerly. It is now made to admit of a small portion of the neck cloth being seen above it; it then descends gradually on the sides of the neck, so as to fall open and rather low in front; the waistcoats are worn both double and single-breasted with collars of moderate heights, and as they are buttoned only half way up, and only two or three of the lower buttons of the coat fastened, they show the drapery of the shirt to much advantage. The breeches come tolerably high up on the hip, and end two or three inches below the bend of the knee, where they sit perfectly close. We notice that waistcoats and small clothes of kerseymere are much more fashionable than silk, which has been gradually declining in favour for many years, and satin which was considered essential to complete the dress of a gentleman, a few years back, has gone out utterly; a pair of satin breeches would attract the observation of every beholder almost as much as a maroon coloured coat."

The following paragraph appeared in a fashion book of 1808:

"Evening dress is invariably black. The coats have constantly collars of the same cloth, and covered buttons : black kerseymere waistcoat and breeches are considered genteel : black silk stockings are necessary in dress parties." Research convinces us, however, that if black was ever recognized as the fashionable colour for evening costume at that period, it had but a brief popularity, light trousers and blue coats gaining ascendency again in the course of the same year.

James Madison succeeded President Jefferson in 1809. He was not only an intimate friend of his predecessor, but to some extent his disciple, and represented the Whigs in opposition to the Federalists. It was said that the barbers were all adherents of the latter party because the leaders of the Federalists wore long queues and powder and thus gave them constant employment, whereas the Whigs wore short hair or small queues tied carelessly with a ribbon (Figure 301). The following anecdote is told by Mrs. Wilder Goodwin in her "Life of Dolly Madison" :

"On the nomination of Madison, a barber burst out : 'The country is doomed ; what Presidents we might have, sir ! Just look at Dagget of Connecticut, or Stockton of New Jersey ! what queues they have got, sir ! as big as your fist and powdered every day, sir, like the real gentlemen they are. Such men, sir, would confer dignity upon the chief magistracy ; but this little Jim Madison, with a queue no bigger than a pipe-stem ! Sir, it is enough to make a man forswear his country.'"

Judging from the numerous portraits painted in 1809, we doubt if the barbers had a good business outlook in any country, for fashion then decreed short hair and no powder, and although a few elderly beaux appear to have worn both until 1810, they illustrated the exception rather than the rule. Another contemporary relates that President Madison " never altered his style of dress. He always wore a plain black cloth coat and knee-breeches with buckles, the hair powdered and worn in a queue behind ; the daily task of dressing it devolved upon his wife who did not think his body servant capable of doing it justice." *

This practice probably gave fresh displeasure to the barbers, but it is not a little surprising to read of the use of powder, which actually went out of fashion in 1794, and according to several authorities was regarded almost as a badge of the Federalists in 1809. The following account of Madison's appearance at his first inauguration is from a contemporary pen :

" Arrived at the Capitol, Madison descended from his carriage and entered the Hall of Representatives, where, until the inauguration of Monroe, the newly elected President took the oath of office. Madison was attended by the Attorney-General and other Cabinet officers. One who saw him describes him as looking unusually well, the excitement of the occasion lending colour to his pale studious face, and dignity to his small slender figure. He was dressed in a suit of clothes wholly of American manufacture, made of the wool from merino sheep bred and reared in this country. His coat was from the manufactory of Colonel Humphreys, and his waistcoat and small clothes from that of Chancellor Livingston, both being gifts offered in token of respect by those gentlemen. At twelve o'clock, with marked dignity and composure of manner, he took the oath of office, administered by Chief-Justice Marshall and, amid deafening cheers, as President of the United States began his inaugural address." †

No history of dress in the nineteenth century would be complete without mention of the celebrated " Beau Brummell."

* Mrs. Seaton's Letters.   † First Forty Years of Washington Society.

> "In Brummell's day of buckle shoes,
> Starch cravats and roll collars,
> They'd fight and war and bet and lose,
> Like gentlemen and scholars." *

His figure, which he always dressed so carefully, is described by Captain Jesse as unusually well proportioned. "Brummell," he says, "was about the height of the Apollo," a rather startling comparison, for it is as difficult to think of one in connection with clothes as of the other without them, "and the just proportions of his form were remarkable; his hand was particularly well shaped. His face was rather long and his complexion fair; his whiskers inclined to sandy and hair light brown. His features were neither plain nor handsome, but his head was well shaped, the forehead being unusually high."

According to another authority, the early part of his career was signalized by the famous pair of gloves to insure the perfection of which two glovers were employed, "one charged with the working of the thumbs and the other the fingers and the rest of the hands, and three coiffeurs were engaged to dress his hair, one for the temples, one for the front, and the third for his occiput. His boots were *cirés au vin de champagne*, and his ties designed by a portrait painter of note."

> "But my beautiful taste (as indeed you will guess)
> Is manifest most in my toilet and dress.
> My neck-cloth, of course, forms my principal care,
> For by that we criterions of elegance swear,
> And costs me each morning some hours of flurry,
> To make it appear to be tied in a hurry;
> My top-boots—those unerring marks of a blade—
> With champagne are polished, and peach marmalade.
> And a violet coat, closely copied from Byng;
> And a cluster of seals and a large diamond ring;
> And *trosièmes* of buckskin, bewitchingly large,
> Give the finishing strokes to the *parfait ouvrage*." †

* London Lyrics.   † Pursuit of Fashion.

Brummell is accredited with the revival of taste in dress among gentlemen which had been conspicuously lacking at the end of the eighteenth century. His first innovation was in the arrangement of neck-cloths. " His collars were always fixed to his shirt and so large that before being folded down they completely hid his face and head; the neck-cloth was almost a foot in height; the collar was fastened down to its proper size and Brummell, standing before the glass, by the gradual declension of his lower jaw creased the cravat to reasonable dimensions."

> " All is unprofitable, flat,
> And stale, without a smart *Cravat*
> Muslined enough to hold its starch—
> That last keystone of Fashion's arch !"

In his dress he was distinguished for great neatness and perfection of fit, but never for singularity or striking combinations.

For morning wear he appeared in Hessians and pantaloons, or top-boots and buckskins, with a blue coat and a light or buff coloured waistcoat, so that his ordinary costume was similar to that of any other gentleman in Europe or America; but, we are told by contemporary authority, it fitted " to admiration the best figure in England." His favourite evening dress was a blue coat and white waistcoat; black pantaloons, which fastened tight to the ankle; striped silk stockings and an opera hat. " He was always carefully dressed, but never the slave of fashion." We need not follow the checkered fortunes of this, for many years, cynosure of style, to their pathetic ending at Caen in 1840. The biographer already quoted says, " Brummell and Bonaparte, who had hitherto divided the attention of the world, fell together." A portrait of Beau Brummell (about 1804) is given in Figure 360.

306

308

307

311

In the early part of the nineteenth century, Doctors of Medicine were distinguished by long black coats and gold-headed canes. Edmund Yates makes the following statement on this subject in his " Reminiscences ": " There are Brightonians yet alive who talk to me of my uncle, Dr. Yates, remembering him with his white hair, snowy shirt frill, Hessian boots, or black gaiters, long black coat and gold-headed cane; a man of importance in the town, physician to the Sussex County Hospital, etc., etc." * Mr. Ashton declares also that during the Regency (1810–1819) " Doctors still clung to their wigs."

Shirts trimmed down the front with ruffles of the finest linen cambric, finished with minute rolled hems, were worn by young and old. The following epigram was printed about 1808, in " La Belle Assemblée ":

<blockquote>
" SHIRTS AND SHIFTS

" Old Musty had married a modish young flirt,
Who, calling one holiday morn for her shirt,
'Why, how now,' quoth Musty, 'what say you,' quoth he,
' What, do you wear a shirt, Moll?'—'Be sure, Sir,' quoth she,
'All women wear shirts'—'Nay,' quoth he, 'then I trow
What has long been a riddle is plain enough now;
For when women wear shirts, it can lack no great gifts
To discern why their husbands are put to their shifts.' "
</blockquote>

Marvels of needlework and feminine patience were the shirts of the first half of the nineteenth century, all made by hand, of course, and with innumerable three-cornered gussets put in to strengthen the seams, and with ruffles of finest linen cambric. Let us hope they were appreciated by the lords of creation who wore them. In the letters of Miss Southgate, the writer speaks of completing a dozen shirts for her father in 1812. A picture of a shirt of 1812 and one of 1830 are given in Figures 337 and

* Reminiscences of Fifty Years.

363.   Happily this painful episode in the history of dress is cast into oblivion by the universal use of the sewing-machine, but the pathetic verses in the " Song of the Shirt " were founded on the true story of many an overworked sempstress in the first half of the nineteenth century :

> " Oh, men with sisters dear!
> Oh, men with mothers and wives,
> It is not linen you're wearing out
> But human creatures' lives !" *

The following amusing advertisements appeared in " La Belle Assemblée " for 1809 :

" Patent Travelling Hair Caps.—Perfectly unique.—This very useful Invention is entirely new, and particularly well adapted for Officers in the Army and Navy, and Travellers in general, who are obliged to wear either a Welsh Wig or Night-cap, which, from their unhandsome or awkward appearance, persons are under the necessity of throwing off when alighting from the carriage, etc.

" The traveller's hair cap, now recommended to the attention of the Public, possesses every comfort of the former, with the appearance of a curled head of hair, and, from its peculiar elasticity, sits perfectly close to the head without any sort of springs whatever, and cannot be put out of order.   The Hair Caps are equally convenient for the Ladies.   They may be had of the Inventors, Robinson and Holmes, No. 1, Essex-street, Strand, Peruke-Makers to their Royal Highnesses the Prince of Wales, Duke of Clarence, and to the Theatre Royal, Covent Garden. Price one Guinea each.   Considerable allowance made to Retailers.   Sailors and Travellers by Sea, will find incredible ad-

---

* Hood's Song of the Shirt.   First published in Punch, 1843.

vantage from the use of the Hair Caps ; and Judges and Gentlemen of the Bar.

" Head-dresses, by the King's Royal Letters Patent, lately
granted for a recent discovery in the art of making Head-dresses,
etc., similar to nature, being so ingeniously wrought as to
imitate the skin of the head and the hair as if implanted
therein.

" Sold only by Vickery, No. 6, Tavistock-street, Covent
Garden."

Men's Apparel
1810–1830

"And he the hero of the night was there,
In breeches of light drab, and coat of blue."

IN the second and third decades of the nineteenth century, we notice that "coats of blue" were still the favoured fashion for both full dress and street costume. In 1810 the tails of coats were rather shorter than in the preceding year, and "did not come lower than within four inches of the knee," according to an acknowledged authority on the subject, "The Repository of Arts." Coats were made, we gather from the same source, with long lappels ending on a line with the hip buttons. The waists were longer too, and the collars, which were cut very high, were slightly padded to make them fit smoothly and were set back about two inches from the neck. Buttons of gilt or silver were worn on both dress and morning coats. Sleeves were made very long. The full dress coat had round cuffs without buttons, and pockets with flaps on the hips. In morning coats the sleeves were slit at the wrist and finished with three large buttons.

Breeches of light drab, made tight-fitting at the hips, and rather long, were in general favour. Pantaloons were made of a material called "double milled-stocking," something like the stockinette of to-day ; and a striped kerseymere, adopted by the Prince of Wales, whose taste in matters of masculine attire was rivalled only by Beau Brummell, became very fashionable in 1810.

Waistcoats were gay at this time. They were made single-breasted and with short regimental skirts, the collar fitting under the coat collar. The favourite material was striped marseilles of various colours.

Green was a popular colour, especially for top-coats which were made double-breasted and trimmed with covered buttons. The tails were wonderfully full and had pockets in the plaits at the back. The shape of the coat shown in Figure 55 was fashionable for many years.

In 1811, hats with low crowns and curved brims were introduced, but not to the exclusion of high hats, which have been unaccountably popular ever since the end of the seventeenth century. Walking coats were not cut away, but buttoned up the front. Light pantaloons reaching to the ankle were a characteristic fashion of that year, and black shoes were universally worn.

The next year, 1812, is noticeable for a change in the shape of the high hats. Brims were made very narrow and drooped very much both back and front, while the crowns were narrow at the top like the sugar-loaf crowns worn in 1850. (See Figure 347.) There was a change in the waistcoats too. They were cut high and close up to the chin, allowing only a small bow-necktie to show. Coats were again short-waisted and cut away, showing the waistcoats. Long pantaloons of cloth were worn with high boots (Figure 95). Pictures of this date show long, close-fitting pantaloons finished with a row of small buttons above the ankle. An illustration is given in Figure 363 of a pair made of buff-coloured duck which were worn in Boston about 1812.

Though, as we know now, pantaloons had come to stay,

1860–1870

FIGURE 312.—1860—Lady in white worked muslin dress over a fashionable hoop-skirt. The dress is made with seven graduated flounces and full bell sleeves. From a plate. Head from a contemporary portrait.

FIGURE 313.—1862—Walking costume of this date. A black velvet pelisse over black silk gown. Black bonnet faced with pink. Muff of chinchilla. From a contemporary photograph.

FIGURE 314.—1864—Gentleman in frock coat suit. From a portrait of this date.

FIGURE 315.—1868—Young lady in a dress of blue Chambéry gauze. Head from a contemporary portrait.

FIGURE 316.—1870—Street dress of dull green silk. Mantilla trimmed with black lace. Small bonnet trimmed with roses. From a plate of this date.

FIGURE 317.—1869—Ball dress of white Chambéry gauze trimmed with white satin folds and blond lace. Worn in this year. Head from a contemporary print.

FIGURE 318.—1870—Gentleman in walking suit of dark blue coat, drab pantaloons, white waistcoat, and grey beaver hat. From a photograph of this date.

1860·312　　　　　　　　1862·313　　　　　　　1864·314

1868·315　　　　　1870·316　　　　　1868·317　　　　　1870·318

much hostility was at first shown towards them.   Taken from the military dress introduced into the army by the Duke of Wellington during the Peninsular war, and at first known as " Wellington trousers," they came into more or less general use at the beginning of the nineteenth century, when the clergy and the fashionable world combined to oppose the innovation. An original trust deed, executed in 1820, of a Non-conformist chapel contains a clause providing that " under no circumstances shall a preacher be allowed to occupy the pulpit who wears long trousers " ; * and we are also informed that Almack's would not admit any one so attired.   The universities were equally firm in their opposition, and in 1812 the authorities of Trinity and St. John's Colleges, Cambridge, decreed that students appearing in hall or chapel in pantaloons or long trousers should be considered absent. †

Whiskers came into vogue in 1800 and were extremely fashionable in 1812.   They are commemorated in the following verses published in a magazine of that year :

> " With whiskers thick upon my face,
>   I went my fair to see ;
> She told me she could never love
>   A bear-faced chap like me.
>
> " I shaved them clean and called again,
>   And thought my troubles o'er ;
> She laughed outright and said I was
>   More bare-faced than before."

A fashion plate of 1814 shows a close-fitting top-coat of green cloth with cuffs and collar of fur.   The back seams of the coat are trimmed with a flat black braid, the tails plaited

* Early Hostility to Trousers, by William Andrews.
† Cooper's Annals of Cambridge.

full and the sleeves long and tight-fitting. With this coat was worn a small chimney-pot hat with drooping brim.

The new king, Louis XVIII, sent M. de Neuville to represent France in the United States and, in the letters of Mrs. Samuel Harrison Smith which have already furnished us with many valuable facts in the History of Dress of her time, we find a description of the costumes of the French delegation.

" M. de Neuville and suite were at Mrs. Monroe's Drawing-room in the most splendid costumes, not their court dress however. Blue coats covered with gold embroidery. The collar and back literally covered with wreaths of *fleurs-de-lys*. With white underclothes and huge chapeaux with feathers. The Minister's feather was white, the Secretaries' black and their dress, tho' in the same style, was not so superb as his."

At the same time Mrs. Seaton wrote the following account of the gorgeous equipage and liveries of the French Minister on the occasion of a reception at the President's house :

" After partaking of some ice-creams and a glass of Madeira, shaking hands with the President and tendering our good wishes, we were preparing to leave the rooms, when our attention was attracted through the window towards what we conceived to be a rolling ball of burnished gold, carried with swiftness through the air by two gilt wings. Our anxiety increased the nearer it approached, until it actually stopped before the door ; and from it alighted, weighted with gold lace, the French Minister and suite. We now also perceived that what we had supposed to be wings, were nothing more than gorgeous footmen with *chapeaux bras*, gilt braided skirts and splendid swords. Nothing ever was witnessed in Washington so brilliant and dazzling, a meridian sun blazing full on this carriage filled with diamonds and glittering orders, and gilt to the edge of the wheels,—you may well imagine how the natives stared and rubbed their eyes to be convinced 'twas no fairy dream."

President Monroe endeavoured to restore some of the stately formalities which had distinguished official life in the capital during the administrations of Washington and Adams. When he sent Mr. Pinckney as Minister to France, the diplomatic dress of our legations at all the foreign courts was very rich and dignified. A portrait of Richard Rush of Philadelphia, who was Minister at the Court of St. James from 1817 to 1825, in the possession of his granddaughter, shows a blue coat richly embroidered with gold. It was lined with white silk and worn with white waistcoat, ruffled shirt, knee-breeches and white silk stockings. A dress sword and *chapeau bras* completed this costume.

The formal tea-drinkings, solemn weekly dinners at the White House, and the " infrequent receptions " of Mrs. Monroe were relieved by numerous card parties and conversation parties. These, we learn, were " very elegant " at the British Minister's, and " very gay " at the French Embassy. M. de Neuville it seems " used to puzzle and astound the plain-living Yankees by serving dishes of turkeys without bones and puddings in the form of fowls, fresh cod dressed as salad, celery like oysters ; further he scandalized some and demoralized others by having dancing parties on Saturday evenings, which the New England ladies had been educated to consider as holy time."

During the last years of the Regency a marvellous variety of cravats were introduced.

" A book on the intricate subject of cravats was published at London in 1818 entitled ' Neckclothitania, or Titania : being an Essay on Starchers, By One of the Cloth.' The fashionable varieties of neck-wear at that time appear to have been the Napoleon, American, Mail-Coach, Osbaldestan and Irish ties ; and another called the Mathematical tie from its triangular form is described as being only one degree less severe than the Oriental tie, which was so high that the wearer could not see where he was going and so stiff that he could not turn his head."

One article of men's attire which has the distinction of an illustrious name and was very popular both in England and America from 1815 to 1850 was the Wellington boot. It was perhaps the most fashionable foot-wear for gentlemen in the first half of the nineteenth century and was popularly supposed to have been designed by the Duke of Wellington, for whom it was undoubtedly named. These boots were made of calfskin and fitted close to the leg as far as the knee and were worn under long trousers fastened with a strap beneath the sole of the boot. (See Figure 343.)

Mr. Richard Rush of Philadelphia was still Minister at the Court of Great Britain at the time of the accession of George IV. In his Memoirs (1817–1825) he describes the gorgeous celebration of the coronation on July 19, 1820. Speaking of the diplomatic corps on that occasion he observes that the box prepared for the Foreign Ambassadors and Ministers was at the south end of the building (Westminster Abbey) opposite the space fitted up for the Royal Family. It was near the throne, affording a good view of the imposing ceremony. The gorgeous costumes worn by the participants in the drama were afterwards reproduced in colour by order of his Majesty and published in a portfolio volume by Sir George Nayler. These costumes must have been very handsome and very hot for a July day. The mantles were of velvet lined and trimmed with fur, and the hats were heavy with groups of ostrich plumes.

In the Memoirs of Lester Wallack, the renowned actor, we find the later history of these same costumes. He says:

" George IV was a most theatrical man in all he did, and

when his coronation took place he dressed all his courtiers and everybody about him in peculiarly dramatic costumes. Dresses of Queen Elizabeth's time. It was all slashed trunks and side cloaks, etc. Of course the dukes, earls and barons were particularly disgusted at the way they had to exhibit themselves and as soon as the coronation ceremonies were over these things were thrown aside and sold, and Elliston bought an enormous number of them. He was then the lessee of the Surrey Theatre where he got up a great pageant and presented the Coronation of George IV."

In the spring of 1820 the Honourable Stratford Canning came to the United States as Minister from Great Britain. In his Memoirs there is an interesting description of the onerous preparations the post entailed. It was considered essential to bring furniture, servants, and all the household equipment he required from England, and it took three days to get his effects on board the ship. He brought over eleven servants, including a French cook. A cabriolet too was brought, but we hear nothing of horses and infer that America was thought capable of supplying suitable steeds for his distinguished use. As he was one of the greatest men England has ever sent to this country, he deserved to be made comfortable, even if his remarks on the manners and customs of the people he met were not always flattering.

He came in a friendly spirit; to use his own words : " The duty imposed upon me by the authorities in Downing Street was principally to keep the peace between Mother and Daughter. It was not easy to keep the peace when the daughter was as vain and sensitive as new fledged independence could make her." Landing at Baltimore, he says : " Fair accommodations awaited me at the Inn, and such native luxuries as soft crabs and cakes made of Indian corn opened a new field to the curious appetite." Of Washington, which he reached the following day, he seems to have received a rather dismal impression. "I know not what appearance the grand seat of government with its Capitol and the celebrated White House present at this period, but when I first saw it forty-eight years ago the Pennsylvania Avenue, extending from one to the other, or nearly so, was the only thing approaching our notion of a street and that for the most part rather prospectively than in actual existence. A low flat space of considerable extent formed the site of the embryo metropolis of the Union."

On the subject of dress he remarks: "Breeches and silk stockings are not infrequently worn of an evening, but these innovations are perhaps confined to the regions of Washington. Even here the true republican virtues have found refuge. At the Foreign Office, trousers, worsted stockings and gaiters for winter. In summer a white roundabout, *i. e.*, cotton jacket, *sans* neck-cloth, *sans* stockings and sometimes *sans* waistcoat. The Speaker of the House in the United States sits in his chair of office wigless and ungowned. I observed several of the members of Congress quite as well dressed as Martin Pitt. The Quakers struck me as being particularly attentive to their persons, their chins close shaved and their hats of the best beaver. Monday, March 9th, when all attended the President's Inauguration in lace coats and silk stockings, was a most wretched day, but as Talleyrand said, 'Nothing is settled in America, not even the climate.' I might be tempted to describe the costume which I assumed since the summer set in, not omitting my white cotton jacket, my umbrella and brimmed hat of Leghorn."

This is Mr. Canning's picture; now let us look on that of Mrs. Seaton from whose entertaining letters we quote as follows:

"The city is unusually gay, and crowded with agreeable and distinguished visitors. Mr. Canning's initiatory ball seemed to rouse the emulation of his neighbours, and we have had a succession of *fêtes*. The British Minister's route was unique. The English are half a century before us in style. Handsome pictures, books, and all sorts of elegant litter distinguish his rooms, the mansion being decorated with peculiar taste and propriety. Mr. Canning is himself a most unpretending man in appearance and manners ; modesty appears to be his peculiar characteristic, which for a foreign minister is no negative praise. The birthnight * ball was brilliant. The contrast between the plain attire of President Monroe and Mr. Adams and the splendid uniforms of the diplomatic corps, was very striking, the gold, silver and jewels donned by the foreigners in compliment to the anniversary festival of our patriot and hero certainly adding splendour to the scene. The captivating D'Aprament made his *début* in brilliant crimson indispensables laced with gold, an embroidered coat, stars and orders, golden scabbard and golden spurs. Poor girls! Perfectly irresistible in person, he besieged their hearts and not content with his triumphs there, his sword entangled their gowns, his spurs demolished their flounces, in the most attractive manner possible ; altogether he was proclaimed invincibly charming. M. de Neuville has adopted a new course since his return. Formerly, his secretaries were remarkably small and insignificant in appearance, but he now appears to have selected his legation by their inches. The most cultivated Frenchman whom I have ever met is in M. de Neuville's family, the Chevalier du Menu. He has resided ten years in America, and is a poet, orator, and scientific man, though still young."

* Washington's birthday.

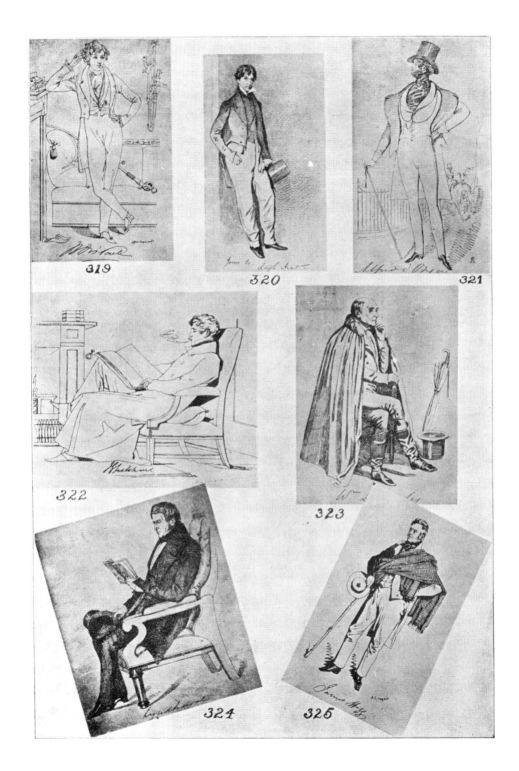

319

320

321

322

323

324

325

In 1820 we notice dark pantaloons were very fashionable, and gaiters, cutaway coats, high stocks and ruffled shirts. There was a slight change in the high hats. They were wider at the top and narrower at the crown, as in Figure 101. Long cloaks were popular. They had a military air and were picturesque when lined with red and ornamented with frogs. Watches were worn with fobs and seals throughout the twenties as will be seen in the portraits of that time. According to the following foolish verses published in " La Belle Assemblée " for December, 1820, pantaloons were worn loose-fitting and shoes with high heels were fashionable :

" MODERN MALE FASHIONS

" Crops, like hedge-hogs, small white hands,
　　Whiskers, like Jew Moses ;
　Collars padded, stiff cravats,
　　And cheeks as red as roses.

" Faces painted deepest brown,
　　Waistcoats striped and gaudy ;
　Sleeves, thrice doubled, thick with down,
　　And stays to brace the body.

" Short great coats that reach the knees,
　　Boots like French postillion ;
　Meant the lifty race to please,
　　But laughed at by the million.

" High-heeled shoes, with silken strings,
　　Pantaloons loose fitting ;
　Fingers deck'd with golden rings,
　　And small-clothes made of knitting.

" Bludgeons, like a pilgrim's staff,
　　Or canes, as slight as osiers ;
　Doubled hose, to shew the calf,
　　And swell the bill of hosiers.

　　*　　*　　*　　*　　*

> " Such is giddy Fashion's son,
>   Such a modern lover ;
> Oh ! would their reign had ne'er begun,
>   And may it soon be over ! "

"Small clothes made of knitting" evidently referred to stockinette.

The inauguration of President Monroe in 1821 (his second term) offers a striking contrast to the coronation of the English King in the previous year. We quote the following description from a letter of Judge Story to his wife in Boston :

" It was, according to arrangement, to be performed in the chamber of the House of Representatives. This is a splendid and most magnificent hall in the shape of a horseshoe, having a colonnade of marble pillars round the whole circular sweep which ascend to and support the lofty dome. The galleries for spectators were about midway the pillars and the seats gradually rise as they recede. The hall was thronged with ladies and gentlemen of the neighbouring cities to witness the ceremony. About 12 o'clock the President came into the hall dressed in a plain suit of black broadcloth with a single-breasted coat and waistcoat with flaps, in the old fashion. He also wore small clothes with silk stockings, and shoes with gold buckles in them. He placed himself in a chair usually occupied by the Clerk of the House of Representatives, facing the whole audience. On his right was the President of the Senate, on his left the Speaker of the House. The Secretaries of all the departments sat in a row on the right, and on the left all the foreign Ministers and their suites dressed out in all their most splendid court dresses and arranged according to their rank. Immediately in front of the President at a small distance were placed seven chairs for the Judges who, upon notice of the arrival of the President, went into the hall in their judicial robes attended by the Marshal. The Chief-Justice was immediately requested to take the chair on the left of the President, who soon afterwards rose, and the Chief-Justice administered the oath of office. The President then delivered his inaugural speech, the Justices, the foreign Ministers, the President of the Senate and the Speaker of the House remaining standing. Altogether the scene was truly striking and grand. There was a simple dignity which excited very pleasing sensations. The fine collection of beautiful and interesting women dressed with great elegance, and the presence of so many men of talents, character and public services, civil and military. I do not know that I was ever more impressed by a public spectacle."

John Marshall was Chief-Justice of the United States on the occasion described above. A portrait of him in his official robes is given in Figure 354, and one of Judge Story in his robes in Figure 303, as specimens of typical legal dress in America. Some idea of the splendour of the costumes worn by the foreign embassies on the same occasion may be gleaned from the descriptions given in pages 384 and 388. The embroidered *fleurs-de-lys*, etc., must have stood out in strong relief against the black robes of the judges and the black clothes of the chief actors in the scene.

In 1825 the court dress of ambassadors is described in a fashion book as a cutaway coat trimmed with gold lace over a white waistcoat and knee-breeches and white stockings. Ruffled shirt and high white stock. A dress sword, white gloves and *chapeau bras* similar to the costume worn by Mr. Rush at the Court of St. James. (See Figure 141.)

Long overcoats with full tails and a deep cape, and finished with a broad collar either of the same cloth or of black velvet, were worn from 1825 to 1830. An illustration of one of these coats is shown in Figure 143 and another in Figure 364, taken from a plate of 1829. The pantaloons reaching to the ankle, but strapped under the stocking, are also shown in the latter picture. They were in the extreme of fashion in 1829. Specimens of the high stocks which were worn at this time are given in Figures 326 and 329. The "stock sentimentale" truly merits its name, and the "stock l'Orientale" evidently derived its designation from the crescent shaped tie beneath the chin.

Men's Apparel
1830–1850

"According to the fashion and the time."

THE period of the thirties was distinguished for a rather effeminate and extremely unpicturesque style of costume for men. Coats were made to fit tight, the shoulders were padded and they were drawn in at the waist line without a wrinkle. The sleeves were very tight and put in at the armhole without any fullness whatever. In fact, the coats of this period which have been lent for our illustrations were all so small in the armhole and tight in the sleeves that a full-grown man could not possibly put them on, and in every instance we have had to make use of young boys for models.

"My love is all that is polite,
He looks so pale and thin;
He wears his boots so very tight,
And pulls so closely in.

"Oh! what a deal in hats and gloves,
In vests and coats he spends;
I call the heart that truly loves,
The tailor's best of friends."

The trousers also were quite tight and produced a slim, genteel effect which seems to have been the beau ideal of masculine perfection at that date.

The hair was worn in loose waved locks over the forehead, and side whiskers were affected by most young gallants of the time (Figures 148 and 307).

We note the description of a suit for summer wear of a dark slate-coloured cloth, made with a collar of black velvet in an American magazine of fashion for 1830, and also the statement that the backs of coats are cut wide across the shoulders and narrow at the waist, the " hip-buttons " being placed about three inches apart. This would naturally contribute to the slender-waisted effect mentioned above. The " latest " in waist-coats, according to the same authority, was white marseilles with large black spots, bound with black galloon and made with a deep rolling collar. The newest trousers were of moleskin, buttoned up the front with a fly, made rather full about the hips, tight from knee to ankle, and cut out on the instep to fit the boot.

The high stocks, which were still universally worn, are illustrated in Figures 330, 367, and 368, Figure 330 being copied from a wedding stock worn in Philadelphia by Dr. William Hunt in 1834. A specimen of the high shirt collars worn in the thirties is given in Figure 327.

A fashion plate for 1833 * shows the extreme of the lady-like dressing of gentlemen at that time. A tight-fitting overcoat tapering at the waist with a broad rolling collar opening wide to show the waistcoat and shirt bosom, a voluminous skirt reaching to the instep. A chimney-pot hat with scarcely any brim. With this peculiar costume, chin whiskers were worn and the general effect is very foolish (Figures 307 and 309).

> " They' ve made him a dandy ;
> A thing, you know, whisker'd, great-coated, and lac'd ;
> Like an hour-glass, exceedingly small in the waist :
> Quite a new sort of creature unknown yet to scholars,
> With heads so immovably stuck in shirt collars,
> That seats like our music-stools soon must be found them,
> To twirl when the creatures wish to look round them." †

* In the valuable collection of the Salmagundi Club, New York.
† Fudge Family in Paris, Thomas Moore.

Palm leaf hats were introduced about 1826 and became so popular in the protracted heat of an American summer that they are often mentioned as typical articles of costume (Figure 371). The following description is taken from "The New England Magazine" of 1831:

"Palm Leaf Hats are manufactured to a surprising extent in New England, but principally in Massachusetts. The manufacturing of them commenced in 1826, in consequence of the encouragement afforded by the duty laid on imported Leghorn, straw and grass hats. It is believed that in this year alone upwards of two millions of hats will be made, the average value of which is about three dollars a dozen, amounting to a half million of dollars. In Worcester County it is supposed half the quantity above stated will be made. The leaf is imported from the island of Cuba; last year six hundred tons, worth fifty thousand dollars, was received. The hats are all made at the dwellings of the inhabitants, by girls from fourteen years old and upwards, are then sold to the country merchants, who collect them together and send them to Boston, New York and other markets. They are made of every quality, varying from 25 cents to $2 each, and suited to the man of fashion or the labourer."

The high hats of 1830 were still of beaver, but not always of black. Grey and white beavers were equally fashionable from 1830 to 1835; the popular shape of that time is illustrated in Figures 148, 307 and 309. Grey hats were worn in the daytime, and black beaver hats in the evening.

In 1830 we read of a new surtout called a Casauba, made with a rouleau of cloth instead of a collar. Dressing gowns of printed cachemire were fashionable too at that time, and a peculiar garment called a redingote vest made of merino reaching almost to

1807–1870

FIGURE 326.—1829—Stock l'Oriental. From a print.
FIGURE 327.—1830—Shirt collar, 1830 and after. From a print.
FIGURE 328.—1840—Stock of black satin of this date.
FIGURE 329.—1829—Stock sentimentale. From a print.
FIGURE 330.—1834—White satin stock worn at this time. (Back and front views.)
FIGURE 331.—1813—Breadman.
FIGURE 332.—1813—Dustman.
FIGURE 333.—1813—Sailor.
FIGURE 334.—1800–70—English workman in smock.
FIGURE 335.—1837—White satin waistcoat.
FIGURE 336.—1838—Old coat of white linen.
FIGURE 337.—1830—White linen shirt worn in Philadelphia at this date.
FIGURE 338.—1825—Militia coat of red cloth faced with brown velvet.
FIGURE 339.—1825—Military coat of dark blue cloth faced with scarlet.
FIGURE 340.—1807—Chapeau bras. From a print.
FIGURE 341.—1850—White beaver hat. Memorial Hall, Philadelphia.
FIGURE 342.—1815–50—Dress boots.
FIGURE 343.—1815–50—Wellington boots.
FIGURE 344.—1800–50—Blucher boots.
FIGURE 345.—1800–40—Hessian boots.
FIGURE 346.—1800–50—Top boots.
FIGURE 347.—1809—Hat with rolling brim.
FIGURE 348.—1850—A black silk high hat. Memorial Hall, Philadelphia.
FIGURE 349.—1865—Picture of a round hat worn by an old man in this year. From a contemporary print.

326

327

328

329

330

331

332

333

334

335

336

337

338

339

340

342

343

344

345

346

347

341

348

349

the knees and fastened with buttons of jet or of white metal, for morning wear.

The following remarks on the various expressions of which a coat is capable were found in an old magazine of the thirties:

"Old coats are the indices by which a man's peculiar turn of mind may be pointed out. So tenaciously do I hold this opinion, that, in passing down a crowded thoroughfare, the Strand, for instance, I would wager odds that, in seven out of ten cases, I would tell you a stranger's character and calling by the mere cut of his every-day coat. Who can mistake the staid, formal gravity of the orthodox divine, in the corresponding weight, fullness and healthy condition of his familiar easy-natured flaps? Who sees not the necessities, the habitual eccentricities of the poet, significantly developed in his haggard, shapeless old apologies for skirts, original in their genius as 'Christabel,' uncouth in their build as the New Palace at Pimlico? Who can misapprehend the motions of the spirit, as it slyly flutters beneath the Quaker's drab? Thus, too, the sable hue of the lawyer's working coat corresponds with the colour of his conscience: while his thrift, dandyism and close attention to appearances, tell their own tale in the half-pay officer's smart, but somewhat faded exterior."

The close relationship between the coat and the wearer has been touchingly expressed by an American poet as follows:

"Old coat, for some three or four seasons
　We've been jolly comrades, but now
We part, old companion, forever;
　To fate and to fashion I bow.
You'd look well enough at a dinner,
　I'd wear you with pride at a ball,
But I'm dressing to-night for a wedding
　My own, and you'd not do at all.

"There's a reprobate looseness about you
  Should I wear you to-night I believe
  As I came with my bride from the altar
  You'd laugh in your wicked old sleeve.

*   *   *   *   *   *

'Tis time to put on your successor,
  It's made in a fashion that's new ;
  Old coat, I'm afraid it will never
  Sit as easily on me as you." *

An English traveller visiting Washington in 1832 was apparently much interested in the appearance and dress of a deputation of Indians which was quartered for a short time in the hotel where he was staying. Several of these, he remarks, " wore only a blanket fastened in front by a skewer, and their hair was adorned with feathers. There were two ladies and several children attached to the deputation, and I desired the waiter if possible to induce some of the latter to pay me a visit. One evening he brought in two, a boy and a girl. The girl's costume consisted of a sort of printed bed-gown without sleeves, fastened close up to the throat ; trousers, moccasins or leggins of deerskin, worn generally by the Indians, and the whole covered by a blanket, the drapery of which she really managed with a good deal of grace. In each ear she wore two large earrings. Fastened to the crown of her head was a piece of blue ribband, which hung down not unbecomingly on one side of the face. The boy was apparently younger by two or three years, and a fine manly little fellow. He also wore a blanket by way of Benjamin, but instead of a bed-gown rejoiced in a long coat, the tails of which reached almost to his heels, and which, being made for some one of form and dimensions very

* G. A. Baker, Jr.

different, was not remarkable for felicity of adaptation. Neither could speak English, but the boy evidently was the leading person, the girl only following his example. Having a bottle of claret on the table, I filled each of them a glass, but the flavour did not seem to meet with their approbation. I then gave them cigars which they appeared to enjoy ; indeed I never saw any one blow a cloud with greater zest than the young lady. The failure of the claret then induced me to try the effect of stronger potations, and I brought a bottle of Eau de Cologne from my dressing table, the contents of which they finished without difficulty or apparent inconvenience from the strength of the spirit. They remained with me about half an hour, during the whole of which time they maintained the sober gravity of demeanour which the Indians consider to be inseparable from true dignity. Nothing seemed to excite surprise, and the only symptom of animation they displayed was on catching a view of their own countenances in a mirror, when they both laughed. At length the boy rose to take leave followed by the young lady, and shaking hands with me they strode out of the apartment with a sort of barbaric grace which well became these children of the wilderness. Before quitting the subject of the Indians whose wild appearance had excited in my imagination a thousand fantastic associations, I must mention one circumstance which I found sadly hostile to their poetical interest. One morning I observed my diplomatic friends lounging and walking about as usual in the gallery of the hotel, but alas, how miserably transmogrified ! Their ‘ Great Father,’ the President, had, it appeared, preparatory to their departure, presented each person attached to the Mission with a new coat, in shape something like that worn by a coachman, and of blue cloth turned up at the collar and cuffs with scarlet. The women wore cloaks of the same colours and materials and my two little friends, whose

barbaric appearance had been delightful, now strutted about in
their new finery with a grand air."

From this strictly American costume let us turn to matters
of dress in England, and read the graphic descriptions of the
apparel worn by different types in the mother country from
1836 to 1846, given by Edmund Yates in his "Recollections
and Experiences."

"Dandies wore high collared coats and roll collared waistcoats, short in the waist; round their necks were high stiff
stocks with 'an avalanche of satin' falling over the chest, and
ornamented with a large pin and a small pin connected with a
thin chain, and high sharp-pointed, almost Gladstonian, shirt
collars. No gentleman could wear anything in the daytime
but Wellington boots (Figure 343), high up in the leg, over
which the trousers fitted tightly, covering most of the foot, and
secured underneath by a broad strap. The great coats of those
days were no misnomers; they were really enormous garments
adorned with capes and deep pockets (Figure 364). They were
Chesterfields, Petershams, Taglionis, Sylphides, and well I
recollect some splendid driving-coats ornamented with enormous mother-of-pearl buttons as big as crown-pieces, with pictures on them of mail coaches going full speed, which were exhibited to admiring crowds in the tailor's windows in Regent
Street. Afterwards came the neat paletot, the blanket-like
poncho, the blue pilot, and the comfortable Inverness. Some
old gentlemen wore cloaks, too, in my youth, and I have a dim
recollection of one kind properly, I believe, called 'roquelaure'
(Figure 323), but known to the London public as a 'rockelow.'"
The latter garment was a survival of the eighteenth century, illustrations of which are given in the earlier volume of "Historic Dress."

The dress of the men of this time (1836–1846) can be studied in the illustrations in " Nicholas Nickleby " and other contemporary publications.

Mr. Yates gives an interesting glimpse of personages once familiar in the streets of London : " The dustman with his call ' Dust O !' and his ever-ringing bell ; the buy-a-broom girl, with her Swiss garb and jödling voice ; the thin Turk, turban-topped, and vending rhubarb from a tray suspended from his neck ; the Jew boys who hung about the coach-offices with their nets of lemons and oranges, and were closely elbowed by the peripatetic cutler, whose knives were always open and constantly being polished and sharpened on a tattered leather glove. Gone is the bag-bearing Jew with his never-ceasing cry of ' Old clo! clo !' Gone are the Quakers, the men broad-brimmed, shovel-hatted, stiff-collared and gaitered ; the women generally pretty with hideous bonnets and pretty dove-coloured raiment. Well do I recollect the introduction, simultaneously I imagine, of the handsome cab, then called 'patent-safety,' and the four-wheeler. People nowadays will smile to hear that for years after their first introduction it was considered ' fast ' to ride in a handsome, and its use was tabooed to ladies. Clean-shaven faces were uncommon ; a pair of ' mutton chop ' whiskers was *de rigeur ;* but a ' pair of Moustachios,' as they were called, was never seen, save on a cavalry officer, a dancing master, or a ' snob,' and the cultivation of a beard was wholly confined to foreigners."

The costume of the policeman, introduced by Sir Robert Peel in 1850, is described in the same volume as follows : " They wore swallow-tail blue coats with bright metal buttons, and in summer white duck trousers and white Berlin gloves. In lieu of helmet they had an ordinary chimney-pot hat, only of extra strength and stiffness and with a glazed oilskin top." Further details are not given by Mr. Yates, but we are left to infer that in winter the English guardians of the peace wore blue cloth trousers, and in summer the same coat was worn with the duck trousers. We are left quite in the dark about the style of gloves they patronized in winter, but are told very decidedly that policemen were not allowed "to grow either moustache or beard."

Another valuable item of English costume is given in the same book. "The general or country postman wore a scarlet swallow-tail coat; the 'two penny' or London district man a blue uniform; a collection for the night mails was made at five P. M. by men who paraded the streets, each armed with a bell, which he rang lustily; many of the despatches and letters from the head office to the various sub-offices were sent by horse-post, the letters being enclosed in leather valises which were strapped behind in post-bags."

Speaking of the familiar characters in the streets of London about 1846, Mr. Yates says: "There in a hooded cabriolet, the fashionable vehicle for men-about-town, with an enormous champing horse and the trimmest of tiny grooms, 'tigers' as they were called, half standing on the foot-board, half swinging in the air, clinging to the straps, would be Count d'Orsay, with clear-cut features and raven hair, the king of the dandies, the cynosure of all eyes, the greatest swell of the day. He was an admirable whip and always drove in faultless white kid gloves with his shirt wrist-bands turned back over his coat cuffs and his whole 'turn-out' was perfection. By his side was occasionally seen Prince Louis Napoleon, an exile too, after his escape from Ham residing in lodgings in King Street."

The white waistcoat affected by Count d'Orsay and other men of fashion soon became very popular. "Punch's" Muse immortalized them in the following parody on the " Roast Beef of Old England ":

"Oh ! the vests of young England are perfectly white,
  And they're cut very neatly and sit very tight,
  And they serve to distinguish our young Englishmen
  From the juvenile Manners and Coningsby Ben ;
      Sing Oh ! the white vests of young England
      And Oh ! the young English white vests.

"Now the old English vest was some two yards about,
  For old England was rather inclined to be stout ;
  But the young English waist is extremely compress'd,
  By the very close fit of the young English vest.
      Sing Oh ! etc.

" The young English white vest upon one little score,
  May perhaps be considered a bit of a bore,
  For it makes the resemblance exceedingly near
  Twixt the young English waiter and young English **Peer.**
      Sing Oh ! etc.

"But what are the odds as concerning the vest,
  So long as felicity reigns in the breast ?
  And young England to wear what it pleases may claim
  Let us hope all the tailors are paid for the same.
      Sing Oh ! etc."

Count d'Orsay, of whom Mr. Yates has given us such a vivid description, was an artist by profession, and is said to have painted the last portrait of the Duke of Wellington. He settled in England in 1821 and assisted the Countess of Blessington to establish a fashionable coterie in London in that year. Bernard Osborne describes him riding in Hyde Park :

    " Patting the crest of his well-managed steed,
      Proud of his action, D'Orsay vaunts the breed ;
      A coat of chocolate, a vest of snow,
      Well brushed his whiskers, as his boots below,
      A short-napped beaver, prodigal in brim,
      With trousers tighten'd to a well-turned limb." *

A manual of etiquette published by him about that time contains the following precepts for the guidance of men of fashion :

* The Chaunt of Achilles.

350

357

358

351

352

353

355

354

356

"It is bad taste to dress in the extreme of fashion and in general those only do so who have no other claim to distinction ; leave it in these times to shopmen and pickpockets. There are certain occasions, however, when you may dress as gayly as you please, observing the axiom of the ancient poet to be ' great on great occasions.' The great points are well made shoes, clean gloves, a white pocket handkerchief, and above all an easy and graceful deportment. Never affect the ruffianly style of dress unless as some excuse you hold a brilliant position in society. Always wear gloves in church or in a theatre. Avoid wearing jewelry unless it be in very good taste and then only at proper occasions. Never leave your hat in the hall when you pay a morning visit, it makes you look too much at home, take it with you into the room." Hints on the art of dancing, card playing and every form of social amusement are given in this little pamphlet which is now almost forgotten. A picture of the author will be seen in Figure 321, copied from Maclise's portrait gallery.

On the subject of hats the following anecdote appeared in the columns of " Blackwood's Magazine " in 1841 :

" There is a great deal in the build and wearing of hats, a great deal more than at first meets the eye. I know a man who in a particular hat looked so extraordinarily like a man of property that no tradesman on earth could refuse to give him credit. It was one of Andre's, and cost a guinea and a half in ready money, but the person in question was frightened at the enormous charge and afterwards purchased beavers in the city at the cost of seventeen-and-sixpence, and what was the consequence ? He fell off in public estimation, and very soon after he came out in his city hat it began to be whispered abroad that he was a ruined man." It is a good story although the moral is hardly commendable.

Men's Apparel
1850–1870

"The coat is the expression of the man."

IT is all nonsense to undervalue dress; I'm no more the same man in my dark green paletot, trimmed with astrakan, that I was a month ago in my fustian shooting-jacket, than a well plumed eagle is like a half moulted turkey. There is an indescribable connection between your coat and your character; and few things so react on the morality of a man as the cut of his trousers," wrote James Dodd, according to Lever, to his friend Robert Doolan during his travels abroad, which were published early in the fifties, a period characterized by rather gay attire in the masculine world.

An American writer mentions that "jewels were conspicuous in men's dressing and gentlemen of fashion were rare who did not have varieties of sparkling studs and scarf pins to add to the brightness of their vari-coloured vests. The latter not infrequently were of the richest satin and velvet, brocaded or embroidered. They lent a desirable note of colour by means inconspicuous to the swallow-tailed evening dress of that time, a note by the by which was supplemented by a tie of bright soft silk and of ample proportions. President Buchanan was remarkable for his undeviating choice of pure white cravats." But we are anticipating; the administration of Buchanan began in 1857.

From the letters of our great historian, Prescott, written during his visit to England in 1850, we glean many interesting items of dress. Although a private citizen and not connected in any way with the Embassy, he was constrained to wear a regulation costume at the Court of Queen Victoria. He describes his presentation in a letter to his wife :

" I was at Lawrence's * at one, in my costume, a *chapeau* with gold lace, blue coat and white trousers, begilded with buttons and metal (the coat buttons up single-breasted to the throat), a sword and patent leather boots. I was a figure indeed, but I had enough to keep me in countenance." This costume is not unlike the suit of an attaché of legation in 1840 shown in Figure 369 which is taken from a coat worn by Robert H. Hale, Esq., of Philadelphia, when he accompanied the Minister of the United States to St. Petersburg.

In another letter, to Mr. Ticknor, Mr. Prescott says : " Do you know I have become a courtier and affect the Royal Presence? I wish you could see my gallant costume, gold laced coat, white inexpressibles, silk hose, gold buckled patent leather slippers." This letter is dated June 26th, and the knee-breeches were probably *de rigeur* for a ball. Later in the same season he writes to Mr. Ticknor of the degree bestowed on him at Oxford.

" On Monday morning our party at the Bishop's went to Oxford where Lord Northampton and I were Doctorized in due form. We were both dressed in flaming red robes (it was the hottest day I have felt here) and then marched out in solemn procession with the Faculty, etc., in black and red gowns through the street, looking, that is, we, like the victims of an *auto da fé;* though I believe on second thoughts the San Benito was yellow."

* Amos Lawrence, Minister from the United States to England.

To Mrs. Prescott (August 24, 1850) he writes of his visit to Lord Carlisle at Naworth Castle.

" This is a fine old place of the feudal times indeed.   In the afternoon we arrived and saw the banners of the Howards and Dacres flying from its battlements, telling us that its lord was there.   He came out to greet us, dressed in his travelling garb, for he had just arrived, with his Scotch shawl twisted about him."

A travelling shawl of this description is shown in Figure 325.   It was a favourite garment in the fifties, being worn in place of a top-coat.

A few days later, while a guest of Lord Carlisle at Castle Naworth, Mr. Prescott described to Mrs. Prescott the visit of Queen Victoria and Prince Albert :

" August 28th, Wednesday.   The Queen, etc., arrived yesterday in a pelting rain, with an escort of cavalry, a pretty sight to those under cover.   Crowds of loyal subjects were in the park in front of the house to greet her.   They must have come miles in the rain.   She came into the hall in a plain travelling dress, bowing very gracefully to all there, and then to her apartments, which occupy the front of the building.   At eight we went to dinner, all in full dress, but mourning for the Duke of Cambridge ; I, of course, for President Taylor !   All wore breeches or tight pantaloons.   It was a brilliant show, I assure you, that immense table, with its fruits and flowers and lights glancing over beautiful plate in that superb gallery.   I was as near the Queen as at our own family table.   She has a good appetite, and laughs merrily.   She has fine eyes and teeth, but is short.   She was dressed in black silk and lace with the blue scarf of the Order of the Garter across her bosom.   Her only ornaments were of jet.   The Prince, who is certainly a handsome and very well made man, wore the Garter with its brilliant buckle round his knee, a showy star on his breast, and the collar of a foreign order round his neck. Dinner went off very well, except that we had no music, a tribute to Louis Philippe at the Queen's request."

During the administration of President Pierce, William Marcy was Secretary of State, and unfortunately assumed charge of the department with the intention of enforcing his plain democratic ideas upon the representatives of our country at foreign courts. Almost the first question he took up, we are told in Rhodes' " History of the United States," was that of diplomatic costumes. From the time of our mission to Ghent until President Jackson's day, " the dress informally or officially recommended was a blue coat lined with white silk ; straight standing cape embroidered with gold, buttons plain or if they can be had with an eagle stamped upon them, cuffs embroidered in the manner of the cape, white cassimere breeches with gold knee buckles and white silk stockings and gold or gilt shoe buckles. A three-cornered *chapeau bras*, a black cockade to which an eagle had been attached. Sword, etc. On gala days the uniforms should be made more splendid with embroidery and hat decorated with a white ostrich feather." Under the strictly democratic administration of President Jackson some changes were suggested in the diplomatic dress in the line of cheapness and adaptability to the simplicity of our institutions. A black coat without a cape and a gold star affixed on each side of the collar, either black or white breeches, *chapeau bras* with cockade and sword were retained.

Mrs. Clay, who was living in Washington at this time, says : " The consequences of Mr. Marcy's meddling were far-reaching. On June 1, 1853, he issued a circular recommending that our representatives abroad should, in order to show their devotion to republican institutions, appear whenever practicable in the simple dress of an American citizen. Our Minister at Berne found the Court of Switzerland quite willing to receive him in his citizen's dress. The Ministers at Turin and Brussels reported they would have no difficulty in carrying out the instructions of the State Department. The representative at Berlin was at once informed that such action would be considered disrespectful. The King of Sweden insisted on court dress at social functions. Mr. August Belmont, at the Hague, received a cold permission from the king to dress as he pleased, and it is recorded (as matter for gratitude on the part of the American Minister) that after all, and notwithstanding, the queen actually danced with him in his citizen's dress, and the king condescended to shake him by the hand and to talk with him! Mr. Mason, at the French Court, could not face the music! He consulted his wife, and together they agreed upon a compromise. He appeared in an embroidered coat, sword, and cocked hat, and had the misfortune to receive from Mr. Marcy a severe rebuke. Mr. Buchanan, at the Court of St. James, having no wife to consult, thought long and anxiously on the subject. The question was still unsettled at the opening of Parliament in February, 1854. Our Minister did not attend—he had 'nothing to wear,' whereupon 'there was quite a sensation in the House of Lords.' 'Indeed,' he wrote to Mr. Marcy, 'I have found difficulty in preventing this incident from becoming a subject of inquiry and remark in the House of Commons.' Think of that! At a time when England was on the eve of war with Russia, all the newspapers, court officials, House of Commons, exercised about the dress of the American Minister! The London 'Times' stated that on a diplomatic occasion 'the American Minister sate unpleasantly conscious of his singularity.' Poor Mr. Buchanan, sorely pressed, conceived the idea of costuming himself like General Washington, and to that end examined Stuart's portrait. He may even have gone so far as to indulge in a private rehearsal, queue, powdered wig, and all; but he seems to have perceived he would only make himself ridiculous; so he took his life in his hands, and, brave gentleman as he was, appeared at the queen's levee in the dress of an American citizen; and she, true lady as she was, settled the matter, for her court at least, by receiving him as she did all others. Mr. Buchanan wrote to his niece, Miss Harriet Lane, ' I wore a sword to gratify those who yielded so much, and to distinguish me from the upper court servants.' Mr. Soulé, at the Court of Madrid, adopted the costume of Benjamin Franklin at the Court of Louis XVI, sword, *chapeau*, black velvet, and much embroidery, looking ' with his black eyes, black looks and pale complexion, less like the philosopher whose costume he imitated, than the master of Ravenswood.' There had been a lively discussion among the Austrian and Mexican Ministers and the Countess of Montijo, the mother of the Empress Eugenia and of the Duchess of Alba, whether or no he should be rejected; but Mr. Soulé did not know this. The queen received him, he wrote to Mr. Marcy, ' with marked attention and courtesy.' "

As we shall see later the reformed diplomatic costume was dropped when a new Secretary of State came into office, who wisely considered it a matter of courtesy, not of state.

From " Things as They Are in America," an interesting book of travel in 1854, we quote the following description of a visit to Congress.

" The House was full. Representatives from California and other distant states were already present—the whole assemblage forming a body of well-dressed persons, such as you would see any day on ' 'Change.' There was little diversity of costume. A black dress coat, black satin waistcoat, and black stock, constitute the general attire—ready for court, dinner, ball, public

359   360   361   362

363   364   365   366

367   369   370   371

368

meeting, or anything. A few wore beards, but clean shaving was the rule. Standing, sitting, lounging, talking, according to fancy, they spent the time till noon. The moment the hands of the clock point to twelve, said my friend, 'Business will commence.' A clerk, seated in advance, and a little below the vacant chair of the Speaker, kept his eye fixed on a clock over the doorway, and accordingly rang the bell when the hour of noon was indicated."

Cutaway coats were known by various names, such as swallow-tail, claw-hammer, and steel-pen. Before 1860 they were worn in morning as well as evening dress, and always had large pockets in the tails. A story is told of a Pennsylvania architect who went to Philadelphia on business carrying in his tail pocket a packet of plans and specifications. He had occasion to cross the river in a ferry-boat from Camden, and on arriving at his destination put his hand in the place where his pocket should have been to take out the plans, but alas, papers, pocket and even the coat tail had been cut off by a venturesome thief in the crowd on the ferry landing. The first lesson in the art of pocket-picking, as taught by Fagan in "Oliver Twist," was to snatch the handkerchiefs and snuff-boxes from the tail pockets of unwary gentlemen in the street. It was even an easier accomplishment than carrying off reticules from the ladies.

White and cream-coloured waistcoats were very fashionable in the fifties. One of cream-coloured silk, wadded and lined with white and fastened with gilt buttons, worn in Philadelphia in 1857, is illustrated in Figure 335.

It was in 1860 that the Prince of Wales, afterwards King Edward VII, visited the United States and was fêted and entertained in all the large cities. At the ball given in his honour in New York an alarming accident happened: a part of the dancing floor gave way. No one was hurt, however, and the progress of his Royal Highness through the country was enthusiastically hailed on every side, and the popular feeling of attachment to the mother country was strengthened thereby.

> " While the manners, while the arts,
>   That mould a nation's soul,
>   Still cling around our hearts,
>   Between let ocean roll,
>   Our joint communion breaking with the sun,
>   Yet still from either breach,
>   The voice of blood shall reach,
>   More audible than speech :
>   ' We are one.' " *

The fashions of the sixties are familiar to every one through the medium of photography. The small *cartes de visites*, as they were called, which were very popular in 1860 to 1870, show long black shiny broadcloth frock coats, rather loose pantaloons and careless neckties. The colours were universally sober. The hair was worn rather short than long and beards and whiskers and moustaches were all popular. In Washington of course, as in all the capitals of Europe, with military and naval uniforms and the costumes of the foreign diplomats, a variety and contrast was noticeable. A diplomatic costume was considered necessary for the representatives of the United States government in 1861.

In Carl Schurz's " Reminiscences " he narrates the embarrassing position he was placed in at the Court of Spain, where he arrived without the diplomatic dress which he had ordered in Paris. By special concession of the Queen, he was permitted to present his credentials in ordinary evening dress, but was stopped at the foot of the staircase by two halberdiers in gorgeous mediæval costume who were guarding the passage to

* W. Allston.

the rooms of state. Evidently fearing the dignity of the Spanish throne was at stake, they crossed their halberds and refused
to let him pass. Finally a high official at the Court was ap-
pealed to and through his intercession admission was gained to
the Queen's presence. The delayed uniform consisted of " a
richly embroidered dress-coat, with correspondingly ornamented
trousers, a cocked hat and a dress sword."

Ugly as men's clothes of this period were, a great deal of attention was bestowed on them everywhere. Poole, the celebrated English tailor, is said to have been accidentally discovered
by King Edward VII while he was Prince of Wales. One night
when the French actor, Fechter, was playing " Robert Macaire "
in a coat apparently of rents and patches, the Prince was looking on and we are told " his keen eye quickly noted that the
garment was singularly well cut. After the play, the Prince
sent for Fechter and asked him the name of his tailor, and
the next day sent for Mr. Poole who from that hour was a
made man."

Looking backward at the pictures of the thirties and
forties we must at least acknowledge that there was something
wholesomely virile about these later day fashions for men. The
small waists, the tight sleeves and close-fitting pantaloons were
effeminate in comparison.

Like his predecessor, George IV, when Prince of Wales,
King Edward was called the best dressed man in Europe, and
although he is universally acknowledged to have been the
greatest statesman of his day, he never lost his earlier prestige
as the " glass of fashion and the mould of form " for men of
English birth. We learn on the best authority that it was etiquette in England for men of fashion to follow the Prince's
lead in the matter of hats at race meetings and " until his
Majesty one year appeared at Goodwood in a round hat, no one

ever dreamed even in the hottest weather of attending these races save in a silk hat and a frock coat. But luckily for the world at large the Prince's popularity and good sense broke through old-world prejudices and now a hot summer afternoon sees Goodwood Park dotted with men in blue serge, white duck, and flannel suits, and the lightest and shadiest of straw hats."

Suitable summer costumes have become a necessity in America, and are certainly much more becoming than the thick winter-like clothing of the sixties.

In the first half of the nineteenth century stage traditions were strongly adhered to in costume. We have already mentioned Mrs. Kemble's dress when she made her *début* in "Juliet." In the Memoirs of Lester Wallack we find an amusing instance of the strong prejudice cherished by stage-managers at that date against what they termed innovations.

" My father was cast for the part of Tressel in Cibber's version of 'Richard III.' Tressel is the youthful messenger who conveys to the King Henry VI the news of the murder of his son after the battle of Tewkesbury. My father, a young ambitious actor, came on with the feather hanging from his cap all wet, his hair dishevelled, one boot torn nearly off, one spur broken, the other gone entirely, his gauntlet stained with blood and his sword snapped in twain, at which old Wewitzer, who was the manager and had been a manager before my father was born, was perfectly shocked. It was too late to do anything, but the next morning Wewitzer sent for him to come to his office and addressed him thus : ' Young man, how do you hope to get on in your profession by deliberately breaking all precedent? What will become of the profession if mere boys are allowed to take these liberties ? Why, sir, you should have entered in a suit of decent black with silk stockings on and with a white handkerchief in your hand.' ' What, after defeat and flight in battle?' interrupted my father. 'That has nothing at all to do with it,' was the reply, 'the proprieties, Sir! the proprieties!' Some of the papers spoke very highly of the innovation, and the audience was satisfied if the management was not."

The hero of this anecdote, James Wallack, was a noted actor in London from 1804 to 1845, after which date he settled in New York and became known as the manager of Wallack's theatre from 1852 to 1864.

The colour harmonies and stage pictures to which we are nowadays accustomed came in with the æsthetic movement in 1860. The success of a modern play depends greatly upon the artistic taste of the stage-manager, who is chiefly responsible for the subtle effects of light and the combinations of colour which contribute largely to the pleasure of the audiences and render them less critical of the histrionic achievements of the actors. In the earlier days, however, very little mention is made in the press criticisms of the scenery or costumes, while every word and gesture of the actors is ardently described.

"Brief as 'tis brilliant, the Actor's fame
    With the spectator's memory lives and dies;
    Out of the witness of men's ears and eyes,
The Actor is a name.

"Yet some so much have stirred the common heart
    That, when they long have past from sight, we find
    Memories, which seem undying, left behind
Of their so potent art." *

CLERGYMEN'S DRESS

Before 1830 a Clergyman of the English Church dressed usually in a suit of black broadcloth and wore a black or white

* To the Memory of Charles Kemble, Punch, 1854.

stock according to his preference. His costume betokened the
college graduate of genial disposition and liberal views. His
profession did not forbid his mingling in the pleasures of the
world when opportunity offered, but a simple domestic life in a
rural parish, where but little thought was given to discussions
of dogma, was generally his lot. In the pulpit he wore the
black academic gown as his predecessors of the eighteenth century had done before him, and read the service in a white surplice, which is still customary. The black gown was worn in
the pulpit in some remote parts of the country as late as 1870.
A Clergyman of the English Church is illustrated in Figure 362,
copied from a print of 1810, when knee-breeches were still worn.
It will be noticed that the coat is made with comparatively
short tails and is not cut away in front.

The Ritualistic movement in the Church of England effected
a revival of the vestments worn during the reign of Edward VI.
The change, however, was not noticed in America before 1860.
Until that date the black Geneva gown had been worn in the
pulpit by Episcopalians, and the white surplice with a black
stole and bands of sheerest lawn were considered indispensable
adjuncts to clerical dress. The High Church party had been
very much in the minority up to that date and the changes
were very gradually introduced on this side of the ocean.

Bishops wore then, as they do now, the white linen rochet
resembling the surplice, but with less full sleeves, the black
satin chimere or outer robe, with lawn sleeves, and black stole.
There is a picture of the General Convention of 1859 assembled
at Richmond, Virginia, which contains portraits of forty-one
bishops of the Church in America. In this group Bishop Hop-
kinson is a noticeable figure, on account of his independence of
established custom. Instead of the usual Bishop's sleeves held
in at the wrist by a black band of ribbon, he adopted the open

sleeves of a priest's surplice. He was also the only member of the Episcopal Bench who wore a moustache and a flowing beard, although many of his brother bishops wore side whiskers.

Other Protestant denominations, Lutherans, Methodists and Presbyterians, all wore the black gown throughout the entire church service.

It is not necessary to describe the vestments worn in the Roman Catholic Church, as they have never changed, and have often been depicted.

In the street, clergymen of all ranks and denominations wore nothing more distinctive than an ordinary frock suit of black broadcloth and a white or black necktie. Trollope says of Mr. Harding, " He always wears a black frock coat, black knee-breeches and black gaiters, and somewhat scandalizes some of his more hyper-clerical brethren by a black neck-hand-kerchief; " and of that imposing dignitary, the Church Arch-deacon, Grantly, " 'Tis only when he has exchanged that ever-new shovel-hat for a tasselled nightcap and those shining black habiliments for his accustomed *robe de nuit* that Dr. Grantly talks and looks and thinks like an ordinary man. A dean or archbishop in the garb of his order is sure of our reverence ; and a well-got-up bishop fills our very souls with awe. But how can this feeling be perpetuated in the bosom of those who see the bishops without their aprons and the archdeacons even in a lower state of dishabille."

Trollope's graphic pictures of English churchmen in the fifties are undoubtedly drawn from life, and numerous illustrations of the bishops' aprons, the shovel hats, the gaiters, and other articles of clerical attire of that period will be seen in the pages of " Punch." " The Warden," etc., was published in 1855, and we venture to say that clerical breeches and gaiters were quite unknown in the United States at that time.

Figure 355, the portrait of a distinguished clergyman of the Episcopal Church in America, the Rev. Henry Morton, of Philadelphia, gives the street garb worn by him in 1865. The surpliced choirs were introduced into America in the seventies. Before that time the church choirs were composed of four trained voices who sang in ordinary costume and usually behind a curtain. Illustrations of the different vestments worn not only by the clergymen of the Anglican Church, but also of the Roman Catholic Church, may be found in the "Encyclopedia of Religious Knowledge." *

UNIFORMS

The Military and Naval uniforms of our own country, from 1800 to 1870, are fully illustrated and described in the government publication of 1889, which may be seen at any public library. For the uniforms of Great Britain the reader is referred to "Her Majesty's Army," † while Lepan's "Armée Francaise ‡ is an excellent authority for the military costumes of France. The illustration of a coat worn in the time of Jackson's famous rescue of New Orleans is given in Figure 339, and a coat which formed part of a militia uniform worn in the United States about 1825 is given in Figure 338.

A unique and most interesting collection of plates showing the uniforms of all nations at different historic periods is in the possession of the Salmagundi Club in New York. It is probably the most complete in this country.

* By Abbott and Conant.
† Her Majesty's Army by Walter Richards, London, 1870.
‡ L' Armée Francaise by Lepan, Paris, 1857.

SPORTING DRESS

" Fox Hunting in England

" Pastime for princes !—prime sport of our nation !
    Strength in their sinew and bloom on their cheek ;
    Health to the old, to the young recreation ;
    All for enjoyment the hunting field seek.

" Eager and emulous only, not spiteful :
    Grudging no friend, though ourselves he may beat;
    Just enough danger to make sport delightful !
    Toil just sufficient to make slumber sweet."

Figure 361 illustrates the riding-dress of a gentleman in 1800–1810, with slight variations in the coat and the hat. It was probably in fashion for at least twenty-five years of the nineteenth century.

The red hunting coats worn in the field by Englishmen throughout the nineteenth century were not noticeable in America, where gentlemen of leisure have ever been in the minority.

" We are off once more !—for the summer's o'er,
    And gaily we take our stand
By the covert-side, in our might and pride,
    A gallant and fearless band !
Again we hear our Huntsman's cheer,
    The thrilling Tally-ho !
And the blast of the horn, through the woodlands borne,
    As merrily onward we go !
            Tally-ho !
As merrily onward we go !"

Although fox hunting has never been a national pastime in the United States, other species of sport have always been popular. The shooting of birds, especially of ducks, woodcocks, partridges and reed birds, is pursued with great zest and regularity at certain seasons. In England we read of some changes in guns and in hunting costume about 1830. From a book on sport in the mother country, we quote the following:

"Gradually welcome improvements were introduced in the muzzle-loading apparatus, as in shooting costume. For it was astonishing how the gentlemen of the ancient school had stuck to the most inconvenient and uncompromising of garments. We see the heroes of many episodes scrambling over the rocks and worming themselves along the beds of the hill streams in high chimney-pot hats and tight-clinging cutaways. Their sons, however, discarded blue evening swallow-tails with brilliant brass buttons, and crimson under-waistcoats, and betook themselves to sensible shooting suits of loose-fitting tweeds and homespuns, and the clever mechanism soon came to the front, going forward hand in hand with the rational tailor."

In Figure 366 a shooting dress of 1832 from an old print is given and another of 1860 is shown in Figure 376.

GLOSSARY

Glossary

Agatha robe.—A semi-classical dress (1800) usually of soft muslin fastened with clasps on the shoulder, open at the left side over a full skirt, close-fitting short sleeves.

Amaranthus colour.—A soft pinkish shade of purple, very fashionable in 1802 and popular for many years.

Angoulême hat.—With a very narrow brim and high fluted crown, named for the daughter of Marie Antoinette in 1815. (See Figure 60.)

Angoulême tippet.—Made of satin trimmed with swansdown ; worn in 1815.

Angoulême spencer.—A new spencer in 1815. Illustrated in Figure 60.

Anne Boleyn mob.—Name given to a fashionable dress cap in 1807.

Arched collar.—A high collar (1814) curved to fit the throat and finished with a slightly flaring turnover.

Armenian toque.—Small turban of tulle and satin trimmed with feathers and spangled with silver, new in 1817.

Balmoral petticoat.—(1860) A woolen underskirt, originally red with black stripes, worn under a long dress looped up for walking.

Balmorals, or Balmoral boots.—(1860) Shoes which lace up the front, worn by both men and women. First introduced for outdoor wear by Queen Victoria at Balmoral, Scotland. Figure 166.

Bands (clerical).—An adjunct of clerical dress worn by Episcopalians and Presbyterians until 1870. Made of sheer linen cambric, worn around the neck with flat ends hanging down in front. Figures 300 and 357.

Beehive bonnet.—(1806) A shape resembling a hive usually made of plaited straw simply trimmed with ribbon and tied under the chin. Figure 59.

Bishop's blue.—A purplish shade of blue, new in 1809.

Blouse.—A loose-fitting bodice worn by women and children in 1820 and after.

Bluchers. — (1814–1850) Popular style of riding boot named for the famous Prussian General who visited London in 1814. It was heavier than the Wellington boot and better adapted for riding and rough weather. Figure 344.

Bonaparte hat.—Shaped like a helmet and decorated with a wreath of laurel ; sometimes worn on one side. Fashionable from 1802 to 1806. (See Figure 243.)

Boot-hooks.—Used to pull on the long boots worn from 1800 to 1870.

Bottle-green.—A dark bluish green worn from 1800 to 1860.

Bouilloné.—Puffed ; 1800 and after.

Brandenburgs.—Ornamental fastenings made of crocheted silk ; 1812 and after.

Brandenburg fringe. — Made of twisted sewing silk ; 1812 and after.

Buckskin. — Popular name for a riding gaiter made of tan-coloured leather ; 1800 and after.

Burnous or Burnouse.—A fashionable cloak worn since 1850, first introduced in France in imitation of the Moorish mantles worn by the Arabs and usually made of an eastern fabric woven of silk and goat's hair.

Bushel.—(Used only in the United States)—To mend or repair a tailor-made garment.

Busheller or Busheler.—A tailor's assistant whose business it is to repair garments.

Cabriolet.—A carriage with two wheels for one horse ; (ancestor of the cab) 1830 and after.

Cabriolet bonnet. — Large bonnet with flaring brim, named for the two-wheeled carriage introduced in 1830. Figures 123, 244 and 279.

Caledonian cap.—A small hat fitting close to the head, trimmed with a profusion of black feathers, worn in 1817.

Caledonian silk.—A new material in 1819. It was very strong and usually of a white ground with a small chequer of colour.

Capot.—An evening hood made of a cardinal silk handkerchief, considered very becoming ; 1816.

Capote or Capotte (same as the Poke bonnet).—A small bonnet with a projecting brim worn by women and children ; 1800 and after. Figure 11.

Capuchin.—A cape with hood, a survival of the seventeenth century ; much worn in 1807.

Capucine colour.—Dark orange or nasturtium colour, fashionable in 1806 and after.

Carmine.—A bright shade of red popular in 1817.

Carrick.—A long loose cloak fashionable in 1817 and after.

Caroline spencer.—Made of white kerseymere with a pelerine cape and trimmed with light blue satin cut bias ; 1818.

Cassock.—A long clerical coat, buttoned in front and reaching to the feet.

Cazenou.—A short sleeveless jacket ; 1855.

Chapeau bras (for gentlemen).—A crush hat of the nineteenth century; quite large when opened but flat when closed. (See Figure 340.)

Chapeau bras (for ladies).—A crush bonnet invented by Mrs. Bell, the foremost London dressmaker; very convenient for concert or opera wear; 1814.

Circassian hat.—Introduced in 1806; something like the Gipsy hat but with a fanciful crown.

Circassian sleeve.—A short sleeve looped up in front; worn by children in 1807.

Clarence.—A closed four-wheeled carriage with curved glass front, and seats for four people inside; 1811.

Clarence blue.—A new shade in 1811, similar to the Cambridge blue.

Coal-scuttle bonnet.—Popular name for the large flaring bonnet, sometimes called Cabriolet, worn in 1830 and after. Figure 272.

Coatee.—A short coat or spencer worn in 1802.

Coburg bonnet.—Bonnet with a soft crown tied under the chin; 1816.

Coburg cap.—Named in honour of the Duke of Saxe-Coburg in 1816. Made with a high crown of silver tissue; fashionable for the opera.

Coburg walking dress.—Named in honour of the Princess Charlotte.

Coiffure à l' indisposition.—Dressy cap made of lace and muslin; worn in 1812 and after. (See Figure 235.)

Conversation bonnet.—Made of chip, with flaring brim; usually lined with soft silk to match the ribbon trimming which was passed around the crown and tied in a bow on top; fashionable in 1807. Figure 23.

Coquillicot feathers.—A stiff little bunch of cock's feathers, fashionable in 1802 and after. Figure 10.

Cornette or French cap.—Fashionable in 1816; like the French bonnet in shape, completely covering the hair and ears; usually made of net or lace. It was tied under the chin with a small bow of ribbon to match the trimming on the top of the high crown. Figure 245.

Cornette à la Diane.—A small bonnet with crescent-shaped front; 1815.

Corset-frock.—Frock with a bodice shaped like a short corset with three gores on each side of the bosom and laced up the back with a white silk cord, short sleeves and short skirt.

Cossack hat.—Hat with a helmet-shaped crown, front turned back and edged with pearls; small feathers at one side; 1812.

Cottage cloak.—Cloak with a hood or cape and tied under the chin; a popular garment throughout the nineteenth century.

Curled silk.—A new material in 1814 used for bonnets.

Curls à la Greque.—Waving locks close to the face; 1802 and after. Figures 9 and 31.

Dandyess or Dandizette.—Popular names for the female dandy in the time of the Regency.

Demi-turban.—Soft scarf of muslin or gauze worn around the head and tied in a bow at the right side; 1800-1812. (See Figures 17 and 33.)

Devonshire brown.—A rich reddish brown like the soil in Devonshire; introduced in 1813.

Dinner cap.—Made of white satin and lace; popular in 1812. Figure 236.

Douillette à la Russienne.—Cloak with a warm lining, usually wadded. Fashionable in 1802 and after.

Dutch bonnet.—A straw bonnet turned up front and back. Fashionable in 1802. (See Figure 31.)

Eau de Veau.—A cosmetic used in 1808.

Egyptian amulet.—A favourite ornament in 1807.

En beret.—An arrangement of the hair with a cap; 1840 and after.

En coulisse.—An arrangement of puffs; 1840 and after.

En manche.—Made with cuffs; 1840 and after.

En ravanche.—An arrangement of flowers and ribbon worn over the left eye.

En tablier.—In apron effect; 1840 and after.

En tout cas.—A small umbrella used for both sun and rain; 1860 and after.

Esprits.—Stiff little plumes worn in hats; 1802 and after. Figure 10.

Eton jacket.—The short coat worn by the boys at Eton; fashionable for women in 1862 and after.

Fatima robe.—Short overgown; sleeves to the elbow; slashed up the front and caught together at intervals with buttons; worn over a muslin gown; fashionable in 1800.

Florence satin.—A thin soft variety of satin much used in 1802 and after.

Flushing hat.—Something like a Gipsy hat in shape, but with a double or under crown supplying the place of a cap; 1809.

Forester's or American green.—A bright green popular in 1817.

French bonnet.—Described in the books of 1811 as made of India muslin with a cone-shaped crown and a deep frill of Mechlin lace around the face and lined with sea-green sarsnet; a large lace bow on top. Figure 76.

French hat.—Another name for the cornet bonnet fashionable in 1815; crown very high and small flaring brim, often trimmed with a group of ostrich plumes.

French net.—A new material for evening frocks in 1807, similar to Brussels net.

Fugitive coat.—A sort of pelisse opening down the front introduced in 1807, a survival of the flying Josie of the preceding century. (See Figure 13.)

Garibaldi blouse.—Loose bodices named in 1859 for the Italian hero. Figure 165.

Georgian cloth.—A light weight broadcloth fashionable in 1806 and after.

Gipsy cloak.—A plain circular wrap, finished with a hood of the material.

Gipsy hat.—A plain hat of straw or chip tied carelessly under the chin with a ribbon; fashionable from 1800 to 1820. Figure 8.

Gossamer feathers.—Downy feathers found under the wings of the goose.

Gossamer satin. — A thin soft-finished satin similar to the Liberty satin of to-day; used for evening gowns in 1813 and after.

Graham turban.—A bonnet of plaid silk with a plume of black feathers; introduced in 1811.

Grecian robe. — A pseudo-classic garment fashionable for evening dress; 1800–1805.

Grecian sandal.—A novelty in footwear in 1812; for evening and street attire. (See Figure 50.)

Grecian scarf.—A graceful adjunct of the toilet illustrated in Figures 48 and 50.

Half boot.—A low shoe for women similar to our Oxford tie; worn in 1812 and after. Figure 48.

Half handkerchief. — A kerchief worn à la Marie Stuart with a point in front; made of net embroidered in gold or silver; very fashionable in 1807.

Hair à la Recamier.—Drawn back from the left eyebrow; 1802.

Hair à la Romaine.—Arranged in coils or braids crossing the head like a coronet.

Head à la Titus.—Name given to the short hair fashionable from 1800 to 1806.

Hessian.—A soft leather boot worn outside the trousers and curved under the knee; usually finished with a tassel at the top; 1800–1850. (See Figure 345.)

Hibernian vest.—A short jacket or spencer of velvet trimmed with fur; 1807.

High-low.—Popular name for a shoe reaching to the ankle; 1810 and after.

Hungarian vest.—A sort of jacket made with a high collar and long sleeves, a scarf hanging from the left shoulder and crossing in the back was caught into a belt; 1807.

Hungarian wrap.—A fashionable loose cloak in 1809, usually made of velvet and lined throughout with a corresponding shade of silk; it was wrapped in folds about the figure.

Huntley bonnet.—A cap of black velvet with silk plumes worn in 1813. (See Figure 49.)

Huntley scarf.—Scarf of Scotch tartan either in silk or wool, the ends fastened on the left shoulder. (See Figure 49.)

Hyde Park bonnet.—Made of white satin and trimmed with four white ostrich plumes. Very fashionable in 1812. Figure 237.

Italian slipper.—A flat slipper without a heel and cut low ; worn in 1812.

Ivanhoe cap.—A cap named in honour of Scott's novel which was published in 1820.

Jaconet or Jaconette.—A thin variety of cambric used for dresses, neck-handkerchiefs, etc., originally made in India; fashionable in 1800 and after.

Jockey bonnet.—A bonnet with full crown and visor turned back from the face ; 1806 and after.

Jockey hat.—Several varieties of hat are known by this name. In 1806 the fashionable jockey hat was turned up in front to show a contrasting colour and trimmed with fur. In 1820 and after a jockey hat had a peak or visor in front and was trimmed with a tassel or small ostrich feather ; while in the sixties the jockey hat, celebrated in a popular song and very fashionable in America, had a small curved brim and round crown and was adorned with a rooster's feather. Figure 169.

Jonquille.—A fashionable shade of yellow ; 1811 and after.

Kilt or Kilted skirt.—A short skirt laid in deep plaits ; a fashion adopted from the Highland costume which became very popular for little boys in 1870. Figure 162.

Knickerbockers. — Loose knee-breeches worn by boys and sportsmen in 1860 and after. Figure 370.

Kutusoff hat.—Named in 1813 for the Russian General who commanded the Allies against Napoleon. Made of cloth and turned up in front with a little corner to the right side ; tied under the chin and finished with a feather ; a full puffing of lace under the brim. Figure 81.

Kutusoff mantle.—Made of cloth to match the hat, with a high puckered collar and a long lappel falling over the left shoulder ; fastened at the throat with a brooch. Figure 81.

Lavinia hat.—A variety of the Gipsy shape, fashionable in 1807. (See Figure 13.)

Levantine.—A very soft velvet with a satin finish used in 1820 and after.

Limerick gloves.—Gloves made of rough kid ; 1807 and after.

Magenta.—A purplish shade of red named for the battle of Magenta in 1859.

Mameluke.—An eastern wrap fashionable in 1806, hanging from the shoulder in full folds down the back.

Mameluke robe.—A full loose gown hanging from the shoulders with a train ; 1806 and after.

Mancheron.—A cap-like trimming at the top of sleeves, often slashed ; 1810 and after.

Manilla brown.—A soft light shade, new in 1811; name derived from Manilla hemp.

Marabout feathers.—Soft and downy feathers found under the wings and tail of the marabout stork; much used for trimming in 1800 and after.

Marie-Louise blue.—A new shade of bright light blue named for the Empress; still fashionable.

Marie Stuart bonnet.—Large in the brim, depressed in front over the brow, and flaring at the sides. For dress occasions it was made of white satin trimmed with lace and coloured ribbons. Figure 32.

Metallic gauze.—A new material in 1820. Gauze with a peculiar lustre and made in all colours to resemble precious gems; emerald, topaz, amethyst, etc.

Minerva bonnet.—Shaped like a helmet with a long ostrich feather across the front; fashionable in 1812.

Moorish boot.—Shoe of coloured kid laced in front; 1807.

Mosaic gauze.—A new variety of gauze popular in 1820.

Nakara colour.—Pearl colour, fashionable in 1812 and after.

Neapolitan head-dress.—Worn for full dress in 1817, made of striped gauze and trimmed with silver.

Nicholas blue.—A new shade in 1817.

Oatlands hat.—Named in honour of the place where the Princess Charlotte passed her honeymoon in 1816.

Oldenburgh bonnet.—Named for the Duchess of Oldenburgh, who visited England in 1814. (See Figure 43.)

Over-alls. — Water-proof leggins worn in 1800 and after.

Pagoda or Chinese.—A parasol fashionable in 1818.

Palatine.—A wrap of black satin made with a hood, and lined with coloured silk.

Paletot.—A semi-loose overcoat fashionable in the second half of the nineteenth century.

Pamela bonnet or hat.—Made of straw, trimmed with a simple band of ribbon and tied under the chin. (See Figure 50.)

Panachée.—Variegated.

Panache.—A bunch of feathers.

Paysanne bonnet.—Another name for the cottage bonnet worn in 1800 and after.

Pea-green.—Very fashionable in 1809 and after.

Pea jacket.—A short heavy coat originally made of pilot cloth and worn by seamen, but copied in finer cloth for small boys; 1850 and after.

Pekin satin.—A heavy satin with a stripe of the same colour; 1802 and after.

Pelisse or Pelice.—A long coat-like garment usually made to fit the figure; in general use with slight variations from 1800 to 1870.

Pensée or Pansy colour.—A delicate shade of purple new in 1841.

Percale.—A soft closely-woven cambric first mentioned in 1812 and still in use.

Persian cap.—A fashionable riding hat in 1811.

Persian scarf.—A Cashmere or silk scarf with a Persian border, a fashionable accessory in 1812.

Pilgrim's hat.—Of Carmelite brown with an ornament in front in the form of a cockle shell ; 1811.

Pistache or Pistachio colour.—A soft light shade of green very fashionable in 1819.

Platoff costume.—Named in 1813 for the daughter of Count Platoff who is said to have offered his daughter's hand to any soldier who would bring him Napoleon's head.

Plume velvet.—Velvet with a narrow stripe of satin of the same colour ; 1820.

Poke bonnet.—Popular name for the capote or close-fitting bonnet which projected or poked over the face. Worn in the early part of the nineteenth century. Figures 11 and 288.

Poland mantle.—New in 1806 ; made generally of light silk and fastened with an antique clasp or brooch on the right shoulder.

Pomona green.—A new shade in 1812 similar to apple green.

Pomposa.—A high-cut slipper laced up the front, worn by children in 1807 and after.

Poussière de Paris.—A shade of light brown known by this name in 1819. It was probably like the Bismarck brown of the present day.

Princess Augusta poke. — Usually of white satin with a feather to match, falling to the left side ; tied under the right cheek with a large bow of soft ribbon ; 1813.

Princess of Wales bonnet.—Made with a round crown and turned up at one side of the front. Named for Princess Caroline in 1812.

Provincial bonnet.—Made of fine straw, fitting closely to the head and flat on top ; trimmed simply with ribbon arranged in a flat bow on top ; 1808.

Redingote.—An outer garment or coat fashionable in 1848.

Regency ball-dress.—A plain round frock trimmed with a bias fold of satin up each side of the front edged with fringe ; an epaulet sleeve edged with fringe and fastened in front of the arm with small satin buttons ; new in 1813.

Regency cap.—Made of white satin trimmed with a rouleau of satin and a bunch of ostrich feathers ; new in 1813. (See Figure 45.)

Regency hat.—Crown made to fit the head and gradually widened to the top ; trimmed with cord and tassel and a feather ; new in 1813. (See Figure 44.)

Regency mantle.—Made of cloth, usually black ; about a yard and a half in length, with a small cape and high collar finished with silk tassels ; a wide band of silk cut bias edged with cord trimmed the garment round the bottom and up the fronts. New in 1813.

Regency wrapper.—New in 1813. Made with a train and long sleeves; was laced up the front with a silk cord, trimmed with a flat band of velvet or sealskin, and finished at the throat with a collar cut in points.

Ridicule.—Popular name for the reticule in general use from 1800 to 1850.

Robe à la Joconde.—A long gown opening over a short petticoat, fastened on the left shoulder with a full blown rose; 1817.

Roman sandal.—Fashionable footwear in 1817 and after.

Rutland poke.—A small bonnet of wadded satin edged with swansdown and tied under the chin with a soft ribbon; an ostrich feather was used as trimming placed very much to one side; 1813.

Saccharine alum.—A popular cosmetic in 1808.

Sardinian mantle.—A scarf made of thin stuff such as net, muslin, or spotted leno. The ends were usually caught into a full knot or rosette and hung down to the knee in front; worn in 1808.

Scoop bonnet.—Popular name for the long narrow bonnet worn in 1840. Figures 125, 131.

Sempstress bonnet.—Made of fine muslin, the crown drawn in with two rows of ribbon and fastened under the chin; 1812 and after.

Sleeve à la Minerva.—A full short sleeve caught up in front with a jeweled clasp.

Snap.—A fastening with a snap clasp used on pelisses and dresses in 1810 and after.

Solferino.—A shade of red named for the battle of Solferino in 1859.

Spa bonnet.—Made of a curiously wrought fancy straw sometimes of two colours, worn without any other trimming; 1819.

Spanish blue.—A favourite shade of dark blue for gentlemen's morning coats in 1809.

Spanish cloak. — Short and full mantle, one end of which was usually thrown over the shoulder.

Spanish coat.—Fashionable in 1814; pelisse with standing collar and epaulettes on the shoulders.

Spanish fly.—A rich shade of dark green new in 1809.

Spanish hat.—A felt hat with soft brim and trimmed with a drooping plume; much worn from 1802 to 1807.

Spencer.—A short jacket with or without tails; 1800 and after. Figure 27.

Surtout à la Sultane.—An overdress with a train worn over a white frock; a new fashion in 1802.

Suarrow boots.—Named for the Polish General; went out of fashion in 1802.

Swiss mountain hat.—Hat with a soft brim drooping over the face and trimmed with ostrich plumes; 1819.

Taglioni.—A short overcoat introduced in the days of the celebrated dancer's triumph; 1830 and after.

Tippet.—A flat collar with long ends hanging down in front. Made of silk, velvet and fur, very popular in the first half of the nineteenth century.

Top boots.—Commonly called "Tops"; fashionable for hunting. They were carefully fitted to the foot and leg and were finished below the knee with buff or white leather tops, whence their name. They came into vogue at the time of the Regency and were worn until the end of the nineteenth century. (See Figures 346, 359 and 361.)

Torsade.—A twisted fringe trimming used in 1840.

Trafalgar dress.—Evening gown of white satin trimmed with silver, named for the battle of Trafalgar in 1806.

Treble or Triple ruff.—Made of three very full rows of pointed lace or of sheer muslin edged with lace, and fastened at the back of the neck; worn in 1813 and after.

Turbans.—Were the most popular head-dresses for women during the first half of the nineteenth century. Many illustrations are given of the different varieties throughout this book.

Turkish turban.—A turban made of folds of silk and gauze; in vogue in 1808.

Vevai cap.—A close-fitting cap of black velvet ornamented with a heron's plume; 1820.

Wallachian cap.—A round cap usually made of dark sable and worn with a tippet to match; 1812.

Washing leather gloves.—Fashionable in 1817 and after.

Wellington boots.—Named for the great General and worn in 1815 and many years after. Figure 343.

Wheel trimming.—Made in 1824 of soft puffings of silk formed into wheel-like circles, each overlapping the other.

Willow green.—Delicate shade of green, fashionable in 1811 and after.

Wraprascal.—Popular name for a loose overcoat used in the first half of the nineteenth century.

Wurtemburg frock.—A frock or dress of 1813, fastened in front under the trimming, which formed a little jacket effect; very long sleeves of lace.

Yeoman's hat.—Felt hat made with triangular points.

York tan gloves.—Made of rough undressed kid without any particular fit; 1807 and after.

Zebra feathers.—Striped in two different colours, fashionable in 1816.

Zephyr cloak.—Long over-garment of lace or net falling in long points to the feet and tied in at the waist by a sash of ribbon.

INDEX
Volume Two

INDEX

Volume Two

AUTHORITIES CONSULTED

Authorities Consulted

The Port Folio, Oliver Oldschool, Philadelphia, 1801–5.

La Belle Assemblée, 1806–24, London.

Letters of Eliza Southgate Bowne ; or, A Girl's Life Eighty Years Ago, New York, 1887.

Our Grandmothers' Gowns, Mrs. Alfred Hunt, London, 1895.

The Dawn of the Nineteenth Century in England, John Ashton, London, 1886.

Follies and Fashions of our Grandfathers, A. W. Tuer, London, 1887.

Forgotten Children's Books, A. W. Tuer, London, 1898.

Old-Fashioned Children's Books, A. W. Tuer, London, 1899.

Diary of Rev. Manasseh Cutler, New York, 1886.

La Vie Parisienne, 1800–1870, Paris.

Letters of William Winston Seaton, Boston, 1871.

Jane Austen and her Friends, G. E. Mitton, London, 1906.

Jane Austen's Letters, edited by Lord Brabourne, London, 1884.

Travels in the United States, 1849–50, Lady Emeline Stuart Wortley.

Court Magazine, 1830–47, London.

American Ladies' Magazine, edited by Mrs. Hale, Boston, 1831.

Evening Fireside, Philadelphia, 1805–6.

Eugénie, Empress of the French, Clara M. Tschudi, New York, 1899.

Private Life of Edward VII (Prince of Wales 1841–1901), by a Member of the Royal Household.

Memoranda of a Residence at the Court of London, 1819–1825, Richard Rush, Philadelphia, 1848.

In Peace and War, Mrs. Pryor, New York, 1904.

Dixie after the War, Mrs. Avery, New York, 1906.

Punch, 1840–1870, London.

Lady's Monthly Museum, 1799–1824, London.

Beau Brummell and his Times, Roger Boutet de Monvel, London, 1908.

Life of Beau Brummell, Captain William Jesse, London, 1886.

Recits d'une Tante, Memoires de la Comtesse de Boigne, Paris, 1907.

Leaves from the Note-Book of Lady Dorothy Neville, London, 1907.

Extracts from the Journal and Correspondence of Miss Berry, London, 1865.

Social Life in the Early Republic, Anne H. Wharton, Philadelphia, 1902.

AUTHORITIES CONSULTED

Fifty Years of London Life, Edmund Yates, New York, 1885.

Things as They Are in America, Wm. Chambers, Philadelphia, 1854.

History of the United States, James F. Rhodes, New York, 1904–6.

Memoirs and Private Correspondence of the Right Hon. Stratford Canning, London, 1888.

Portraits of the Sixties, Justin McCarthy, New York, 1903.

A Belle of the Fifties, Mrs. Clay, New York, 1904.

A Southern Girl in '61, D. G. Wright, New York, 1905.

Latrobe's Journal, New York, 1905.

First Forty Years in Washington Society, Mrs. S. Harrison Smith, New York, 1906.

Slight Reminiscences of a Septuagenarian, Countess Brownlow, London, 1867.

Memoirs of Lady Dorothy Neville, London, 1908.

Ladies' Magazine, Boston, 1829–1834.

Harper's Magazine (Vol. 15), New York, 1857.

Sartain's Magazine, Boston, 1849.

Moniteur des Dames et des Demoiselles, Paris, 1855.

Little Memoirs of the Nineteenth Century, London, 1902.

Letters from England, Mrs. Bancroft, New York, 1904.

Diary of a Lady in Waiting, Lady Charlotte Bury, London, 1908.

Mrs. Fitzherbert and George IV, W. H. Wilkins, New York, 1905.

Memoirs of Fifty Years, Lester Wallack, New York, 1889.

Memories of Seventy Years, edited by Mrs. Herbert Martin, London, 1883.

Reminiscences, 1819–1899, Mrs. Julia Ward Howe, New York, 1899.

Two Centuries of Costume, Alice Morse Earle, New York, 1903.

Directoire, Consulat et Empire, Paul Lacroix, Paris, 1884.

Dix-neuvieme Siecle en France, J. Grand-Carteret, Paris, 1893.

Le Costume Historique, A. Racinet, Paris, 1888.

The Quaker, a Study in Costume, Mrs. Francis B. Gummere, Philadelphia, 1902.

The History of Fashion, G. A. Challamel, London, 1882.

Modes and Manners of the Nineteenth Century, from the German of Max von Boehm, 3 Vols., London, 1910.

Chats on Costume, G. Woolliscroft Rhead, New York, 1906.

Collection of Fashion Plates, 7 Vols., 1810–1890.

Godey's Lady's Book, 1830–1870, Philadelphia.